CITY CINDEREL

CITY CINDERELLA

The life and times of

Mercury Asset Management

Peter Stormonth Darling

TEXERE

LONDON · NEW YORK

Copyright © 2000 Peter Stormonth Darling

First published in Great Britain in 1999 by Weidenfeld & Nicolson

This edition published by

TEXERE Publishing Limited
71–77 Leadenhall Street
London EC3A 3DE

Tel: +44 (0)20 7204 3644
Fax: +44 (0)20 7208 6701
www.texerepublishing.com

A subsidiary of

TEXERE LLC
55 East 52nd Street
New York, NY 10055

Tel: +1 (212) 317 5106
Fax: +1 (212) 317 5178

A CIP catalogue record for this book
is available from the British Library.

ISBN 1–58799–035–0

Typeset by Deltatype Ltd, Birkenhead, Merseyside
Printed in Great Britain by
Butler & Tanner Ltd, Frome and London

*To my three beautiful daughters,
Christa, Iona and Arabella,
so that they may know what was
going on all those years.*

Ah! What avails the classic bent
And what the cultured word;
Against the undoctored incident
That actually occurred?

Rudyard Kipling, 'The Benefactors'

CONTENTS

ILLUSTRATIONS

Between pages 80 and 81.
Siegmund Warburg
Eric Korner
Henry Grunfeld (*Financial Times*)
30 Gresham Street
Eric Roll (*author's photograph*)
Siegmund Warburg in Switzerland (*author's photograph*)
Warburgs' Chairman's Committee in 1980 (*Jacques Lowe*)
Andrew Smithers (*author's photograph*)
The 'gang of motorcar salesmen' (*Roger Hutchings/The Observer*)
David Price, PSD and Stephen Zimmerman (*Institutional Investor*)
The Prince of Wales opens Mercury's Youth Enterprise Centre
David Price (*author's photograph*)
Cartoon of David Price (*Paul Hyman*)

Between pages 176 and 177.
Stephen Zimmerman with Nick Faldo
David Rosier (*author's photograph*)
Leonard Licht (*Mike Pattison*)
Andrew Dalton (*author's photograph*)
Cartoon of Andrew Dalton (*Paul Hyman*)
Leon Levy (*author's photograph*)
PSD and Hugh Stevenson (*Warburgs' newsletter*)
Brian Lara, sporting his Mercury outfit (*Allsport Photographic Ltd*)
David Scholey, PSD and Hugh Stevenson at Templeton College,
  Oxford
Hugh Stevenson, Carol Galley and Stephen Zimmerman
Herb Allison and Carol Galley (*Mercury's newsletter*)
David Komansky and Hugh Stevenson (*Mercury's newsletter*)
Satvinder Maan (*author's photograph*)
33 King William Street (*Paula McColl*)

INTRODUCTION

There's no business like show business, and no business which is not in some way a branch of show business. In this respect, business is not very different from Parliament, the judiciary, the church, the military, the monarchy or professional wrestling.

So it was that on 19 February 1998, David Komansky, chairman of the giant investment banking firm Merrill Lynch, hosted a reception for 1400 people in the grand hall of Earls Court in south-west London. Full-page advertisements in the newspapers that morning had heralded the occasion with a picture of the sun rising behind the planet Mercury and the caption 'Merrill Lynch on aligning with Mercury'. It was a multimedia extravaganza with morale-boosting speeches, giant screens, laser-beamed lights and funny hats. Acrobats, clowns, jugglers and stiltwalkers mingled with members of Mercury Asset Management and Merrill Lynch as they drank champagne to celebrate the purchase of Mercury by Merrill Lynch for £3.2 billion, or about $5 billion ($5000 million).

For Mercury it marked the beginning of a new era, and the culmination of some fifty years of hard work, joyous successes and bitter disappointments. I wondered what the ascetic and eccentric founder of Mercury, Sir Siegmund Warburg, would have made of it all. He was not unknown for a certain type of theatrical behaviour himself, but he was not one for celebrations, or 'stupid cocktail parties' as he called them.

When I was appointed Mercury's chairman in 1979, he said to me, 'Your first task as chairman, Peter, is to get rid of it.' Mercury was then the investment management arm of the merchant bank which carried his name, S.G. Warburg & Co. (usually referred to as Warburgs) and was called Warburg Investment Management (WIM). In his eyes it had become an embarrassing and worthless appendage which damaged the elitist reputation of his bank, and he had lost patience with it. It was Warburgs' Cinderella. 'I don't care what you get for it,' he said. 'You can give it away.'

Fortunately, no one seemed to want Cinderella* then. The business grew, and Mercury became a separate and partly independent company in 1987 when Warburgs sold 25 per cent of Mercury's shares through the London Stock Exchange. It achieved full independence in 1995 following the sale of Warburgs to Swiss Bank Corporation, and the price at which Mercury was now being sold to Merrill Lynch was nearly four times that paid by Swiss Bank Corporation for Warburgs itself.

There were many people who contributed to this fairy tale, and certainly a number who played a more important role in it than I did. But, as a director from the first day of WIM's incorporation in 1969 until Mercury's last as an independent company in 1998, and as chairman from 1979 to 1992, I had an unrivalled front-row seat throughout. It was indeed the stuff of theatre much of the time, a mixture of comedy and tragedy interspersed with a touch of farce and the occasional descent into pantomime. Experienced entertainers realise the value of theatre as a medium for communication; we had a number of them and at least one who might have been nominated for an Oscar.

*

The key player was, of course, Siegmund Warburg, without whom Mercury would never have existed. As a member of the management committee of Warburgs, I had every opportunity to observe this endlessly fascinating person over a number of years. His legendary achievement in building from scratch, in one generation, London's most successful and feared merchant bank has been thoroughly documented in numerous newspaper and magazine articles, in several books and even in a rather less than accurate French television series which the Warburg family attempted unsuccessfully

* Other analogous characters for Mercury might have been Hans Christian Andersen's Ugly Duckling which became a beautiful swan, and Little Orphan Annie, heroine of a popular American strip cartoon that first appeared in 1924. Annie's guardian and mentor was Daddy Warbucks, whom I was for a while tempted to believe could have been based on one of the rich socialite American Warburgs of that period. However, despite the Broadway musical *Annie* in the late 1970s and the 1984 film of the same name that starred Albert Finney as Daddy Warbucks, and a revival of the musical in London in 1998, Annie is less known in the UK than in the US. Moreover, while Daddy Warbucks had some qualities in common with Siegmund Warburg – affection for children, kindness, financial acumen, power and dynamism – he was very different in other respects. Warbucks was right-wing, he was an industrialist and he was new money.

to prevent from being shown. I have tried to avoid straying into such well-covered territory in the pages that follow.

Assessments of his character, on the other hand, have seemed to me to be wide of the mark. Jacques Attali, luxury-loving socialist and adviser to President Mitterrand, better known perhaps as the first head of the European Bank for Reconstruction and Development who spent more on the bank's lavish fittings than he gave out in loans, wrote a biography of Siegmund Warburg in 1984. It was titled *A Man of Influence* and, although it was unauthorised, was largely hagiographical. His acquaintance with his subject was brief, and his book was full of errors and was not taken seriously by anyone who knew Siegmund.

In a highly readable 800-page epic history of the Warburg family, *The Warburgs* (1993), Ron Chernow examined Siegmund's character in minute detail. Chernow never met Siegmund, but his research was comprehensive and he conducted a large number of interviews with former members of the bank. Some of these, however, had scores to settle. The impression left by Chernow was of a neurotic and tempestuous dictator plagued by internal demons and given to vindictiveness, machiavellian manipulation and explosive tantrums. As Henry Grunfeld, Siegmund's most trusted partner and friend commented, you felt from Chernow's book that Siegmund was someone you would not want to meet. Chernow gave too little emphasis to the benevolent and attractive side of Siegmund's character. Ironically, the Warburg family and the senior people at Warburgs gave full co-operation to Ron Chernow, but withheld it from the more favourably disposed Attali.

Chernow made amends in a subsequent book, *The Death of the Banker: The Decline and Fall of the Great Financial Dynasties and the Triumph of the Small Investor*, in which he was adulatory about Siegmund Warburg's achievements, and appeared almost to apologise for mentioning that some people found him devious.

Two former senior directors of Warburgs have written about Siegmund in books that came out in 1998. In *I Spy: The Secret Life of a British Agent*, an account of his father's life in espionage, Geoffrey Elliott refers to his days 'under the watchful, hooded eye of Sir Siegmund Warburg'. His comments are amusingly scurrilous but hardly friendly, although he does concede Siegmund's 'moody but mercurial' genius. A more even portrayal is given by Peter Spira in his engaging memoir *Ladders and Snakes*. As a one-time heir apparent in Warburgs who fell out of favour with Siegmund, Spira had every reason to feel aggrieved by him, but he is wise enough to have seen that Siegmund's qualities of generosity and creativeness outweighed his obvious flaws.

In a delightful memoir, *Footfalls in Memory*, published privately in Canada in late 1998, Tony Griffin writes even-handedly about his thirty-year friendship with Siegmund. He describes him as a gifted personality with a volatile temperament who had an 'exotic air about him'. Griffin noted also his capacity to blow hot and cold on people, but he had a great admiration for Siegmund, and writes warmly of the debt he owes to his memory.

Siegmund Warburg himself did not publish any memoirs. He did, however, write a number of autobiographical notes and essays, which, as far as I know, were never circulated, some under the title 'Expensive Lessons'. These are revealing about his childhood, his fierce German patriotism – which initially took precedence over his traditional Judaism, but finally gave way to disillusion – his attitude to Jews and Jewishness, his attachment to England and the British, his time working for N.M. Rothschild & Co. in the 1920s, his leftish and somewhat idealistic political views and his precocious but justified fears as a young man for the future of civilisation in Germany. Honest as these surely were – they show only too clearly his inability to hide his chronic worrying and introspection – such musings inevitably suffer from an unconscious wish on the part of the writer to present himself as he wants to be seen, and in his case, they fall far short of giving a complete picture.

It would be presumptuous of me to believe I could put the record straight as to the nature of such a complicated person, nor has this been my intention, but in setting out my impressions I have tried to balance the shade in his personality with the sometimes less obvious light. My feelings may have been influenced by my having got to know Siegmund well only in his later years, when he had mellowed to some extent; my initial apprehension of him changed gradually to a warm if wary affection and a deep sense of gratitude for the many occasions when he influenced my life in a helpful direction.

*

The story which follows is, I suppose, mainly a business story with a corporate rags to riches theme. I have preferred, however, to think of it in terms of the human aspects. My aim has been to write a deliberately subjective, somewhat intimate, occasionally confessional and frequently anecdotal memoir describing the principal characters inside and outside Warburgs and Mercury Asset Management who had a part in the formation, growth and ultimate sale of Mercury. If my account is often superficial, I take refuge in the saying that if something is worth doing, it's worth doing superficially.

The story of Mercury was punctuated by many unexpected incidents, some happy and others less so, in every instance brought about by the actions of people, whether by design, neglect, dishonesty or arrogance. I have described such events only where I know about them through some degree of personal involvement. I have not sought to write a complete history of Mercury, or to rectify gaps in my knowledge about certain periods of its life, including a ten-year stretch from 1968 to 1977 when I was engaged either full time or part time in other areas of Warburgs' business.

Siegmund Warburg would not, I feel, have been at all happy with the sudden, and still largely unexplained, sale in 1995 of Warburgs to a quietly jubilant Swiss Bank Corporation for a price no more than the value of its tangible assets, even though, at the time of the sale, it was not generally known that Swiss Bank Corporation had become richer through holding gold seized by the Nazis from German Jews. Swiss Bank Corporation thus paid not a penny for the Warburg name, which it wisely continues to use today in Warburg Dillon Read, or for a reputation which had been built through sixty years of sweat and toil since the firm's foundation in 1934 as the New Trading Company. I was no longer an insider in Warburgs in 1995, although I was recalled to its board in the final stages of the sale for a brief period which included the last board meeting. I have, however, been unable to resist venturing some observations on the virtual demise of the Warburgs we once knew.

It was my intention to focus mainly on the large number of unforgettable people whose paths I crossed in a 42-year career in Warburgs and Mercury. I have found that some lapses into autobiography have been almost unavoidable in providing an element of continuity in what might otherwise have become a recital of disjointed events involving unconnected people, and in explaining the perspective from which I viewed things. I hope this indulgence will be forgiven.

*

To avoid tedious repetition, I have generally referred to Sir Siegmund Warburg as Siegmund, the name that he invited a number of us to call him from quite an early stage of acquaintanceship despite a considerable age gap – a practice which was not quite so common thirty years ago as it is today. I have used the designation Warburgs to describe both the original merchant bank, S.G. Warburg & Co., and the publicly quoted holding company which owned it, S.G. Warburg Group, which, confusingly, was previously called Mercury Securities. In its early days, Mercury Asset Management was known successively as the investment department (of Warburgs), the investment division and Warburg Investment Management, and I have used these designations, or occasionally just Cinderella, in covering the period up to 1985. Thereafter, Mercury Asset Management is described as Mercury in preference to its more colloquially and frequently used designation of MAM. I have always felt that the acronym had overtones of subservience and maternalism which came uncomfortably close at times to the reality of the relationship between Mercury and Warburgs.

PART ONE
Old Warburgs

CHAPTER 1

A Visitor to Canada

I first met Siegmund Warburg in 1957 in Canada, a country he didn't really like much, perhaps because he felt he had been snubbed in the once proudly gentile, but nowadays more politically sensitive Toronto Club, which he visited as a lunch guest. He made a striking impression in the rather provincial atmosphere of Toronto's Bay Street financial community of the 1950s with his British clothes, European manners and German accent.

His reputation as the financier to watch in the City of London preceded him, and I had done a little extra homework. I knew that he was always immaculately dressed, usually in a dark-blue suit with well-polished black shoes (brown shoes were frowned upon in his circle, and so were brown suits, let alone green ones – the worst crime of all was to wear brown shoes with a blue suit). If he wore an overcoat, it was black, and he sometimes had a Homburg hat of the same colour pulled down at a rakish angle. His complexion was sallow, his hair dark then, and his sharp eyes seemed to penetrate right through you.

He had a magnetic charm and was always courteous except in moments of anger. He treated everyone, whatever their role in life, with equal civility. He was meticulous in preparation and precise both in speech and in writing. He disliked sloppy punctuation and all abbreviations, and would not have been happy with my frequent use in this book of three-letter acronyms (TLAs). He was rarely late for an appointment, unless he was trying to make a point of putting some less than wholly welcome visitor in his place, and he was seldom early; he believed that arriving more than a minute before a meeting was due to start gave the impression that you didn't have enough to do. And, despite a powerful self-discipline, he had a fearsome temper that could erupt without warning.

His banking firm, Warburgs, was still viewed with suspicion by many people in the City of London then; it was seen by the City establishment as an upstart, even as a bit of a credit risk. 'I'd be careful if I were you', a well-regarded lawyer to whom I had mentioned that I wanted to work for the firm said to me. 'What will it look like on your curriculum vitae if they go bust?' This reaction made me even keener to join.

A few years earlier, under the leadership of a supremely charming and internationally minded Canadian, Tony Griffin, Warburg had started what he described as a 'financial laboratory' in Canada with initial capital of $1 million. He always liked to have prestigious partners, and for the Canadian venture he had brought in Helbert Wagg, a British merchant bank subsequently taken over by Schroders; Kuhn Loeb, a top-drawer American investment banking firm with close Warburg family connections of which he was himself a partner; Lehman Brothers, another eminent Wall Street firm; and some Canadian individuals. The company was called Triarch, and it engaged in a modest way in corporate advisory activities and investment management for a few clients.

The largest investment client was the Trust and Loan Company of Canada, which had been formed in 1842, very old by Canadian standards, to lend money on mortgage to British immigrants settling farms in Upper and Lower Canada (later Ontario and Quebec) and in the prairie provinces. As time went by, mortgages were paid off or farms were repossessed, and by the 1950s the company, which had changed its name to the Toronto and London Investment Company, was an investment trust with assets of around $15 million (probably the equivalent of about ten times that amount today). We called it T and L.

The shares of T and L were quoted on the London Stock Exchange and traded for a while at minus values (i.e. you were paid to buy the shares) because of the company's right to call up more money from its shareholders. In the early 1950s, Warburgs had bought a controlling position in the company and had passed the management responsibility to Triarch. Now Triarch was looking for an investment manager, and I was a candidate for the job.

I had gone to Canada in early 1957 to join some friends from Oxford who were already there, and in search of my own eldorado. I travelled by sea to New York on the *Queen Elizabeth* in steerage with Jeremy Pinckney – we will come to his eldorado shortly – and thence by train on my own to Toronto via Lachine, Quebec.* I was

---

* So named because the French explorer Champlain thought he had reached China when he

working in a small investment management and advisory company in Toronto which published a weekly newsletter, to which from the very first days of my employment I was contributing a column of investment advice on Canadian oil stocks. Since I had no qualifications whatsoever for this assignment, it has made me cynical ever since as to the level of expertise contained in many investment advisory and research reports.

Anxious to improve my scant knowledge of the oil industry and its investment prospects, I frequently found myself working beyond the 9 a.m. to 5 p.m. work day which most other employees of the company appeared to find congenial and to observe rather precisely. One day the boss came to my desk at about 5.15 p.m. and asked me why I was staying late, reminding me that he paid me to work only from 9 until 5. This came as something of a surprise in the light of a memorandum he had sent me sometime earlier, from which the following is an extract:

> This year will be a more difficult one for the financial community and our firm will be no exception. Under the circumstances we shall be forced to pay more attention to punctuality and absenteeism than we have done in the past. We are prepared to overlook occasional tardiness and sickness has been more prevalent than usual this winter.
>
> Your record is as follows:–
>
> In the past 15 working days you have lost 78 minutes through lack of punctuality. This is the equivalent of 1,480 minutes in a working year of 287 days. This is the equivalent of $3\frac{1}{2}$ working days.
>
> We would appreciate a greater effort on your part to be punctual and to be at your desk ready to work at 9 a.m. and at 1.30 p.m.
>
> Your co-operation will be appreciated.

Soon after my encounter with the boss, another Englishman working in the company, who was later to become a junior minister in James Callaghan's Labour government and is now a member of the House of Lords, received similar guidance from him not to stay beyond 5 p.m. Sharing my curiosity as to the reason for our employer's unusual attitude, and having rather more nerve than I, he locked himself in the office lavatory one evening and sneaked out of it at 5.30 p.m. to see if there was some hidden agenda. Peering into

arrived there at the end of the sixteenth century.

the open-plan office, he observed our boss in an intimate encounter with his female vice-president on an office table. Years later I learnt that, where a similar act had been witnessed in a London stockbrokers' office, the table in question was thereafter called 'the yield table'. At the time, it seemed such an improbable occurrence that we found it funny. Now, however, it is apparently commonplace. According to *The Guardian* in 1999, a poll showed that 28 per cent of men interviewed and 13 per cent of women had had sexual encounters in the office. The preferred location is their own desk, but failing that, the boss's desk will do.

*

I responded readily when Tony Griffin asked me one day to come round for an interview with Siegmund Warburg, who was in Toronto for a short visit. Tony, today an elegant and extremely amusing octogenarian still actively skiing and playing a fine game of tennis (though slightly less reliable golf), had been recruited by Siegmund from the Canadian Department of External Affairs. When I arrived in Canada I had a letter of introduction to him from Alfred Wagg, a senior partner of Helbert Wagg and a gentleman who saw it as his duty to be helpful to young people embarking on their careers – a characteristic, incidentally, which was shared by both Siegmund Warburg and Tony Griffin.

Tony knew of my keen interest in the job of investment manager at Triarch, and here was my opportunity. I had already met Ernest Thalmann, a taciturn but, as I subsequently discovered, delightful person who was one of Siegmund's early partners in London. Like Siegmund, Thalmann was a German Jewish refugee living in England. He interviewed me in the sitting room of his suite at the Royal York Hotel in Toronto, then the tallest building in the British Commonwealth, in a silk dressing gown, thus giving a fleeting impression of Noel Coward until I learnt that he was confined to his room with a cold. His wife, Edith, whom I later came to know very well, found an excuse to come into the room so that she could have a look at me too.

Thalmann asked me if I was a chartered accountant, which I was not, and whether I was an investment analyst, which, supposedly at least, I was. He then questioned how I could possibly be an investment analyst if I was not a chartered accountant. I was stumped for an answer to what seemed to indicate an unrealistic expectation of investment analysts, who were then a lowlier breed than accountants and were generally either not clever enough or not patient enough to want to study accountancy for five years. I clearly failed to convince Ernest Thalmann that I was the right man for the job, but he kept the door open and it was decided I should meet Siegmund Warburg on his next visit to Toronto.

*

A trim figure then, in his mid-fifties, Siegmund Warburg eyed me intently. He greeted me with old-fashioned courtesy, expressing not altogether convincing gratitude that I was taking the time to see him. It did little to calm my nerves. There was not much small talk thereafter, and he seemed diffident and may even have been a little shy in those days. He invited me to suggest a Canadian investment that would do well over the next few years. I blurted out the name of some rather speculative Canadian oil company which he had never heard of, and immediately regretted it.

He then asked me what I had been reading lately. It was a question he put to everyone he interviewed, but I was not forewarned. I must have given a pretty unintelligent response because the books and magazines I read at that time were mostly low-brow and frivolous, but his question provoked me afterwards to do something about my reading habits in case he was ever to ask me again. I became a committed reader, and this is one of many things for which I am grateful to him. I was nevertheless surprised, and relieved, when in an interview that Siegmund gave more than twenty years later to *Institutional Investor*, a sort of parish magazine of the international investment banking world, he described me as 'extremely well read', together with David Scholey, later to be my chairman at Warburgs, and Martin Gordon, an orientalist who is one of the world's greatest exponents of the art of remembering birthdays.

This was a gross exaggeration in my case, and the sort of deliberate flattery in which he might indulge when you were in favour. However, once again it spurred me to greater efforts to justify his comments, and I started to read more of one of the novelists he liked best, Anthony Trollope. I had become addicted to business stories and biographies, which were not quite what Siegmund had in mind, but I found that they often contained a huge amount of practical wisdom for anyone making a career in the investment business. I was to discover that one of the best business stories of all is Trollope's *The Way We Live Now*, published in 1873, which should be essential reading for anyone who needs to be reminded that there is nothing new in the realm of human nature or trickery. Greed, wickedness and, above all, gullibility are just some of the qualities exemplified in Trollope's tale which feature prominently in the real world of business today.

Siegmund himself was a voracious reader at a loftier level and in several different languages, and he often gave books as presents. Other than Trollope, some of the writers he liked best where Thomas Mann, George Eliot, Dickens, Balzac, Tolstoy, Stendhal, Shaw and Ibsen. He also enjoyed biographies and history. Books on economics bored him.

Despite my stumbling responses, Siegmund offered me a job 'in my London bank', which was not what I was looking for then. He appeared unimpressed that I wanted to remain longer in Canada. I found this disappointing because his initiative in starting a financial business in Toronto suggested a favourable view of the opportunities there, while my own wish to stay at least demonstrated, I thought, a desire to learn about business in a capitalist society rather than in the environment of high taxation and excessive red tape then prevailing in the UK. I hoped he might commend my attitude, but it was not so. He was a committed internationalist, and I am sure he felt, with some justice, that London, for all its faults and despite the exchange controls which inhibited British investment overseas until 1979, was likely to remain a much more important international financial centre than Toronto.

*

Finally, having given Tony Griffin my word that I would remain in Canada for at least five years, I got the job I wanted in Triarch in the summer of 1958. Tony had observed that a number of Englishmen came to Canada in the 1950s for a year or so, only to return home after some useful training at someone else's expense – a trend that was exemplified by a number of my own friends who were there at the time.

From their point of view, at least, their Canadian experience appeared to help them in their subsequent careers. Alick Rankin became chairman of Scottish and Newcastle Breweries, Oliver Fox-Pitt started a successful brokerage firm specialising in American bank and insurance investments, and James Rockley became chairman of

Kleinwort Benson. John Craven, who came to Canada around the time I was leaving in 1963, was later chairman of Morgan Grenfell and then occupied the hot seat at Lonrho (renamed Lonmin in 1999). Tim Renton became a member of the House of Commons and Chief Whip during Mrs Thatcher's government, and was later a member of the House of Lords. Jeremy Pinckney took control of a company called J.H. Vavasseur ('Vava-who?' to some), whose shares had a meteoric rise, enabling him to own for a while Trafalgar (pronounced with the emphasis on the third syllable), a beautiful eighteenth-century mansion in Wiltshire. John Abell, Angus Ivory, Chris Taylor-Young and Gurth Hoyer Millar were others who had successful careers after their return to the United Kingdom. I hope there was, after all, some reflected glory for those who gave them jobs in Canada, and in one or two cases more tangible reciprocation too.

Another friend, David Scholey, was in Canada working for a Lloyd's insurance broker. I had known David at Oxford, where he was one of a small group who organised late evening roulette games. I was an usher at his wedding in Ottawa in 1960. His attractive and artistic bride, Sandra, was the daughter of George Drew, who had been Canada's High Commissioner in London. The Canadian Prime Minister, John Diefenbaker, was a guest at the wedding. Diefenbaker, who sometimes had the appearance of a startled turkey, was a radical anti-Establishment conservative from western Canada, with the manner of an evangelical preacher, who presided over a generally constructive period in Canada's economic development from 1957 until 1965.

David Scholey has a phenomenal memory. He also shares with me an instinct for collecting trivial and useless information about all sorts of matters, including American sports. What other Englishman, I wonder, can tell you the last occasion when a 'bases-loaded in the park homer' was hit in a professional baseball game? I used to visit the Maple Leaf Gardens in Toronto to watch ice hockey and, more shamingly, a carefully choreographed entertainment described as professional wrestling. One evening, I took David with me to see the latter, an eye-opener then into an aspect of North American culture.

Many years later, to my astonishment, David was able to remember the names of the wrestlers: Whipper Billy Watson; Koko Bonk Brazil (whose name confusingly referred to no more than an inclination to butt with the head); Haystacks Humphrey, who weighed 600 pounds (no known connection with the British wrestler of a later generation with similar dimensions, Giant Haystacks, 'the gentle giant'); Lord Atholl Layton of Surrey, England, who was accompanied into the ring by his butler Seymour carrying a silver tray with a pot of tea; Little Beaver, a pugilistic midget; and Gorgeous George with his peroxide hair and ambiguous body language.*

Although the amount of money I began looking after at Triarch, some $25 million altogether, was not large by today's standards, even after adjusting for inflation, I was the sole investment manager and I had to learn fast. I was courted by all sorts of stockbrokers who believed that Warburgs' laboratory in Canada was bound to grow. One of these was an old timer who had entered the business at the time of the 1929 crash – an experience that had moulded his outlook on investments for ever. 'I wouldn't touch stocks if I were you – much too scary; stay with bonds.' He was not alone in this view – stocks in those days yielded more than bonds, reflecting a perception of greater risk, and this situation was not reversed for a few more years. Happily for me, my colleagues at Triarch advised me to pay no attention.

I did not see much of Siegmund Warburg during the next three or four years. He was a director of T and L, but he never liked board meetings and seldom came to any during the five years I managed T and L's portfolio in Canada. From time to time, I received a letter from him out of the blue commenting in fulsome terms on some not very consequential comment I had made in one of my weekly investment commentaries. I was to find out that this was one of his ways of letting you know he was keeping an eye on you.

---

* No doubt David has followed, as I have, the arrival of the wrestling world in the realms of government with the election of Jesse ('the Body') Ventura as Governor of Minnesota in 1998. The Body used to enter the ring wearing lycra and a pink feather boa. Now, as Governor, he wants lower taxes and legalised marijuana, which may or may not explain the 'pot-luck lunch' he gave on New Year's Day, 1999.

CHAPTER 2

A Phantom Offer

Toronto in the 1950s had not yet fully escaped from its Calvinistic heritage. There were no Sunday newspapers, and more worryingly for someone who came from London, restaurants were not allowed to serve alcoholic drinks – not even a glass of wine. We had to look for other forms of entertainment.

At lunch times I would sometimes go to the street-level offices of a brokerage firm dealing in penny mining stocks, named T. A. Richardson and Sons. One of the attractions was a team of decorative mini-skirted young women who chalked up the prices of shares from an elevated gallery in a large open pit, where we would stand and watch. I met a young broker there, Bert Applegath, a smooth talker with an urbane style, who advised me to buy shares in something called New Mylamaque Mines, which were selling at 39 cents a share. It had a promising copper prospect and the shares were sure to double.

From Bert I learnt a great deal about the manipulation of penny mining stocks by stock 'promoters'. They would patiently accumulate shares of their chosen company when the price was languishing at a low level as a result of investors' disillusionment from a previous run-up. This phase was followed by the announcement of the acquisition of some new mining claims in a distant part of frozen northern Canada. The next step was the issue of options on the shares at current and higher prices to one or more brokerage houses, to give them an incentive to recommend the shares to their clients, and thereafter the spreading of rumours about promising core assays with highly prospective amounts of gold or copper.

The share prices sometimes multiplied several times during this process without any genuine or substantive reason, and the promoters sold their own shares before the truth materialised that the assays had, after all, proved uneconomic. The public investor – the mug punter, you might say – ended up holding shares that were once again worthless. It was a pattern repeated over and over, but somehow the punters were always there to be taken for the next ride. It was much worse than a casino game because the odds were heavily stacked against the outsider.

Bert Applegath liked to think he could outsmart the promoters by keeping in contact with them and trying to anticipate their moves, but his ambition was to become a promoter himself. He had me in and out of New Mylamaque several times, sometimes with a small profit, but more often with a somewhat larger loss. On one of the occasions when we were briefly in profit, he invited me to a barbecue dinner with his beautiful Mexican wife and suggested we all go for a holiday at a house he owned in Zihuatanejo, on the Pacific coast of Mexico. Unfortunately, or perhaps fortunately, I was denied this experience by another collapse in New Mylamaque shares.

I soon learnt that my attempts to get rich quickly were proving counter-productive. I had been gambling in all sorts of shares, not just the penny mines, with far too little understanding and not much success. By contrast, the money that we managed for our clients, including T and L, was invested conservatively, and I could hardly fail to notice that it seemed to perform much better than my own far riskier investments.

Speculation – by definition, short term in nature – may be all right for some, but I was beginning to realise that, for my temperament, stocks of companies with good management and prospects of growth that you expected to hold for a very long time were the place to be. As Warren Buffett, the much acclaimed American investor, has put it, the best way to get rich is very slowly. These were useful lessons which it took me a while to absorb fully, but my experiences put me on guard against excessive claims of future profits, which are still commonplace today in some areas of the stock market. Although ethical standards have improved and regulation has been tightened, manipulation of share prices, usually intentional but sometimes naively unintentional, has not been and never will be eliminated.

Many years later, I learnt that Bert Applegath was the main promoter of a mining company called New Cinch Mines, whose shares rose from $2 to $29 in two weeks in November 1980 before it transpired that its assays had been contaminated (or 'salted'), whereupon the price collapsed. An employee of the assay laboratory in Texas who knew of the salting was murdered, but the crime was never solved. Applegath denied any knowledge of these happenings, and indeed I found it hard to conceive that the nice Mr Applegath with his sweet wife and his Mexican hideaway could have been involved in such goings on.

*

My main contact in the investment department at Warburgs in London was Julian Earl, with whom I was required to exchange weekly notes on investment matters. Communication was by mail, or occasionally by the more expensive route of telex, the long superseded predecessor of fax. International telephoning, while theoretically possible, was in reality useless. Calls from Canada to London took hours to get through and were frequently cut off, and it was usually difficult to hear the person at the other end. It was not until 1960 that Xerox introduced the first dry photocopier (Xerox's sales increased more than ten times in the next five years). Before that we had to make carbon copies of everything that was typed; it was a cumbersome and dirty task for the secretaries.

Julian was supposed to keep an eye on my ideas for the portfolio of T and L in which Warburgs clients held the majority of the shares. I thus became a *de facto* member of the investment department of Warburgs in London, which I visited for the first time in late 1958 in its offices at 8–13 King William Street. My recollection is of a sparsely decorated room with about half a dozen people seated at austerely handsome leather-covered tables that served as desks. They were managing money for private clients and one or two small investment trusts. Corporate pension funds did not become clients for investment management until about a decade later; they were mostly managed in those days by insurance companies or by the company's own finance director, and were substantially invested in government bonds, known in the UK as gilts.

Julian, who was a great-nephew of Somerset Maugham, was one of the fund managers. An Etonian with a languid manner, he was an expert on wine and opera who on occasion led the booing at Covent Garden, and was also an accomplished skier and golfer. As an investor, he was original but erratic, something of a gambler and sometimes too confident in his strongly held opinions. He was an early believer in the talents of George Soros, and a director of Soros's Quantum Fund from its inception. Julian left Warburgs before I joined it in London in 1963, and sadly he died young.

Ernest Thalmann took a fatherly interest in my progress and looked after me on my London visits. I was in his office one day when he heard the unmistakable and slightly uneven footsteps of Siegmund Warburg coming down the corridor. He was in some awe of Siegmund, who by then disapproved of smoking (he had been an occasional smoker). He hastily stubbed out his cigarette in an ashtray which he kept for just such a circumstance in a drawer in his desk. Unfortunately he did not quite complete the task, and a minute or so later, smoke started coming from the drawer. 'Ernest, I think your desk is on fire', Siegmund commented with some enjoyment.

It was a loss when Ernest Thalmann, never in robust health, died at the age of 64, a year before my return to London. Together with Henry Grunfeld and Eric Korner, he was one of the 'uncles' – a designation given to Siegmund's older partners who kept on coming into the office and seemed likely to do so indefinitely. We referred to him as Uncle Ernest, while the uncles addressed each other by their surnames. I remained in close touch with his widow, Edith, until she died at 93 in 1986. She was a generous and amusing hostess and a helpful interpreter to me of Warburg ways and wiles.

*

Jet travel between Europe and North America only began on a regular basis in about 1960. Until then a traveller had to take a five- or six-day ocean voyage from Southampton to Montreal or New York. Appropriately coinciding with the arrival of the jet age, the responsibility within Warburgs for Triarch passed to Ronnie Grierson, Siegmund's confidant and jester and a consummate networker. Ronnie is one of the more colourful characters in the Warburgs story. If there were Guinness Book of Records prizes for long distance travel, long distance telephoning or the number of people known personally, he would hold all three. I once took him to a cocktail party in Toronto given by friends of mine, at which there were some fifty to sixty people present of whom I knew a handful. Ronnie was able to tell me at dinner afterwards that he had spoken to all of them, and he could recount each of their names and what they did. Moreover, I am sure he remembered it all years later.

Ronnie is a kind man with great charm and a fund of amusing stories and observations. However, he is allergic to airline staff, which is unfortunate for one who is a member of the intellectual jet set and travels as much as he does. In his memoir, A Truant Disposition, published in 1992, there is a photograph of him engaged in heated discussion with a policeman who had just prevented him from lying down on the runway to stop an aircraft taking off on a flight he had missed.

Many years later, he and I were travelling together one day from Chicago to New York in first class. The stewardess came round to ask passengers their names and their choice of drink. Ronnie clearly resented the intrusion into his reading and his privacy. I gave my surname and first name, as requested by the stewardess, whereupon the following conversation ensued between her and Ronnie who continued to look at his newspaper throughout:

STEWARDESS: Can I have your name please, sir?
GRIERSON: Closet.
STEWARDESS: And may I have your first name please, Mr Closet?
GRIERSON: Water.
STEWARDESS: And what would you like to drink after take off?
GRIERSON: Water, please.

I was not entirely surprised to see a tabloid newspaper headline in 1995: 'Raging GEC tycoon Sir Ron is thrown off plane.' Apparently Ronnie, then vice chairman of General Electric Company (GEC) and knighted for his services to the South Bank theatre complex, had refused to sit in the seat assigned to him and had created a noisy scene. 'I fly off the handle', he explained to the paper afterwards. 'My wife claimed I did not go to English public school long enough to learn how to bear frustration.'

Now in his mid-seventies, Ronnie remains active in business and socially, and has a travel schedule that would exhaust most people half his age. He said recently that he gets 'frightfully annoyed' when someone asks him, 'Are you *still* skiing?' In 1998, he was described teasingly by his friend Barry Humphreys, in his guise as Dame Edna Everage, with whom he was working on a charity performance, as 'that appalling social bulldozer and card-carrying menace'.

*

My job at Triarch continued to provide me with a useful investment education, which increased exponentially with the New York stock market collapse of 1962, known as Blue Monday. One of our close colleagues in the investment banking firm Kuhn Loeb in New York, a man with considerable experience of the market, was in despair as prices tumbled, but when I went into my boss Tony Griffin's office at the end of the afternoon and told him how much the market had fallen, Tony sat back, paused to reflect for a moment and just laughed. This was not because he had anticipated the crash or had sold his own investments – he had not. It was his way of keeping the event in perspective. I am sure it was the right way to react.

It was a useful lesson and it helped me to view with some equanimity subsequent market collapses such as those in 1974, 1987 and 1998. Depressing as it is to stand by helplessly and see the prices of your shares tumbling day by day, the correct investment response to a market crash, I learnt, is to do nothing. Neither a seller nor a buyer be. Don't sell – it's too late. Don't buy – you'll have sleepless nights. And most of all, don't let it get to you. Don't let it disturb your night out at the opera. Sooner or later the market will recover.

I also discovered that some people lie about their investments as others do about their sporting or sexual prowess. The day after Blue Monday there was a board meeting of T and L, at which I had to tell the board that our portfolio had suffered a sharp decline in value. One of our London directors, a member of another well-known banking family and a seasoned market player, castigated me in front of the board for my gross stupidity in not anticipating the crash. Any fool could have seen it coming, he said, and he had sold everything except his government bonds. The same day he attended a dinner party with people I knew, who subsequently told me that late in the evening he had sunk into depression and confessed to them that he had experienced huge losses both for his clients and personally.

*

In 1962 I met Siegmund Warburg again in the offices of Kuhn Loeb in New York. My appetite for joining Warburgs in London had been whetted not only by the exposure I had already had to a number of people in the firm who seemed interesting and friendly, if in several cases unconventional, but also by some graffiti which could not fail to catch my eye in a New York subway car. Someone had written in crude black paint, 'Warburgs financed the Russian Revolution'.

The fantasy of an international Jewish conspiracy, with the Rothschilds and the Warburgs at the heart of it, has been around since the 1920s and persists to this day. In the 1960s, a Ku Klux Klan leader named Shelton, who was at least a Grand Dragon if not the Imperial Wizard of the order, contrived to blame the Bolshevik Revolution in 1917, the great depression of the 1930s, two world wars and the assassination of President Kennedy on 'the international concern of Kuhn and Loeb and their interests in England and Switzerland and so forth'. The American Civil War, according to Shelton, had been financed by the Rothschilds.*

In a paperback book entitled *None Dare Call it Conspiracy*, published in 1971, a writer named Gary Allen introduced a new twist by accusing the Warburgs of helping to finance Adolf Hitler – a neat reversal of the Nazi propaganda of the 1930s – and stated categorically that Max Warburg had financed Lenin and the Bolshevik Revolution.

A similar theme was propagated once again in the early 1980s by Lyndon LaRouche, a deluded but well-financed former Marxist and US presidential candidate. LaRouche and his supporters were much in evidence at the International Monetary Fund and World Bank meetings in Toronto in 1982. Their particular target of hate was Henry Kissinger, whom they accused, improbably, of homosexuality. A copy of LaRouche's organisational diagram of perceived conspirators, which was shown in an article in the *Observer* in October 1982, included some unlikely collaborators, such as the British royal family, Mrs Thatcher, Gianni Agnelli and Siegmund Warburg. (In 1998, LaRouche was publishing a journal, *Executive Intelligence Review*, which claimed that the Queen was the world's top drug dealer and by 1999 he had a conspiracy website.)

Currently, Louis Farakhan, leader of the Nation of Islam, who arranged the Million Man March in Washington in 1995 to protest discrimination against blacks in the US, has called Hitler a very great man. He has been banned from entering the UK, but some 200 of Farakhan's followers paraded in Trafalgar Square in 1998 to mark the anniversary of the Million Man March. Farakhan himself is currently laying the blame for many of the world's problems on the Rothschilds and the Warburgs.

In 1962, however, the suggestion of a Warburg-led conspiracy was entirely novel to me, and it was enough to spark a frisson of curiosity. Obviously the firm I hoped soon to join must be even more powerful and mysterious than I could have imagined.

I was excited when Mr Warburg invited me to move back to London to take charge of his investment department, of which he

---

* In the 1990s, the Klan has affected modernisation. Jews are now divided into two categories: ordinary Jews, who are capable of reforming, and those descended from Cain, who are beyond redemption.

was openly critical. In the event, the offer proved to be illusory. When I came to London in late 1963 to take up his offer, I found that someone else still had the job and no one had told that person that a change was contemplated. This, I discovered, was the sort of ploy that Siegmund Warburg used deliberately to create tension and competition among his subordinates.

CHAPTER 3

The Investment Department Chieftains

There can be few starker architectural contrasts than that between Wren's beautiful restored Old Jewry church in Gresham Street in the City of London and the functional office building immediately across the street at number 30, which Siegmund Warburg's most trusted partner, Henry Grunfeld, once described as 'that awful mauve building'. The restoration of the former and the building of the latter took place within a year or so of each other in the late 1950s. Warburgs moved from King William Street into 30 Gresham Street in 1961 and stayed there for the next twenty-four years before moving on to a more substantial, newly built octagonal building, once again in King William Street. This became Mercury's headquarters following its separation from Warburgs in 1987 and remains so today.

My arrival in the mauve building in November 1963 was full of surprises. The first was to discover that Milo Cripps was running the investment department and that he had decided I was to man the North American desk – not quite the assignment that Siegmund Warburg had proposed to me, but one that I nevertheless welcomed when I reflected on my limited experience and ability to take charge of twenty or so prima donnas, most of whom I knew only superficially.

Milo is an intelligent, irreverent and amusing, if complex, person. I had come to know him when he managed the portfolio of a small investment fund that Triarch had formed to enable some of its Canadian clients to invest in European shares. It was widely believed that the character Milo Tindle in Anthony Shaffer's acclaimed play *Sleuth*, later also a film starring Michael Caine and Sir Lawrence Olivier, was based on him – at the time, the unit trusts of a company called Tyndall were managed by Warburgs' investment department, and Milo was the chief individual manager. On my arrival and subsequently, he was politeness itself and clearly had no inkling that Siegmund had offered me his job. In the event, I was glad of Milo's ignorance.

The second surprise, which took a few more days to surface, was to find out that in reality Milo was perhaps not in charge of the department after all, but that there were at least two senior directors, Eric Korner and Gert Whitman, who acted as if they were. It was Eric Korner, I learnt, who had actually started the investment department as a one-man show in 1935. He used to telephone his clients in the evenings so as not to disturb them at work. Warburgs had opened for business in London the previous year under the unexciting and even misleading name of the New Trading Company, which was not changed to S. G. Warburg & Co. until 1946.

Charles Sharp was another senior director who was a member of the investment department. And even that might not be the end of it. In those days, everyone in Warburgs was supposed to take an interest in all of the bank's activities, and there were times when it seemed from their directives to Milo that either Henry Grunfeld or Siegmund Warburg himself might be in charge of the investment department. At least we knew that Peter Spira was not. He had been offered the job before I was, and had turned it down, to the intense fury of Siegmund, on the grounds that it was not his scene and he could do a better job for the bank on the corporate finance side.

*

Eric Korner, an irrepressible and energetic man with a large bald head and a mischievous twinkle in his eye, was a youthful (a word he confusingly pronounced in his heavy Austrian accent as 'useful') 70-year-old. He had been an officer in the Austrian cavalry and then a banker in Berlin before coming to London in 1934. His manners and customs were old-fashioned European. On his first post-war visit to the United States, he put his shoes outside his hotel room to be cleaned as he always did on his frequent visits to Vienna. The next morning, to his horror, he discovered that the hotel had thrown them out.

He made his powerful presence felt both inside and outside the firm; through a mixture of intimidation and charm, he could sell almost any investment idea, often without a full understanding of what it was he was selling. He applied to the selling of shares the principle which Sydney Smith, the nineteenth-century cleric, philosopher and wit, espoused in the reviewing of books: that he 'never read a book before reviewing it: it prejudices a man so'.

We called him Mr Korner and he addressed me, in the old-fashioned manner, by my surname with no prefix. He was one of only three people in the firm who called me 'Darling', the others being Henry Grunfeld and Mary, the tea lady. In her case, the connotation was different, and I was not the only person she greeted in this way. Another was Steve Ross, head of Warner Communications, the entertainment company (now Time Warner), who later achieved some notoriety when his annual bonus was well over $100 million – a figure that seemed preposterous in the climate of twenty years ago. Ross was an engaging person with film star looks and a regal style, who once asked me if I could arrange, whatever the cost, for Heathrow to stay open past midnight so that he could arrive in his private jet.

Steve Ross was in our office one day in the 1970s to tell the London investment community about the prospects for Warner at a lunch which Warburgs was to host and I was to chair. This process was commonly known as a 'roadshow', although one of our American colleagues, Stephen Lash, who had all the American jargon, preferred to call it a 'dog and pony show'. Ross was accompanied by several aides, including his personal coiffeur, and we were meeting to discuss arrangements for the lunch. Mary came into the room and asked Ross if he would like 'some coffee or tea, darlin'?' Ross snapped back, 'Say that again!', whereupon an unnerved Mary apologised and enquired if she had offended our important guest. 'Not a bit', said Steve Ross. 'But I'd like to audition you for a part in my next movie.'

Mr Korner was a lovable character who took an interest in the young and had me to dinner at his flat in Queen's Gate on several occasions. Over the years he had assembled a wonderful collection of medieval illuminated manuscripts at a cost far below that at which they were sold at Sotheby's after his death, and he also had some exquisite pieces of silver, mainly German, from the sixteenth, seventeenth and eighteenth centuries. When it came to the stock market, however, his judgement as an investor did not always match his skill as a salesman. He had a habit of selling too soon any shares that had made a profit, while holding those with losses indefinitely – a pattern which defied both conventional wisdom and common sense, which are not always synonymous in matters of investment strategy. 'That's an old one', he would comment to a client who was seeking an explanation for an investment that had reduced in value to a fraction of its cost, as he rummaged through file drawers for the records of the client's holdings. 'And that's another old one', he would continue as he looked at the next holding, hastily shoving it back in the drawer before finding a less disastrous one on which he could linger.

He had an incomplete understanding of English syntax, and his accent at times perplexed his listeners. Some of us would occasionally tease him in a schoolboyish, but I hope not too unkind, way, and I like to think that with his puckish sense of humour he was aware of it and went along with it. 'What are the news?' he would ask when he came to one of our desks, to which we might reply, 'The news, Mr Korner, are that . . .'

In 1962, Korner had persuaded a number of his banking friends on the Continent to invest in a new offshore fund called Selected Risk Investments with an initial capital of $3 million (subsequently renamed Mercury Selected Trust, it was to become Mercury's flagship offshore fund, and by 1999 its capital had increased to over $6 billion). Siegmund Warburg was its first chairman, but after a while he resigned in favour of Korner – to make way, as he put it rather nicely, 'for a younger man'. Eric Korner was nearly ten years older than Siegmund.

One of my first activities was to join the investment committee of Selected Risk, the other members of which were Eric Korner, Gert Whitman and Milo Cripps. The weekly meetings of the committee were constantly interrupted by telephone calls, which Korner always took, and by discussion of extraneous matters – an experience untypical of most other Warburgs meetings. Because of this, and partly I suspect because he found it hard to take Korner's investment decisions and ideas seriously, Gert Whitman stopped coming to the committee meetings after a while, and sometimes in the afternoons he would instruct the dealers to sell the very shares which Korner had told them to buy for Selected Risk in the morning.

Milo and I soldiered on with the meetings with Eric Korner. One day Korner told us that his son had a school friend, the Nizam (which he pronounced 'Nitsam') of Hyderabad, who, he explained, was what sounded to us like a 'Morehammedan', to which Milo enquired, 'Do you mean as opposed to a Lesshammedan, Mr Korner?'

For a while I used to go once a week in the morning to a hair specialist in Mayfair, grandly labelled a trichologist, who was going to prevent me from going bald. This sometimes made me a bit late for our Selected Risk meetings, and, moreover, on those occasions my hair had a frizzy appearance following a succession of washings and electric shock treatments. Milo knew the signs and remarked, 'Oh, Peter, I see you've been to your hair doctor again.' Korner, greatly intrigued, demanded to hear about it and requested that I should let him know if it worked. However, my hair continued to disappear, and I was unable to recommend him to go for what I notice is now called a trichocheck, let alone to try any trichotherapy. (Recently, when I had my hair cut in a well-known hairdressing establishment in the City and remarked on the high price being charged for a few minutes' work, I was told that part of it was a search fee.)

I had difficulty sometimes understanding Eric Korner's pronunciation of his holiday destinations. He would ask me to take care of some of his clients in his absence. The conversation seemed to my ear to go like this:

KORNER: Darling, I'm going on holiday next week, I'm going to Essen.
PSD: Mr Korner, you can't be going to Essen for a holiday, no one goes to Essen for a holiday.
KORNER: (*Impatiently*) No, Darling, not Essen. Essen.
PSD: Why on earth do you want to go to Essen, Mr Korner?
KORNER: (*Even more impatient*) Not Essen, Essen – where zey have ze Parsenon [Parthenon].

Another holiday destination sounded to me as if it was Pakistan, and we went through the same conversational routine. It turned out to be Bad Gastein.

He also had some original pronunciations for some of the shares he was dealing in. British Oxygen, for example, came out with the 'x' sounding like an 'h', as in the way a Spanish speaker might pronounce Mexico. English Sewing Cotton was English Sueing Cotton, Tennessee Gas was Kelly Cigars and Wilkinson Sword was Wilkinson Sward.

Eric Korner continued to work in Warburgs until he was 87, and he died in 1980 soon after leaving. I missed him and his humour, conscious and unconscious. I also enjoyed his observations on human nature. 'I'm always suspicious', he once said to me, 'when somebody tells me that he has made a lot of money.'

*

Gert Whitman was quite another sort of person, though equally likeable. A German banker before the war, he went to live in the United States, where he worked in Wall Street. He moved to London and joined Warburgs in the late 1950s, and he became one of the designers of the Eurobond market, for which he was inadequately recognised.

He knew the American stock market well. Unfortunately, as with a number of refugees from Nazi persecution, he had a deeply pessimistic view of the world and distrusted the market. We had daily conversations about it, but we could seldom agree because I had by then developed a conviction that one should at all times be fairly fully invested in shares. Market timing, I had discovered, was for the birds.* Several years after we commenced our dialogue on these matters, during which period the stock market had risen 150 per cent or more, it took a sharp tumble one day, falling perhaps 3 or 4 per cent. 'I told you so', Gert rang me to say triumphantly. 'I told you, I warned you, but you wouldn't listen.' Like the proverbial stopped clock that is momentarily correct every twelve hours, the prophet of the market apocalypse will have his moments.

Charles Sharp was an entirely different character. Born Karl Spitz in Austria, he was a gentle and scholarly man with an abundance of wisdom and a well-developed sense of the ridiculous. We all called him Mr Sharp, except the uncles to whom he was just Sharp, and he in turn addressed us formally. When an American broker whom he hardly knew breezily called him Charles, he reacted with 'Mr Sharp will do', and when the bursar of an Oxford college which was a client invited him to call him by his first name, Sharp confessed that he did not know what it was. He continued to come to work beyond retirement age in order, he said with affection, to get away from his wife's hoovering. He told me once that he had been to a reception given by a Japanese bank and found himself 'ze only Englishman in ze whole room'.

Sharp and I shared an office in Gresham Street at one time some years later. One day Siegmund Warburg opened our door, looked in

* I am indebted to Charley Ellis and his brilliant book, *Winning the Loser's Game* (earlier editions were entitled *Investment Strategy*) for the clearest exposition of the perils of market timing judgements. The reality is that no one can predict the market's short-term behaviour. As Yogi Berra, New York Yankees baseball star, famously observed, 'Prediction is dangerous, especially about the future.'

and greeted us with a rather cryptic 'Good morning', and slowly went away again. Perceptively Sharp said to me, 'That's all very well, Mr Darling, but when Mr Warburg says "Good morning" what does he really mean?'

Another member of the small board of Warburgs when I joined was Lord Gladwyn, a distinguished retired diplomat, who as Gladwyn Jebb had been the first (acting) Secretary-General of the United Nations in 1947, then British ambassador to the UN, and later, as Sir Gladwyn, the British ambassador in Paris. An articulate spokesman for western interests as the UK's representative at the UN in the early days of confrontation with the Soviet Union, he became a world figure and briefly ranked above Marilyn Monroe in the popularity league tables in the United States. He sat in the House of Lords as a Liberal, and he was a prominent Europhile and a member of the Establishment if ever there was one. A kind-hearted but rather unworldly person, Gladwyn's understanding of banking and investment matters was minimal, and he gave the impression of one who was disdainful of the City and those who worked in it.

One day, no doubt because he was reminded of the Warburgs rule that he should not entertain lunch guests at 30 Gresham Street on his own, he invited John Morgan, a colleague in the investment department, and me to join him for lunch when his guest was Sir John Russell, who was in between ambassadorial appointments in Ethiopia and Brazil. The conversation throughout lunch was entirely diplomatic gossip, and neither John Morgan nor I said a word. Then, as he lit his cigar, it seemed to occur to Gladwyn that he should bring us into the conversation. Leaning back in his chair, he said, 'Russell, now Morgan here [pointing to me] and Darling here [pointing to Morgan], young men in the investment department, I'm sure they'd be interested in what investments you'd recommend in Ethiopia – would it be shares or bonds or perhaps preference shares?' Sir John tactfully explained that no investments of any type were available in Ethiopia.

CHAPTER 4

The Bus Queue Recruits

Milo Cripps once jokingly told me that Siegmund Warburg recruited fund managers by approaching people in bus queues and asking them if they would like to join his bank's investment department. By contrast, those joining the corporate finance department were likely to be chartered accountants, Jews or Old Wykehamists according to Raymond Bonham Carter, a much loved former colleague who has borne with enormous courage and humour a partial incapacity resulting from an unsuccessful operation. He might have added Scots, and there was also a surprising number of Old Etonians; Siegmund liked to have a few 'English gentlemen' to give a bit of tone and some useful contacts. On the other hand, he did not think much of professional economists, management consultants or business school graduates, who, he considered, came with a built-in arrogance as to their own value.

If the chieftains in the investment department were mostly German or Austrian Jewish émigrés, the fund managers, when I arrived in 1963, were an equally eccentric group, mirroring the diverse natures and backgrounds of our seniors, and likewise they were all male. Their number had grown three or fourfold since my visit five years earlier, to about twenty, but we all sat together in a large open-plan room on the second floor of 30 Gresham Street. Altogether we managed about £100 million worth or so of investments, mainly for private clients.

There was an unusual mix of backgrounds. Ronald Gurney, who had been a friend of mine at Oxford, had impeccable connections with the aristocracy in England and abroad, and an excellent bedside manner with his clients. Christopher Burney had been in solitary confinement in Paris in the war and had written a book, *Down from Ararat*, about his experiences; he did not enjoy the investment business and soon left. Howard Guinness would get up at 5 o'clock in the morning to milk his cows in Hampshire. Bob Arnheim, a younger refugee from Germany and an unusually good fund manager, addressed his fellow Germans in English with a German accent and the rest of us without one. Peter Chudleigh, correct and methodical, had a surname that baffled Eric Korner, who called him Chadburn. Andrew Smithers, Nick McAndrew and Leonard Licht were starting in the department around that time, Leonard filing the Extel company information cards. All were bright and fun to be with, if perhaps we were somewhat disrespectful at times in our imitations of the German and Austrian 'uncles'.

Only a small number of clients gave us full discretion to manage their portfolios in those days, and our function was therefore not very different from that of a stockbroker's private client department, with the exception that we charged a fee based on the value of the clients' portfolios, whereas the brokers instead earned commissions on every buy or sell transaction. We had to telephone the client each time we wanted to make a new investment in his or her portfolio. David Price, of whom more later, tells of an occasion when an inexperienced fund manager tried to explain to an upper-class English lady who lived rather grandly in Italy the reasons he wanted to buy a certain mining share for her. 'I'm afraid I don't understand a word you're saying', she told him. 'I'm going to pass you on to my dog.'

Officially at least, the minimum size for a private client account was £100,000, equivalent to more than £1 million in today's money, and it remained at that level for many years. We lived in a less prosperous world then, income tax was up to 80 per cent and tax on so-called unearned income (i.e. investment income) was even higher, so the market for our services was limited to a fairly small number of people. There was a story, surely apocryphal, which of course related to a competitor and not to us, of a person who gave a merchant bank £150,000 to invest for him. The performance of the portfolio was terrible, and a year or so later he received an impersonal and unsigned communication from the bank asking him to remove his funds as 'they are valued at £95,000 and we only manage accounts of £100,000 or more'.

Investors with smaller amounts could buy unit trusts which we managed for a Bristol-based company, Tyndall, which was then our largest client. Before my time, Warburgs had managed the unit trusts of Unicorn, a group developed by Edward du Cann, a pioneer in the unit trust movement. He was later for a while chairman of Lonrho and was well known as a Conservative MP before ultimately experiencing financial difficulties. By comparison with other merchant banks, we were hopelessly under-represented in the management of investment trusts. We managed just two trusts, Keystone and Abchurch, each with assets of a little more than £1 million. They were later merged, and today Mercury Keystone Investment Trust, with assets of £200 million, has one of the best performance records among UK investment trusts.

There was no system to separate the functions of underwriting issues of securities and managing investments, and if Warburgs was either leading or underwriting a new issue of shares, a good proportion of it was 'placed' with the clients of the investment department. No concept of a conflict of interest attached to this neat arrangement. To the contrary, many of our clients came to Warburgs for investment management with the main aim of being able to participate in the bank's underwritings, which they expected, usually quite correctly, to rise in price after the issue was completed. Pricing procedures were less competitive than they are now, and issues were deliberately priced to sell, i.e. at a price below that at which it was anticipated they would trade in open market dealings.

Investment decisions were left to the individual fund manager, as a consequence of which the composition of clients' portfolios, and their performance, varied greatly from one fund manager to another. Investment meetings were held each Tuesday at 4.30 p.m. They were free-form in nature, and were described by Charles Sharp as resembling debates in the House of Commons except that all present belonged to the opposition. No agreed investment strategy emerged; nor did anyone take much notice of the ideas put forward by anyone other than themselves.

Some attempt was made around the time I arrived in London to establish a research department. It consisted of just two people. The first of these was Arthur Winspear, a blunt Yorkshireman and former journalist who had acquired a reputation for independent views and trenchant commentary on financial matters as the columnist Lex on the *Financial Times*. He used to call Siegmund 'old stooping deadpan' because an article about him in the *Financial Times* had opened with the words, 'Stooping, deadpan Siegmund Warburg . . . .' Perhaps Arthur had written it himself.

The other was John Morgan, who had worked with a firm in Cambridge engaged in investment analysis. Twenty-five years later John was to become the head of the Investment Management

Regulatory Organisation (IMRO), in which capacity he fined Mercury £50,000 for a rather minor technical breach of rules, which we reported to IMRO and from which no one suffered except ourselves. It was a small fine in comparison to today's levels, but it set a new record at the time. John apparently kept a 'Roll of Honour' in his office of firms that IMRO had fined. Mercury was a high-profile scalp, and it is not impossible that he enjoyed a wry smile when he was able to put our name at the top of the roll.

*

The prevailing view in Warburgs, I soon learnt, was that investment management was a boring and inferior occupation which was only slightly more demanding than a clerical job. Anyone with even a modicum of intelligence could handle it easily, it was believed, and if someone in the department seemed to have more than average brainpower, he was moved to the more prestigious corporate finance side, which engaged in activities such as advising companies on raising money and take-over strategy. Corporate finance is the 'consummate art of the investment banker', as Ken Costa, a Warburgs corporate financier, described it in 1998.

Arthur Winspear was one who was moved. In the opinion of the uncles, he had too good a brain to be wasted in the investment department, and he was whisked away to deal with more weighty matters. He was to gain another reputation as a skilled practitioner in the field of corporate take-overs. With his departure from the investment side, the notion of a separate research department gradually gave way to a policy of having each fund manager assume an area of research responsibility – a policy that has survived in Mercury to the present day.

The information available to use as fund managers then was a fraction of what it is today. We did not sit at work stations with multi-coloured screens; nor did we have access to instantaneous stock market prices. There were no computers or even electronic calculators. If you needed to do a sum, you either worked it out yourself, or you could use a manual calculator called Facit with a keyboard like an ancient typewriter and a handle you turned to get the result. It was the only piece of technology on our desks other than two old-fashioned black telephones, one for the outside world and the other to contact the dealers. Eric Korner, for some reason, had an extra telephone, which only complicated his life because when one of them rang he never knew which of the three it was. 'Hello', he would say into the first one, 'Hello', he would repeat into the second, and finally 'Hello – oh zere you are', he would say into the third.

The ethos of corporate transparency and dissemination of information was just beginning to reach the United Kingdom from North America, while in continental Europe only a few leading multinational companies gave out anything more than rudimentary bulletins to their shareholders. In the UK, turnover did not have to be reported until 1967. In France and Belgium, directors could report for profits whatever figure they chose; in consequence, the reported profits were often enough to cover the dividend, but only a fraction of the true profit. Meanwhile in Italy, it was widely believed that even publicly quoted companies kept three sets of accounts – one for the tax inspectors, one for the shareholders and one with the correct numbers to be seen only by the directors. Profits were, literally, a matter of choice.

These practices gave rise to guessing games among investment professionals as to the size of hidden profits, and provided excellent opportunities for insiders to accumulate shares they knew to be undervalued, and to sell those that were overpriced.* Even in the UK, the concept of shareholder relations was in its infancy. An analyst wanting to meet a company had to arrange it formally through the company's broker, and only a minority of companies agreed to meetings. Analysts were viewed with suspicion and were in any case thin on the ground. Still less did companies talk to their institutional shareholders. In our own case, we were usually able to talk to companies which were corporate finance clients of Warburgs, but few others. Annual general meetings of shareholders were formal and routine affairs, with virtually no information given out, let alone tea and cakes.

Research into the prospects of companies and their shares, although well recognised in the USA and Canada, was still quite primitive in London in the 1960s, but some stockbrokers were waking up to the need to upgrade the status of their statistical department to a research department; Joe in stats was becoming Joseph in research. The notion of shareholder value, whereby

---

* Market professionals refer to an 'inefficient' market where prices of shares are based on less than full disclosure of all relevant information. Regulations requiring full disclosure of information and improvements in accounting standards have virtually eliminated inefficient pricing in most major markets, thus creating greater fairness among investors.

companies take steps aimed solely at maximising the value of their shares, such as buying in their shares or narrowing the focus of their activities to those they believe will meet the approval of the investment community, was unheard of then. It became fashionable only in the late 1980s and the 1990s.

*

Measurement of investment performance was perhaps equally unsophisticated, but even if our clients received valuations irregularly and often many weeks late, I like to think that the results we achieved for them were at least as good relative to the performance of the markets as they are today. We were natural beneficiaries of a much lower rate of turnover of shares within the portfolios we managed then. The vast amount of information available to fund managers today, the volatility of markets and the requirements of pension fund and other institutional clients for quarterly performance measurement collectively induce an urge to make frequent switches in clients' portfolios, always at some dealing cost and often to the detriment of long-term performance. In the 1960s, we had no such temptations, and the incentives not to change the portfolios were greater than those to do so; you bought your shares in Marks and Spencer, ICI and Shell, you held them and over time you did very well thereby.

If life was less user-friendly for fund managers in the absence of today's technological aids, it was at the same time simpler and conducted at a more civilised pace. To obtain a quotation on a share during market hours, we had to telephone our dealers – we were early in having a central dealing department – who in turn would telephone a broker at the Stock Exchange. It took a few minutes to process an order. Vincent Tweedie, our head dealer, would walk round the investment department at the close of market hours to report the bargains completed for each of us.

The London Stock Exchange had not yet started to report figures for the volume of trading in shares. We did not have the opportunity to deal in derivatives, which existed only in the most elementary forms, and we had no knowledge of betas, co-variances, standard deviation, econometric modelling, investment methodologies or even benchmarks, all of which are common usage in the jargon of professional investment management today, although not necessarily of any additional use in picking the right investments.

There were no seductive emerging markets in south-east Asia, the

Mediterranean countries or eastern Europe, although some adventurous people were beginning to look at Japan. Japanese shares sell today on high price/earnings multiples, 40 or 50 or more, but in the 1960s you could buy the shares of growth companies like Canon Camera, whose cameras were then little more than cheaper copies of the well-known German brands such as Leica and Zeiss, for as little as two or three times earnings. Those who did so, and held them for the next twenty years, made a fortune.

Latin America was considered highly speculative. One London broker did visit Venezuela and recommended some shares in that country, but I never heard of anyone who bought them. We should have listened when Hugh Barton suggested modestly, after joining Warburgs as a director in 1965, that we should consider some shares in Hong Kong. An immensely likeable and gregarious Irishman, Hugh had joined Jardine Matheson (the *Noble House* of James Clavell's novel) as a tea taster in Shanghai before the war, and had ended up as its 'taipan' in Hong Kong. In his time, this position carried with it the chairmanships of Hong Kong and Shanghai Banking Corporation, Hong Kong Land and the Hong Kong Jockey Club, added to which he was, to those who know about such matters, the inventor of the famous Mandarin Hotel in Hong Kong. In his own words, Hugh persuaded his fellow directors at Hong Kong Land 'with a few minutes of Irish blarney' to build the Mandarin rather than an office building.

Foolishly, and to our great long-term cost, we ignored his advice to invest in the leading Hong Kong companies. The working environment there, as in Singapore and other areas of south-east Asia, as well as in the sun belt states of the US, was beginning to be transformed by the advent of efficient air conditioning. This, together with cellular telephones, computers, credit cards, jet travel, photocopiers, the pill, satellite television and more recently the astonishing revolution in information technology, all of which we take for granted, has done so much to change lives and attitudes during my working lifetime.

There were no junk bonds with high yields to attract our attention. Venture capital, later known as development capital and now as private equity, as its practitioners have given it a less racy image over time, was just starting. We got involved in it when we invested some of our clients' money in a new ten-pin bowling company called Excel Bowling, which, after a promising start, produced very disappointing profits, way below the level forecast at the time of the issue. Warburgs conscientiously decided to repay its clients the full cost of their investment, and thereafter such private investments were off limits for us for several years.

We invested mainly in high-quality quoted shares, with the largest proportion naturally going into the UK. Most of our clients liked to have a participation in America and, for a stake in natural resources, something in Australia and Canada. Continental Europe was viewed with caution in part because of the lack of reliable information. Bonds were considered boring, all right only for the short term if you were sure interest rates were going down, and so we were always fully invested in equities. In this we were probably ahead of our time, and it meant that our clients had large gains in their portfolios until the long-drawn-out bear market of 1973 and 1974.

*

Siegmund affected mild disappointment, but no surprise, that I had not been more assertive in taking control of the investment department, but he let the matter drop. For my part, I was the specialist in American and Canadian investments, about which I had some knowledge, I was being paid £3000 a year (it seemed a lot at the time) and I was content. Being at Warburgs was stressful enough in itself and I did not need any extra pressures, and that remained the major part of my job for the next five years or so.

Sometime during this period, it was decided that the designation 'department' had implications of a bureaucracy and that we should be called the investment 'division'. This was supposed to confer a more exalted status. It did not take long to realise, however, that in the eyes of almost everyone in other parts of the bank, we in the investment division were, rename it what you will, second-class citizens. We were the Cinderella, and our new title made no difference to that.

I noted that Siegmund himself took little interest in the investment division except as potentially fertile recruiting territory for corporate finance. When he telephoned me, he would ritually ask, 'How's the market?', but he paid not the slightest attention to my answer other than to see whether I knew. If I told him it was up when it was down, he was in no position to correct me; nor did he care. Somehow, though, one could seldom escape the brooding presence of this strange person whom I got to know over the years that followed, but never fully to fathom. It was impossible to be indifferent to him or to his contrasting moods. One soon experienced his less agreeable qualities – the world-class rages and sulks and the constant personal reminders that he was in control of you. It took longer to learn of his capacity for generosity, kindness, friendship and inspiration.

CHAPTER 5

The Observer from Outer Space

While I had seen or heard (the decibel level could be very high) some of Siegmund Warburg's more standard rages, directed as often as not at other extremely senior members of the firm, it was not until two years after I joined Warburgs that I was to experience an eruption of truly volcanic proportions. Its unlikely target was an attractive young woman, and it happened in New York.

Shortly after he gave up his partnership in the American Warburg family firm Kuhn Loeb at the end of 1964, Siegmund opened a small office for Warburgs in New York in Rockefeller Center. There was a staff of four headed by David Mitchell, a friendly and thoughtful banker whom Siegmund had recruited from Chemical Bank. I was seconded there for three months, during which time Siegmund came for a visit of two weeks or so.

The office manager, who also deputised as David's secretary, was a pleasant and efficient American woman in her twenties, but not always the tidiest of people. Her desk, which was in full view of any visitor, was usually strewn with papers, files, used ashtrays and other accoutrements. One morning Siegmund happened to pass her desk when it was in a worse than usual mess and flew into a terrific rage, shouting at the unfortunate woman at the top of his voice, with occasional lapses into German. 'We are a banking house, not a butcher shop!', he screamed. After what seemed an age to the rest of us, witnessing the incident with rather cowardly vicarious sympathy, the office manager, still seated at her desk, pulled out a Salem filter-tipped cigarette, tapped it, lit it casually, blew out a long trail of blue smoke, looked him in the eye and said, 'Gee, Mr Warburg, you gotta be insecure.'

The effect was dramatic. Without a further word, the great man turned on his heels, stalked off and slammed the door of his room. He emerged about an hour later, walked slowly and one might guess somewhat abashedly to the office manager's desk and, with no reference to his earlier tirade, asked her in his most pleasant manner if she could kindly supply him with some pencils. It was his way of apologising. (Another time, having thrown a tantrum at one of the secretaries in London, he told her the next day what exquisite shoes she was wearing.)

Only an American of that age, I felt, could have both the psychoanalytical insight and the courage to respond to his outburst as she did. And her analysis may have been at least partially correct. It can be a surprise to discover that successful people are often insecure until one reflects that it was probably their insecurity which drove them to succeed in the first place.

In Siegmund's case, he might have attributed his tremendous ambition more to a strong sense of duty, which was instilled into him from an early age by his mother, to whom he was devoted. Whatever the spur, he saw it as his mission to restore to its rightful position the Warburg banking name, which had been taken away by the Nazis during their terrible persecution of the Jews in Germany in the 1930s. Although it had to be bailed out of financial difficulties arising from bad loans in the 1930s, M.M. Warburg and Company in Hamburg was one of the best-known private banks in Germany in the nineteenth century and the first part of the twentieth, and now S.G. Warburg & Co. in London meant everything to him. He was determined that it should succeed and that those who worked in it should live up to the standards he expected of them. When they failed, his frustration was quick to surface. He suffered from being a perfectionist. As his friend Isaiah Berlin once said, 'The search for perfection does seem to me a recipe for bloodshed, no better even if it is demanded by the sincerest of idealists.'

On the worst occasions, Siegmund would throw telephones and directories at the target of his rages, or at the window. Fortunately, he had neither the arm nor the aim of a sportsman, which was as well from the point of view of the firm's expenses. When I read recently of the existence of Anger Management courses, it was difficult to avoid thinking that Siegmund might have been a good candidate for one, except that he would inevitably have become angry with the instructor and it would have ended in tears.

Some of his tantrums were faked. After the diminished and shaken victim had left the room, Siegmund might turn to those present as if to ask, 'How did I do?' But mostly they were real. Either way, while generally short-lived, they were exceedingly unpleasant for their recipients and only slightly less so for witnesses. Moreover, they occurred often enough to constitute a self-destructive behaviour pattern which invited unfriendly comment even from his greatest supporters.

*

Siegmund's great interest, apart from the firm, was people and their behaviour. People were his hobby and his work. In his own words, the most important things to him were 'first, human beings; second, books; third, the sun; and fourth, music'. In later years, he described himself as 'an observer of human nature from outer space'.

He believed quite simply that all activity was initiated by people and that, in any business, people were paramount. Obvious as that may seem to most of us, it has not always been the accepted wisdom. The careers master at my school told us that we would have to choose between working with people, money or things, as if they were mutually exclusive. There are those, including a recent chairman of one of the UK's leading industrial companies, who believe that the keys to success in business are good products and access to markets. And I can remember an American investment analyst once saying that Coca-Cola, with its unique products and worldwide distribution system, largely put in place to support the US military in the Second World War, would be a successful company even if managed by orang-utans. But if Siegmund was asked his opinion on, for example, a proposal for a new business venture and was presented with plans, projections and prospects, he would typically reply, 'It all depends on the people – have you got the right people?'

He was a wonderful listener and a father confessor to a number of us in the firm. He talked to you in some detail about his own concerns in such a way as to make you feel you were his most trusted adviser, and you found yourself responding by confiding in him some of your innermost secrets. He was always available and responsive and, however busy with more important matters, he somehow found the time to talk over any problem you had. I always thought he would have made a superb professional psychoanalyst. People would have flocked to his consultancy rooms in Zurich or London, and would have paid large fees for an hour of his time. He would, of course, also have been an extremely interesting candidate for some other psychoanalyst's couch.

Younger members of the firm might be surprised to get a summons to his room, usually late in the day, for an hour or more of conversation in which he asked their views on all sorts of matters, mostly unrelated to business, and reflected often amusingly on some of his own experiences. None of them was likely to forget those occasions. When David Price was called for one such session, he answered Siegmund's question as to what he was reading by mentioning a biography of Dr Johnson by John Wain. Siegmund looked at David as if he thought he was making a show business joke. When their conversation was over, David rushed to check that he had the author's name right, which fortunately he had. A few days later he received a note from Siegmund telling him how grateful he was to have been told about the book and how much he had enjoyed reading it.

Siegmund seemed to have a sixth sense as to one's mood swings, somehow knowing when you needed a word of encouragement or when you should be put in your place. He was greatly helped in his assessments of people by his secret weapon, his cousin Theodora Dreifuss, a graphologist as well as a trained psychologist. He was a convinced believer in handwriting analysis, as all of us became as we saw the remarkable accuracy of the reports we received. To many people, graphology is on a par with astrology or tarot readings, but none of us in Warburgs viewed it that way, and I am happy to say that it is still considered a vital aspect of recruiting by the top people in Mercury today. What matters is the interpretative skill of the individual graphologist, and Mrs Dreifuss was the practitioner *par excellence*.

From time to time, Siegmund might give Theodora Dreifuss a fresh sample of our handwriting to see why we had, as he might have said, 'deteriorated'. In late 1965, during a period when I had private worries and my performance was disappointing him, I was summoned by Siegmund to attend some relatively unimportant business meeting in Zurich. I had declined a promotion to the Warburgs board that year because I did not feel ready for it – a decision he found perplexing.

He suggested that I should stay over at the Baur au Lac Hotel on the evening of the meeting, so that we could have dinner together. I was to discover that all this was a pretext for Mrs Dreifuss, who joined us for dinner, to look me over with a view, no doubt, to giving Siegmund a detailed psychological update afterwards on my deterioration. I had not met her before and I was taken aback when she greeted me with 'Mr Darling, I'm very glad to meet you. I know you so well.'

After a pleasant dinner in the hotel restaurant, we returned to Siegmund's sitting room to play 'little mental games' which provided Mrs Dreifuss, as well as Siegmund, with further insights into my psychological condition. She invited him and me each to imagine ourselves lonely and lost in a dense forest with darkness setting in. Exhausted and cold, we saw a pretty little house with smoke coming out of its chimney, but to reach it we would have to cross a wide river in a small but leaky boat. Prowling on the other side of the river, protecting the house, were two extremely fierce Rottweiler dogs. What would each of us do? Siegmund's artful and premeditated response, delivered with much assurance, was 'I go straight ahead', thus affirming to his two-person audience that no obstacle would ever be allowed to stand in his way. I am afraid my reaction was more timid.

There were examples of such an attitude on his part in real life. A taxi driver once told me that he had driven Siegmund to a meeting, on the way to which they got stuck in total traffic gridlock, unable to move in any direction. Desperate not to be late for his meeting, Siegmund hysterically ordered the poor cab driver to 'Go on, man, go on, drive on, drive on, now, now, drive on.' It amused me later to discover that one of the epigrams Siegmund composed began, 'Life and imagination are always in continuous conflict with one another.'

*

A manifestation of Siegmund's talent for influencing people was the extraordinary assembly of outstandingly able senior colleagues he had persuaded to join the firm. As a businessman, Siegmund was capable of coming up with innovative and imaginative ideas, often involving changes of people in some way, but he was not an expert in matters of technical banking detail. For these he relied especially on Henry Grunfeld, a financial genius with a resourceful solution to every problem. He too had left Germany in the 1930s, but having been arrested and imprisoned by the Nazis, he was less forgiving of the Germans than Siegmund, and less trusting of people in general.

Henry Grunfeld was austere and meticulous, and some of us were a little frightened of him for his obvious intellectual superiority and his almost magical ability to know what you were doing or supposed to be doing. He had the wonderful gift of cutting through to the heart of any problem, however complex, and explaining it in comprehensible terms and without condescension to those of us with lesser intellects. He also had an uncanny nose for trouble ahead. He was years ahead of others in warning of the dangers inherent in leveraged buy-outs and derivatives. In 1994 he predicted in an interview that the so-called hedge funds (very few of which are actually hedged) would come unstuck, which indeed a great many of them did, although not until 1998. His definition of emerging markets was that when there was an emergency they did not pay – one only has to look at Russia in 1998 to see how right he was.

As Siegmund's troubleshooter, Henry Grunfeld was the perfect complement to the great man, and he has rightly been given a very large share of the credit for the success of Warburgs. The reality was that during Siegmund's lifetime, while he deferred to Siegmund on people decisions and overall direction, Henry Grunfeld ran the firm. His humour reflected his intellect. When Martin Gordon, as a young member of Warburgs, asked whether we could underwrite a share issue of Playboy Enterprises, he was told by Grunfeld that no bank should underwrite a company that made its money from gambling.

There were others who were crucial to the success of Warburgs. Eric Roll, who joined the firm in 1967, is an indefatigable traveller with innumerable contacts around the world, who was of great value to Warburgs in its international business. Now in his nineties and still with an apparently iron constitution, he continues his travelling on behalf of Warburg Dillon Read. At Eric's ninetieth birthday party at the Bank of England in 1997, David Scholey noted that Eric had never knowingly passed an airport without going into it. I have more to say about Eric in another chapter.

Geoffrey Seligman, always a pleasure to work with, was someone who was tireless and successful in building relationships with a number of major companies which became clients both in the UK and US. Geoffrey came from a distinguished German Jewish family. His grandfather Isaac started Seligman Brothers in London in 1864, while shortly afterwards two of Isaac's brothers formed the Anglo California Bank in San Francisco, which eventually became part of Wells Fargo Bank. It was the merger of Seligman Brothers with Warburgs in 1957 which brought Warburgs into the inner circle of London merchant banks. Seligman Brothers, which Geoffrey joined in 1934 and of which he was a partner, was a founder member in 1914 of the Accepting Houses Committee, whose members' credit was acknowledged by the Bank of England as being as good as its own. As such, it was at the heart of the established merchant banking community. Siegmund seemed to be resentful of Geoffrey for this, rather than grateful for it, and at times he treated him with a disdain that gave scant recognition to his contribution to Warburgs' business over a long period.

Frank Smith, who had joined the firm in its early days, was another formidable figure and a well-known City personality. An accountant by background, with a razor-sharp mind and a knack of spotting the essentials in any proposal, he acquired a reputation as a skilful and aggressive practitioner in the take-over field. I recall being summoned by him one day to have it pointed out to me with a withering look that the sums in one of my notes did not add up. All right, he would say, the error is small this time, but that was my good luck, and next time a misplaced digit, or a wrong addition, could cost the firm or its clients many millions.

In younger generations, Ian Fraser, Peter Spira, David Scholey and John Craven were just some of the other talented merchant bankers who contributed to Warburgs' growth and reputation over the years.

Another powerful ally to Siegmund was his very competent senior secretary, Doris Wasserman, who also played the roles of nanny, psychologist and benevolent headmistress. Despite her loyalty to Siegmund and her access to his private thoughts, she was always considerate and helpful to the rest of us, or at least to those she liked. There were times, for instance, when I might receive a telephone call from her asking if I really intended to include such and such a sentence in my latest note to Sir Siegmund, the implication being that it might save an upset on both his part and mine if I were to amend it. She is today a trustee of Siegmund's charitable trust, a guardian of his archives and a leading upholder of his tradition.

Siegmund was not only a superb chooser of people, but also a great persuader. When he wanted you to do something, he turned on his full panoply of charm and flattery and simply refused to take no for an answer. John Heimann, until recently a vice-chairman of Merrill Lynch, tells of a meeting in which Siegmund was trying to convince him that he should join Warburg Paribas Becker. In 1974, Warburgs had bought a 20 per cent interest in a Chicago-based investment banking firm, A.G. Becker, with our partners, Paribas, buying a further 20 per cent. The name was changed to Warburg Paribas Becker, and Siegmund saw it, rather late in his life, as the opportunity to make his rightful mark on Wall Street. Some twenty minutes into the meeting, one of Siegmund's secretaries came in to tell him that the Governor of the Bank of England was on the telephone. The conversation continued as follows:

WARBURG: Tell him I will telephone him shortly.
SECRETARY: Oh, but he says it's important, Sir Siegmund.
WARBURG: Well, he may think it's important, but for me nothing is more important than my discussion with Mr Heimann.

It has never occurred to me, of course, that there was any possibility of the intervention having been planned in advance.

Siegmund had a wide circle of friends, and even more admirers among those with whom he had had some brief contact, or others who knew him only by reputation. And as a true fighter for his beliefs and for his firm, he also had quite a number of enemies. Some were competitors whom he had outmanoeuvred in some business transaction, while others were former members of the firm who felt he had treated them badly. Virtually all of his detractors, however, admitted to a healthy degree of respect for him. An exception was one of his cousins in New York, Paul Felix Warburg, better known as Piggy, a banker and playboy who dismissively described Siegmund as 'a horse's ass'. Another who could speak of Siegmund only in the most scathing and hateful terms was Cy Lewis, legendary senior partner of Bear Stearns, a major American investment banking house, of whom more later.

*

Among Siegmund's less attractive qualities was his constant need to remind you that you were working for him at all times. In today's terminology, he was a control freak. Despite avowals to the contrary, he did not like dissent or disagreement on any matter on which he had a strong opinion. Henry Kissinger, an admirer and close friend of Siegmund, once commented that he was an easy person to get along with if you just said 'yes'. Peter Spira is someone who cannot hide his refreshingly honest views and as a result he often crossed Siegmund, and he paid the penalty. When it became apparent that Siegmund had designated David Scholey as his ultimate successor, Peter left the firm and took up an invitation to become finance director at Sotheby's.

The control aspect of Siegmund's leadership could sometimes be extremely intrusive. Christmas was a bad time for Siegmund because the office was closed, and he knew that members of the firm would be engaged in entertainments that he felt were frivolous. He made a point of walking round the bank's office late in the afternoon on Christmas Eve to see if anyone had left early, as people did in most other firms. Needless to say, we were all at our desks. It was not one of those occasions on which to leave a second coat on the back of your chair to give the impression you were still there if you were not.

On Christmas Day in 1964, when I had been back in London from Canada for just over a year, Siegmund telephoned me at home at 12.30 p.m. when we were getting ready for a family lunch. The conversation went something like this:

WARBURG: I do hope I'm not disturbing you.

PSD: Oh no, Mr Warburg, not at all.

WARBURG: Well, it's about your note dated 22 December on the American stock market. Do you have a copy in front of you?

PSD: Er, no, I'm afraid my copy is in the office.

WARBURG: Well, let me remind you of your second sentence in the fifth paragraph . . . I think there should be a comma after the word 'development'.

PSD: Er, yes, there should be. I'm sorry.

WARBURG: No, no, I didn't mean to trouble you, I just thought I should point it out. Perhaps you can send out a correction as soon as you are back in the office.

PSD: Yes, of course I will. I'm so sorry.

WARBURG: Not a bit. I wish you and your family a very happy Christmas.

It was done, of course, with great politeness. But the message was clear, as it was when he rang me on New Year's Day at 8.30 a.m. when I was staying with my brother in Scotland. We had gone to bed only a few hours before, as he would have guessed. His familiar opening line of 'I hope I'm not troubling you at an inconvenient time' was the prelude to an all too obviously concocted comment on a minor matter.

Each time he made his point. He was the boss, and you didn't easily forget it. It was a behavioural technique not unknown in other powerful people. President Lyndon Johnson, according to his biographers, employed the same trick of contacting his subordinates on some manufactured pretext at times he knew were inconvenient for them. So did Andre Meyer, the formidable French American banker and head of Lazard Frères in New York, whom Siegmund greatly respected. Another practitioner was Emperor Haile Selassie of Ethiopia, and there is even an expression for it in Amharic – *shum shir* – the raising and lowering of subordinates' status so as to maintain their loyalty without letting them become too powerful. Anyone thinking of practising *shum shir*, however, should note that Haile Selassie's army mutinied against him, and he spent the last year of his life as a prisoner in his own palace.

*

A meeting in the early 1970s between Siegmund and Ross Perot, the American billionaire and presidential candidate, was an encounter between two controlling people who managed to get together only with the utmost difficulty.

Perot, through his company Electronic Data Systems (EDS), had acquired control of the Wall Street investment banking house Du Pont Glore Forgan in the belief that EDS's knowledge of information technology systems would enable them to solve Du Pont Glore Forgan's back-office chaos. A number of Wall Street houses had been caught unawares by large trading volumes in shares, and their settlements departments had been unable to cope. The New York Stock Exchange was forced to close every Wednesday and there was the prospect of a complete halt in trading unless the backlog could be sorted out. The Stock Exchange had approached Perot, the acknowledged wise man of the computer software industry, and he thought he saw an opportunity to save a major firm and make a lot of money in the process. He sent his right-hand man, Mort Myerson, then not much more than 30, to New York from Texas to take charge of Du Pont Glore Forgan.

Myerson had a healthy disrespect for Wall Street bankers and few connections with them. He turned for help to Siegmund Warburg, whose reputation as the man who had broken the mould of London's merchant banking scene was by then well established. Myerson arranged an introduction to Siegmund, and they met and got on well in a sort of father–son relationship. Siegmund was interested at the time in finding a suitable New York firm with which Warburgs could strike an alliance, and he asked me to spend a week or so with Myerson in New York to form an opinion as to whether we should join EDS in investing in Du Pont Glore Forgan. (My recommendation was negative.)

During this time, Ross Perot decided that he himself should meet Siegmund, who in his turn had developed an intuitive and correct feeling that Perot was not the sort of person with whom he would be wholly compatible. The clash of egos was reflected in an exchange of messages by telex, in which Siegmund proposed times for a meeting in London that he knew would be inconvenient for Perot, who responded in similar vein. After this long-drawn-out game of telex tennis, a meeting was finally fixed at our office at 11 a.m. one morning, with Siegmund insisting that he would only be able to see Perot for half an hour. When Perot arrived, Siegmund, plainly available, told me to go in and 'Keep Mr Perot happy. I'll be with you soon.'

It was not an enjoyable assignment. I did my best to make conversation with the restless, crew-cut Perot, who was pacing the room and looking pointedly at his watch. After about twenty minutes of this, Perot demanded that I go and find out where Mr Warburg was and remind him that Ross Perot was a busy man too. I found Siegmund in his room, relaxed and enjoying the little game he was playing. I pleaded with him to rescue me, but he sent me back with the promise that he would join the meeting within a minute or so. Shortly after, he entered the room, greeted Perot with a big smile and said, 'I've been so much looking forward to meeting you, Mr Perot. You must pay my dear friend Mort Myerson as your personal public relations adviser, so warmly does he speak of you.' With the wind thus taken out of his sails, Perot listened attentively to Siegmund's every word as they talked for the next forty-five minutes. It was a familiar pattern; Siegmund was one up on Perot. He was in control, and it was obviously important for him.

As far as I know, they never met again. Many years later, in 1992, I was taken to a large dinner in New York by Andy Blum, a much-liked Wall Street character and an anglophile, and his beautiful wife Flis, at which Perot, then a candidate for the American presidency, was a guest speaker. Perot is without doubt a brilliant businessman. He sold EDS to General Motors for $1 billion in 1984, and as soon as his non-compete agreement with GM expired in 1988, he started Perot Systems. It has been equally successful and has many active relationships in the UK today, with the government and with

Mercury among others. I recall the succinct but wise advice he gave to businessmen on that occasion: 'Listen to your customers and listen to your employees.' I was introduced to Perot at the dinner and reminded him of the meeting at Warburgs twenty years earlier. He told me that Siegmund Warburg had been a good friend whom he admired greatly.

CHAPTER 6

Not a Subscriber to Playboy

Despite a somewhat puritanical manner, Siegmund was no prude. On the contrary, I believe he had a powerful interest in erotic matters. While I was living in New York in 1969, and was still on rather formal terms with him, I came across a copy of *Playboy* with a lengthy and well-informed article on graphology. I sent him a copy of the magazine with the following personal letter:

Dear Sir Siegmund

I do not expect that you are a subscriber to the American magazine *Playboy* and you may not therefore have seen the enclosed article on graphology, which appeared in the November issue. I think it might interest you, as well as Mrs Dreifuss. The cartoons which appear alongside parts of the article should perhaps be viewed separately.

In case you are jumping to potentially damaging conclusions, I should hasten to add that I am not a subscriber to *Playboy* either.

Yours ever
Peter

His reply showed that he was not without a sense of humour in such matters.

Dear Peter

I have received your letter of the 3rd December, with enclosure, for which I thank you. You are right in assuming that I am not a subscriber to the *Playboy* magazine, and I equally understand that you are not a subscriber. Like you, however, I suffer from considerable curiosity and on rare occasions I look at *Playboy* copies when I have too much waiting time on my hands at airports.

It is very thoughtful of you to call my attention to the article on graphology in the *Playboy* magazine, which I shall read with much interest and I shall send a photocopy of it to Theodora Dreifuss.

Yours ever
Siegmund

Some years later, he was talking to me about the politican and broadcaster Robert Boothby, who had at one time bombarded Siegmund and others in the firm with somewhat crack-pot financial ideas that reflected his impractical nature (Richard Oldfield was once having a drink with Boothby to obtain careers advice when Boothby produced an egg whisk in lieu of a bottle opener). Word of Boothby's affair with Lady Dorothy Macmillan was reaching the public domain, but Siegmund told me that Boothby was also 'a great homosexual'. When I expressed mild surprise, Siegmund insisted, 'Oh yes, a *very* great homosexual.'

Siegmund was fiercely loyal to one of our board colleagues who was caught out in a minor scandal. George Jellicoe, an amusing extrovert who enjoyed life to the full, was an active non-executive director of Warburgs. He had a brilliant war record as a commando, winning the DSO, MC, Légion d'Honneur and Croix de Guerre, and afterwards, following a short period in the Foreign Office, he became a minister in the Macmillan and Heath governments. He was, in short, a man of many parts, and he had a wide circle of friends.

In 1963, at the time of the Profumo scandal, George had criticised the 'niggling, sneaking, smearing frame of mind' prevalent in the UK, and ten years later he was himself involved in a peripheral way in a scandal involving Lord Lambton and a call girl, Norma Levy, and promptly offered his resignation to the Prime Minister, Edward Heath, who accepted it. He probably made the same offer to Siegmund, but Siegmund was steadfast in his support of George, who continued to be a productive and popular member of the board of Warburgs.

*

It was Ron Chernow who first disclosed, in his book *The Warburgs*, Siegmund's affair with the Ballet Russe prima ballerina Alexandra Danilova in the period before the Second World War when both Siegmund and Danilova were in their thirties. There were those among Siegmund's admirers who thought Chernow should have kept his knowledge to himself – hardly a realistic expectation for a modern-day biographer of Chernow's quality and thoroughness. The alternative view is that Chernow did us a favour by illustrating that the ascetic Siegmund was, after all, as human as the rest of us.

Danilova was discretion itself. She never talked about their affair and avoided any mention of it in her memoirs written fifty years later. It was ended under pressure from Siegmund's delightful Swedish wife, Eva, who threatened to move with their two children to Paris. Siegmund terminated his relationship with Danilova with a formal and less than sympathetic letter, and that was the end of it. He did not see her again. Chernow tracked her down, however, in an apartment in New York while researching for his book. He found her forgiving and understanding of both Siegmund and Eva. Danilova died in 1997. An obituary in the London *Times* contained no reference to Siegmund.

In 1991, there was a mischievous, and to the best of my knowledge entirely fictitious, suggestion in a $4\frac{1}{2}$-hour French television series, based on Jacques Attali's biography of Siegmund, that he had once had an affair with one of his secretaries. A distraught Eva Warburg is shown asking Henry Grunfeld if Siegmund had taken the lady in question with him on a business trip. 'Does it matter to you?' asks Grunfeld. 'Yes, of course', replies Eva Warburg. 'Then he did not take her', Grunfeld replies reassuringly.

The affair with Danilova must be seen within the context of an enduring and from most accounts largely happy marriage between Siegmund and the loyal Eva, to whom he was devoted, although, goodness knows, he must have tested her patience many times. I always found Eva Warburg gracious and totally charming. She was well informed of what took place in the bank, because Siegmund gave her copies of all his correspondence and internal notes. Shortly after Siegmund died in 1982, Eva Warburg asked me to take an umbrella of his to New York on my next trip to give to John Heimann, who had joined Warburg Paribas Becker and who she remembered had admired the umbrella on a visit to London. It was a thoughtful gesture that John will never forget.

Siegmund was an avid collector and composer of epigrams. It was a pity they were never published, although Henry Grunfeld's view that they would have shown him as excessively introspective, cynical and gloomy was justified. The epigrams he wrote himself provide a telling insight into his views on fidelity. 'Loyal is not the same as faithful in friendships or in marriages', he wrote in 1965. In another from the same period, he noted that 'dignified adultery', performed without shame but with honesty, was often a precondition for the 'happy and healthy functioning of married life'. It is likely that at the time these were written, adultery was almost *de rigueur* in some circles, but it is difficult not to imagine that there were elements of self-justification and guilt in these thoughts.

*

I was the beneficiary of Siegmund Warburg's generosity on many occasions. As a keen amateur doctor who spent a lot of time with members of the medical profession, and a hypochondriac, he was preoccupied with matters of health and took a great interest in anyone who was ill. Once when I was threatened with an immediate operation on my larynx while living in New York, he insisted that I fly the next day to London for a second opinion from his own favourite specialist. There may have been a controlling aspect in his action, but his concern and friendship at such a time were welcome none the less.

He was a gracious host. A reputation for having 'a monkish indifference to ephemeral pleasures' was not fully warranted. It is true that he had been brought up by his mother in a spartan atmosphere, and he had an aversion to any conspicuous display of wealth or lavish entertainment. But he enjoyed giving small dinner parties, usually involving clients and younger members of the firm, which might be at his flat in Eaton Square or at one of his favourite hotels, such as the Savoy or the Stafford.

If he chose the menu, it tended to have a familiar ring to it of smoked salmon, rack of lamb and chocolate soufflé, with only minor variations. As to wines, Hugel's Alsatian *gewürztraminer* was an old standby for the first course, usually followed by a good claret, such as Château Haut Brion. I remember an excellent Château Latour 1961 which was served at Siegmund's seventieth birthday party at Grosvenor House. If a dinner was just for members of the bank, he could be abstemious and ask for 'a little cold chicken and a Ryvita biscuit', but this was largely to show up the rest of us for our relative extravagance.

He was not averse to the odd indulgence in certain rich foods such as chocolates, and he sometimes put on more weight than he liked. One summer's day, at a house that he had for a few years at

Roccamare on the sea and not far from Rome, he was entertaining an American investment banker to lunch outdoors and had invited me along. There was a large bowl of dark cherries which he was finding hard to resist. He picked up the bowl and placed it at the far end of the table out of his own reach, but thereafter he got up from his chair every few minutes to gather another handful of the cherries, while chatting away merrily in the erroneous belief that the investment banker and I were thus distracted from noticing what he was doing.

Even when entertaining clients to the theatre, which he did quite often, Siegmund was thinking about business. He asked my first wife Candis and me to join him and Eva and a French banking friend to see Joan Littlewood's *Oh! What a Lovely War*, a popular but provocative musical depicting the sacrifices of the First World War and the costly mistakes made by the British generals, which was later made into a spectacular film by Richard Attenborough. 'Oh! What a War', he called it. As soon as the curtain went up, Siegmund took out a memorandum pad and ceaselessly made notes, in the dark, until the interval. This may explain his inviting us to 'Oh! What a War' twice more in the next few weeks with different guests. He seemed to have no recollection either that he had seen it before or that Candis and I had.

*

Money, Siegmund said, was of 'utterly secondary importance' to him. The black American author James Baldwin, whose work Siegmund liked, once wrote, 'Money it turned out was exactly like sex. You thought of nothing else if you didn't have it, but of other things if you did.' I am sure money did matter to Siegmund during his early days in London, when he did not have enough to pursue the sort of comfortable but inconspicuous lifestyle he wanted. When he arrived in London in 1934, he allegedly had less than £5000 and he, Eva and their two children, George and Anna, lived in a flat in Roehampton. But I am equally certain that once he had enough it mattered little to him. He justifiably contrasted his own attitude with that of some of his banking friends, noting that Andre Meyer had an erotic relationship with money – a lust for money presumably – while Louis Franck, the dominating influence at the London merchant bank Samuel Montagu, played with it as a form of sport.

To Siegmund money was no more than a means to an end. He was casual about his own investments, which were managed for him by

Charles Sharp. The latter complained that it was difficult to arouse in Siegmund any interest in his personal financial affairs. Partly by conviction and partly by default, and conveniently moderating the opinions he expressed in other contexts, he took a relaxed and positive long-term view on his portfolio, and through his benign indifference and Sharp's astute selection of shares, it increased in value substantially over the years. Perhaps there was an aspect to his pessimism which feared the optimists might be right. His view on investments was pragmatic, if cautious. 'My personal experience over a long life', he wrote, 'has been that if one expects miraculous results from investment management this is the best way to do badly and in the long run the most favourable achievements are obtained on the basis of modest anticipations and by way of policies which rather err on the side of being solid and pedestrian than original.'

He had none of the trappings of wealth – no car, no chauffeur, no country house. He liked to live simply and distrusted possessions, regarding his friends as his best possession. An exception was the extensive library he had in his house at Blonay, overlooking Lake Geneva. Each book was carefully arranged by subject matter and by language, with its dust jacket folded and placed inside the cover. He had read every book at least once, some many times, and made pencilled notes on the cover page of points which particularly struck him. He never travelled without at least two or three books, even on the shortest journey when every minute was likely to be taken up with appointments.

After his death, Eva Warburg arranged for his library, consisting of some 3500 books, to have a permanent home at St Paul's Girls School in London, where his daughter Anna had been a pupil from 1945 to 1949. It is housed in an annexe to the school's main library. Some of the rare books went to his family, but the remaining treasures include a 1778 edition of *The Plays of William Shakespeare*, a first edition of *Little Dorrit*, a beautiful set of the works of Blake and a first edition of Kipling's *Jungle Book* of 1894.

Siegmund's attitude to money took on almost comic dimensions when it came to tipping. Before leaving the Drake Hotel in New York after one of his stays of a week or so in the 1960s, he asked the office to provide $300 in notes, worth much more today. His reputation for exceptionally generous tipping was well known among the Drake staff and on the morning of his departure there was an unusual number of doormen, receptionists, barmen, housekeepers and chefs in the lobby as he checked out. Five-dollar and ten-dollar bills were dished out by Siegmund regardless of whether he recognised the particular member of staff who was so fortuitously in attendance. Even some of the guests arriving to check into the hotel could scarcely avoid becoming the surprised beneficiaries of his largess.

*

Siegmund's relations with the press were complicated. While he genuinely disliked self-promotion, his carefully cultivated reputation for being publicity shy was, I have always felt, artificial. It was as if he had arranged for stories to be spread about his reticence as part of what Eric Roll described as the 'aura of mystery' which Siegmund consciously created. He appreciated the power of the press, and he courted a number of the leading financial journalists of the day, such as Nigel Lawson, Patrick Sergeant and Anthony Sampson, and later Gil Kaplan and Cary Reich of *Institutional Investor*. He wanted coverage, but only if he had a substantial influence over its content.

There was, for instance, the matter of Siegmund's perceived reluctance to agree to be interviewed. In a generally well-informed article on Warburgs in *The Spectator* in October 1992, Martin Vander Weyer mentioned that Siegmund had only ever given one interview to the media. Such was the myth, but in fact he gave interviews to the *Sunday Telegraph* (1970), *Investors Chronicle* (1973), *Business Week* (1974), *Euromoney* (1980) and *Institutional Investor* (1980). The last was reprinted in *Now*, a short-lived magazine financed by Jimmy Goldsmith and intended as a British answer to *Time*. Seductively entitled, 'The Confessions of Siegmund Warburg', and written by Cary Reich, that interview was more revealing than the earlier ones, but Siegmund gave it only on condition that he would have a chance to edit his answers before publication and after Reich had agreed to submit to a graphological test.

He co-operated wholeheartedly with Joseph Wechsberg in a lengthy and detailed profile in the *New Yorker* in 1966, and with a contemporaneous book, *The Merchant Bankers*, by the same writer. Siegmund himself published a pamphlet that year entitled *The Case for Sterling: The Case for a Rejuvenated Britain*. Quite often he wrote letters to *The Times* about the British economy or the political

situation in the Middle East. It was hard to accept that all these were
the actions of someone who shunned publicity.

*

That Siegmund Warburg had moral courage was evident from his
reaction to kidnapping threats in 1970, during one of the worst
periods in the long struggle in the Middle East. As a Jew who was
thoroughly assimilated in England, Siegmund was never a Zionist,
and his attitude to Israel was ambivalent but well disposed, not least
because his daughter Anna was married to an Israeli and lived there.
He had been honoured by the Weizmann Institute and had put
money into the Israel Corporation, a sort of investment trust which
invested in Israeli companies. But he disliked nationalism in general,
and felt that Israel in particular had fallen prey to it.

At a time when kidnappings by Arab fanatics were occurring not
infrequently, Siegmund became one of their possible targets because
of his prominence as a European Jew who had helped Israel. He
circulated a memorandum to some of us in the bank, commanding us
under no circumstances to pay a penny of ransom if he were to be
kidnapped. He meant it and would have been horrified if we had
disobeyed him. Fortunately, we were not put to the test.

Another example of his resolution in the face of adversity was
shown by his reaction to the now long-forgotten Arab boycott,
which had its impact on the investment banking scene for about
three years from 1974 to 1976. The Arab banking houses in Kuwait,
Saudi Arabia and the United Arab Emirates, wallowing in money
from their oil riches, were active purchasers of new issues of
eurobonds. However, they refused to participate as underwriters in
any issues in which the underwriting group included firms that
actually or allegedly had dealings with Israel. Rothschilds, Banque
Bruxelles Lambert and some of the Lazard houses were among those
blacklisted by the Arabs in addition to Warburgs.

Warburgs had invented the eurobond market and was one of the
leading houses in originating and underwriting new issues. However,
we did not have the same capacity to absorb large amounts of bonds
as the Arab banks, as a result of which many of the other traditional
lead managers, from both the United States and Europe, started
to prefer the Arab houses and exclude us from their underwriting
lists. We could have accepted underwriting on an 'undisclosed basis',
but the possibility of participating furtively in such a manner was

totally rejected. Another option would have been to roll over resignedly and accept the situation, thereby not embarrassing our non-Jewish banking friends, with whom normal business would no doubt resume in due course. At least one prominent so-called Jewish bank in London did just that. But Siegmund despised appeasement and refused to give in to blackmail. He was determined to protest against those houses that chose to leave Warburgs out of their underwriting lists.

Looking back on the situation ten years later, David Scholey commented to *Institutional Investor*, 'there were many occasions when people would say to us in arranging an issue for a borrower whom we knew, "I'm sure you'll understand that we can't invite you into this because we have Middle Eastern bankers in the management groups." And we always said: "We don't understand, we don't think it's right and we don't think you should accept that sort of limitation."'

In short, thanks to Siegmund's leadership, we made a thorough nuisance of ourselves over an extended period of time. It required a lot of guts on his part to put principle ahead of expediency. Our policy was largely successful, and we were eventually removed from the blacklist, which in any case became ineffective over time as the relative importance of the Arab banks declined.

*

Above all, Siegmund liked to be thought of as a teacher, and he sometimes told us he wished he could have spent his life as a teacher rather than a banker. He would have made a superb professional teacher, although I preferred to visualise him as a psychoanalyst. I have read that some people in the firm and outside it referred to him as the headmaster. I never heard that expression used, just as I never heard anyone who knew him well call him Siggy, a nickname that found favour with some sections of the British press, who thus pretended greater familiarity than was justified. Apparently, some of Siegmund's American cousins had teasingly called him Siggy behind his back. He did not like it, and he was not too keen on some of those cousins. 'God gives us our relatives; thank God we can choose our friends' was another of his epigrams.

He had a generally pessimistic view of the world. In the post-war years, he believed that communism would prevail over capitalism, and in his interview with *Business Week* in November 1974, he predicted a worldwide depression far worse than that of the inter-war years. He rationalised that pessimism was preferable to opti-mism because you might have some pleasant surprises, and he liked to be thought of as a 'cheerful pessimist'.

Enthusiasm is not usually associated with pessimists, but he was an enthusiastic person none the less and this, combined with a natural wisdom, made him an inspirational leader. He had a grand vision for the bank, and he communicated it, and through a combination of encouragement and chastisement, usually mild, he knew exactly how to get the best out of you in his pursuit of that vision. Criticism was good, he believed, when it was warranted, but it had to be balanced with praise.

I learnt from him that in any business, but especially one like Warburgs, the management of people is that business's single most important aspect. It involves spotting, recruiting, selecting for the right position, listening, caring and motivating, and Siegmund spent much of his time, far more than anyone else in the firm, on these activities. It was, of course, impossible to emulate the skills he had with people or his intuition, but at least one could observe the master in action.

Many business executives today utter platitudinous proclamations about people being their company's most valuable asset, and then pass recruiting and career management to the director of human resources, as he or she is now called. Siegmund believed that such matters were too critical to delegate.

Equally important were the values he taught us. Collectively, they constituted a set of rules for the conduct of business, which could be copied with advantage by almost any business today. We tried to perpetuate those rules in Mercury following its separation from Warburgs in 1987, not always completely successfully, and they are followed as much as possible there today under the leadership of Carol Galley and Stephen Zimmerman. They frequently involve not doing what other firms are doing, and do not always come naturally to a younger generation more readily inclined to follow fashion. I have more to say about these values in Chapter 26.

The decline of Warburgs in 1994 and 1995 and, just thirteen years after Siegmund's death, its sale to Swiss Bank Corporation for a knock-down price, was brought about, I believe, largely because those at the helm in Warburgs forgot to follow some of Siegmund's most basic rules. Most of all, he sought to guard against the complacency that followed success and which he sensed could too often lead to what he called 'expansion euphoria'.

CHAPTER 7

Night Club in the City

There was never a dull day at Warburgs. To people working in other financial houses in the City, however, the long working hours and spartan office surroundings seemed uncivilised and showed an excessive preoccupation with business at the expense of fun. After all, the marginal rate of tax on income was 80 per cent then, so why bother to go the extra mile?

While executives in other merchant banks in the 1960s came in for a leisurely start not much before 10 a.m., had a long lunch with at least two different wines followed by port, sometimes of a pre-war vintage, and not surprisingly after that, returned home around 4.30 p.m., we were at our desks before 9 a.m. and often did not leave until 7 p.m. Our hours may not seem so demanding to the modern observer, accustomed to the marathon all-night sessions that nowadays take place regularly in lawyers' and bankers' offices in the City, and I confess to having felt a certain degree of inferiority on learning that one of Mercury's new chieftains, Herb Allison, until recently president of Merrill Lynch, was often at his desk at 7 a.m. and did not go home until 8 p.m. But our hours were thought long enough at the time for us to be called the Night Club in the City.

When I joined it in 1963, Warburgs was 100 per cent owned by Mercury Securities (later S.G. Warburg Group), a public company whose shares were quoted on the London Stock Exchange. It was a holding company which also owned an advertising firm, a metals trader, a pension benefit consultancy, a general insurance company and a polling organisation. These other interests had been acquired because of Siegmund Warburg's distrust of the banking business following the nearly disastrous collapse of his family bank, M.M. Warburg, in Hamburg in 1931, when it had to be rescued by the Warburg cousins in America. It was for the same reason that he wanted a different name for the holding company from that of the bank, S.G. Warburg & Co. His fear was that a stock market collapse could cause a loss of confidence in the bank if the quoted company and the bank carried the same name. In the event, however, the bank, through the strong growth that followed its successful challenge to the City establishment in the first major contested bid, for British Aluminium in 1958, became the dominant factor in Mercury Securities. The other businesses were gradually sold off in the 1970s and 1980s.

To convey the image of a private bank, there was nothing to identify the mauve building in Gresham Street other than the street number. There was no sign proclaiming that this was the office of S.G. Warburg & Co., not even a name plate. Inside, the aim was to create an atmosphere of 'dignified austerity'. The décor was sparse. Visitors were shown to small rooms with just a desk and chairs but no wall decoration, where they were left with the door closed to protect confidentiality – it would not do to be seen in a common waiting room by your competitor or by someone who might be curious as to why you were meeting Warburgs. The only pictures I can remember, apart from two Dufy prints of New York given to the firm by Kuhn Loeb, were a collection of prints of old China, which hung in the corridor bordering the dining rooms. In each one, Chinese peasants were labouring away at some manual activity, milling, spinning, weaving, lifting, preparing meals and so on. No doubt they were carefully chosen to imbue us with an appropriate work ethic.

Warburgs was indeed an acquired taste. We did work hard, the intellectual level was high, and business was taken more seriously than in most other City houses, certainly than in many of the other merchant banks, where talented amateurism was still largely the order of the day and the office was regarded as something that should take second place to social events like Ascot, Wimbledon and Lord's. It was frowned upon in Warburgs if we took the day off for such occasions. Holidays were permitted, with some reluctance, and on condition that you left a telephone number where you could be reached. All business travel had to be at weekends whenever feasible, so as not to miss any working time.

Those were the days of the grand establishment merchant banks, such as Barings, Hambros, Hill Samuel, Kleinworts, Lazards, Morgan Grenfell, Rothschilds and Schroders, most with roots in continental Europe. (In the 1990s, thanks to the City of London's open-door policy, several of these have been sold to continental European banks, thus providing a variant of the Wimbledon effect,

in which Britain has the best tennis tournament but few of the top
players: the City is the best arena for international merchant
banking, but the main firms are now owned overseas, even if they do
still employ mostly British talent.) Partners of those banks were
expected to have the right background or at least to acquire the
manners and ways of those who did, and few could be found at their
desks in August, many preferring the grouse moors or the Côte
d'Azur. Siegmund, however, disliked all sporting activities and
seldom took holidays. He even disapproved of skiing, allegedly
because it resulted in so many accidents and thereby days missed at
work, but possibly more accurately because, as Eva Warburg once
told me, he had tried it once and completely failed to get the hang of
it.

The atmosphere in the bank was European. In addition to
Siegmund and the uncles, who were, of course, as much at home on
the Continent as in London, there were a number of German or
Austrian refugees in the firm and always a few 'volunteers' from
foreign banks spending a year or so with us. Then there was the
German-born but English-educated Ronnie Grierson, who spoke
fluently at least half a dozen languages and probably more, and our
charming Italian counts, Carlo di Robilant and Gian Luca Salina. It
was sometimes joked that it might be useful to put up an 'English
spoken here' sign in some of the more obviously cosmopolitan areas
of the bank. One quickly became adept at pronouncing more or less
correctly the names of such companies as Rheinische Westfalische
Elektrizitätswerke and Nederlandsche Handelsbank Maatschappij. It
was only in later years, as my interest in shares took on a wider
geographical aspect, that I discovered such intriguingly named
companies as Kinki Nippon Railway (Japan), Grupo Industriel
Bimbo (Brazil) and Arcelik (Turkey).

The dress code, unwritten but widely observed, was dictated by the
example of the inconspicuously but immaculately Savile Row
tailored uncles ('think Jewish, dress British'). Bowler hats were going
out of style when I returned to London in 1963, thank goodness, so I
was spared having to wear one of those uncomfortable adornments,
now sported mainly by clowns at the circus or Orangemen in
Northern Ireland. They were, in any case, considered démodé and
eccentrically English in the environment of Warburgs, and the only
members of the firm I can remember wearing bowlers were the ex-
journalist Arthur Winspear, who was more English in his outlook

than most, and Solly Brandenberger, an older Swiss-born foreign exchange dealer, who had assumed English attitudes and customs.

For similar reasons, school, club or regimental ties were not worn. They were a sign of class consciousness in a firm that was meritocratic before it was fashionable to be so, and they stood for a world that the uncles did not much respect and only partially understood. Getting into the firm might have been serendipitous, but getting on was on merit, provided it was accepted that the firm's style ranked ahead of the individual's. Anything remotely flashy was thought to be in bad taste. The uncles were upset when, as a young member of the investment division, Leonard Licht showed up in a Rolls-Royce. And it was Charles Sharp, never sartorially inclined himself, who once commented, 'If you notice a banker's tie, he's wearing the wrong tie.' (It is now almost impossible to buy any tie which would meet Mr Sharp's test: he would not have passed those colourful modern numbers with koala bears, tortoises, dolphins or cartoon characters.)

When I joined the firm, the total complement of people, including administrative and clerical staff, secretaries, messengers, tea ladies and cleaners, was no more than 150. For some twenty-five of us, the formal part of the day started with the so-called 9.15 meeting, sometimes referred to as 'morning prayers' (which, curiously, began at 9.20 a.m. on Mondays). Issues of day-to-day business interest were raised and debated briefly under the weekly chairmanship of each director in turn; that director also took the minutes, which had to be circulated by lunchtime the same day. The uncles attended the 9.15 meeting, but not Siegmund, who was presumably thinking about less mundane matters. Levity and long-windedness were heavily discouraged, in contrast to the unstructured weekly meetings of the investment division.

Board meetings in the old Warburgs were perfunctory affairs. They were held quarterly and lasted less than an hour. We were presented with a list of business transactions completed during the previous three months, and a short commentary was given on some of the more important ones. It was not the done thing to ask questions, except of the respectful 'Can the Prime Minister confirm that the United Kingdom economy has been performing along the right lines?' variety. One day a newly appointed director who had achieved eminence as the finance director of one of the country's leading industrial companies enquired about the firm's profits for the

year just ended, before there had been time for Henry Grunfeld and
others to decide what level of profit would be shown to shareholders
for that year. He was greeted with amazed stares like a man in an
H.M. Bateman cartoon, and he was shortly to find himself removed
from the board altogether.

At one board meeting, Geoffrey Elliott and I noticed Ronnie
Grierson registering his boredom by nonchalantly reading the
Financial Times. Geoffrey, who has a keen eye for the absurd, asked
me in a whisper what the reaction would be if he were to bring in a
copy of *Penthouse* for the next meeting.

It was a policy that at least two members of the firm should attend
every meeting with a client or guest, as well as every lunch, and the
most junior person present had to write a full and accurate
memorandum afterwards. We were forbidden to take notes during
meetings, so that the guest would not be inhibited in what he told us,
but you had nevertheless to be sure that your account was accurate
because there was always someone who would correct it if it was not.
It was good training for concentration and memory.

All memoranda were later summarised by a small team of ladies
under the leadership of Elsa Iglich, who, although her first language
was German, had a remarkable facility for capturing the essence of a
memorandum in just a few lines. Her summaries, which included all
incoming and outgoing correspondence, were circulated daily to
executives of the bank, so that a diligent reader had every
opportunity to be thoroughly informed of the bank's business. We
could never complain of inadequate internal communication.

Sometimes, Miss Iglich engaged in little games. Once a member of
the investment division went on what he explained as a marketing
trip to Ireland, and on his return wrote fifteen separate notes on the
fifteen visits or contacts he had made. A more usual way of reporting
such a trip, and a more considerate one both for potential readers
and the summariser, might have been to incorporate it all into one
note, Miss Iglich's summary of which might have read, 'Note of
meetings held with prospects in Ireland'. As it was, fifteen different
such summaries had to be made. They were brief, but we noted that
a sixteenth was given fuller treatment. It was a letter from a Dublin
hotel informing our colleague that he had left his golf clubs behind.

Siegmund himself was a prolific writer of notes to members of the
firm, exhorting us to be more self-critical, not to rest on our laurels,
to cry over spilt milk and to cross that bridge now rather than when

you got to it. His entreaties reached a crescendo when the firm had a notable success in some transaction, or was generally performing very well; at such times, he was more than usually fearful of complacency. He recorded in writing all his meetings, his lunches and dinners, and a good many of his telephone conversations. His notes didn't always come out quite right in English, despite his comprehensive knowledge of the language and its literature. 'I had Mr Hamburger for lunch today', he once wrote.

Lunches were abstemious by comparison with those of other financial houses. The food, although plain, was of good quality, as was the cooking, but no wines were served, which was most unusual in the City at that time. A glass of sherry was offered before lunch, but there was not enough time to drink it before lunch arrived. Beer or water was the choice at lunch. Some guests no doubt complained behind our backs about this enforced abstemiousness, and there were even some who refused our invitations because of it. But mostly I believe our clients were left with the impression that we were a sober bunch and that we cared about their affairs. 'The longer the lunch, the shorter the story' might have been our credo.

In later years, cider was added as a third choice of drink at lunch, and the waiting staff would ask the guest if he would like 'Beer, cider or water, sir?' Sometimes the question came out in a mumble with the 'or' getting lost. This elicited a response one day from an American guest of 'Oh, I'd really like to try the cider water, I haven't had that before.'

It was a requirement of the carefully thought-out style for us not to start talking to our neighbour at lunch, but to defer to the host, who would conduct a single conversation. The subject matter was definitely business, in contrast to some other City houses where it was still considered unBritish and bad form to 'talk shop' at lunch or dinner. To facilitate discussion in which everyone could participate, the number present was generally not more than five or six, and most of the dining room tables were oval or round. One of them had a small war wound made by a piece of shrapnel during the blitz, when the New Trading Company had its small office in 8–13 King William Street.

CHAPTER 8

An Unpleasant Lunch

The uncles and other seniors were extraordinarily good in inviting younger colleagues to join their lunches and dinners with illustrious guests, who might be politicians from the United States or France or Germany as often as they might be businessmen from the UK or Japan or elsewhere. Thanks to the wide range of friendships of Siegmund, Eric Roll and George Jellicoe in particular, most of the senior British politicians of the 1960s, 1970s and 1980s, including Margaret Thatcher, lunched at 30 Gresham Street at one time or another.

Our older colleagues were also willing to join lunches to which we had invited someone whom they felt could be an interesting connection for the firm. It was on one such occasion that I managed to incur the wrath of Siegmund and to experience its full and frightful impact. It happened in 1968 and it was the only time I was myself the direct and sole recipient of one of his rages.

I was still manning the American desk in the investment division, but had by then branched out into other areas of business, including the eurobond market. This was a natural progression because a larger number of American companies issued eurobonds that were convertible into their shares. While I was not an expert on the credit-worthiness of the issuing companies, I was supposed to have an opinion on the attractiveness or lack of it of their shares. I therefore took part in helping to price the convertible bonds of American companies, in the process receiving and meeting executives from the companies who came to Europe to help market the issues. I was in due course to graduate to travelling for Warburgs in the US to seek mandates for us to manage new convertible issues.

The eurobond market is a huge and largely tax-free offshore bond market which developed from the pool of dollars held outside the US, which became known as eurodollars. These originated from the cumulative American balance of payment deficits, and they were mainly invested in short-term dollar deposits with European and other banks outside the US. They could not be legally owned by American citizens.

It was a mark of the creative genius of Siegmund Warburg, closely aided in particular by the very able Gert Whitman, and on the technical side by others including Ian Fraser and Peter Spira, that he saw an opportunity to arrange an issue of long-term bonds to the holders of these deposits, and in 1963 Warburgs managed the first eurobond issue, $15 million of 25-year bonds at $5\frac{1}{2}$ per cent, for the Italian motorway authority, Autostrade. The market has grown exponentially ever since, and it has now reached a size of around $3 trillion.

In 1968, over $3 billion worth of eurobonds were issued, more than half of them by way of convertible bonds of American issuers. The United States government had enacted legislation aimed at improving its balance of payments, which in effect required US companies to raise money overseas for the expansion of their operations overseas. Thus they became major borrowers through eurobonds, almost always convertible into their shares. The policy did not meet its objectives and was abandoned after a few years, but the US government had unintentionally done a huge favour to the City of London. The market for expatriate dollars, including the gigantic eurobond market (not to be confused with the new euro currency of 1999), is today firmly entrenched in London.

Convertible bonds, common in the US, were almost unheard of in Europe in the 1960s, but it did not take long for British and other European investors to latch on to their attractions. They offered downside price protection through the bond element and the prospect of capital appreciation through the possibility of converting the bonds into shares once the share price had reached the conversion price, usually some 15 to 25 per cent above the price at the time of issue. One Swiss banker described convertible eurobonds as 'God's gift to mankind'. More accurately, he should have said God's gift to mankind except for nationals or residents of the United States.

It was indeed a God-given opportunity for both European bankers and investors. In 1968 alone, some $2 billion worth of eurobond convertibles were issued by American companies, including such well-known names as Standard Oil of California (Chevron), Chrysler, Eastman Kodak, Firestone, Reynolds Metals and Texaco. While the Americans dominated the field, the Dutch companies Philips

Lamp and KLM, and the British company Beechams (later Smith-Kline Beecham) were among a small number of others that were able to find a place in the rush to issue convertible bonds.

The drawback was that it became a rich man's game with bonds going to the clients of the underwriting banks, or to the banks themselves, which saw a chance to make money by holding on to some of the bonds. This practice was frowned upon by conservative firms such as Warburgs, which did not regard buying bonds as principals as an appropriate part of the underwriting function, but it was too tempting an opportunity for many others to forgo. It meant that the retail investor, the man in the street, was being shut out by the banks. His only chance to get bonds was in the secondary market, where he usually had to pay a price several points above the issue price.

I had been fascinated by convertible bonds from my days in Canada, and in particular recalled a story I had read in *Business Week* in about 1960, concerning two young Wall Street traders who had started a firm to deal exclusively in convertibles. They were able to persuade banks to lend them large amounts of money against the security of their positions in convertibles. The convertibles were bonds, after all, and banks traditionally have been happy to lend generously against the collateral of bonds. The two traders in turn stood to make large profits on their geared positions through the conversion feature if the underlying shares rose in price. They made $20 million or so between them in just two or three years in business, and retired to go farming in Connecticut.

Encouraged by this knowledge, I had the idea of forming an offshore fund to hold only convertible eurobonds, the shares of which would be sold to retail investors. I received tremendous encouragement from Eric Korner, who loved to sell investments, or 'place' them, as he would have preferred to describe it (stockbrokers sell, but bankers place, the latter being a euphemism for the same thing). He was excited at the prospect of engaging in some enjoyable selling of shares in the fund to his banking friends, who in turn would distribute them to their clients. Korner brought in the Bank of London and South America as a co-manager under our lead, and needing a brokerage firm with a strong retail distribution network in continental Europe, we turned to the American brokers Bache, which met that requirement.

We named the fund 'The Convertible Bond Fund'. It was

incorporated in Curacao, thus giving it offshore and tax-free status, and its shares were listed in Luxembourg. We raised $50 million, a large amount for an offshore fund in those days. It compared with the initial size of Selected Risk, Warburgs' only other offshore fund at that time, of $3 million in 1962, which was increased to $8 million in 1963 through a second issue. I was to formulate the investment ideas, but the management of the fund had legally to be provided by our Swiss banking subsidiary, which in reality had none of the relevant expertise. They were the managers, while we in London were merely the advisers. This complicated and rather absurd arrangement was necessary to reassure overseas investors that there was no danger of their investment income or capital gains being taxed in the UK – a fear they might justifiably have had if Warburgs in London had been the manager.*

*

Eric Korner and I were delighted as we shared our new plaything. We issued the first report to shareholders in burgundy and navy blue, thus foreshadowing the colours we chose for Mercury many years later. We found ourselves being courted by prospective issuers who wanted to test our appetite for their bonds, and by bankers who wanted to place new issues with us. I was invited to many roadshows for the issuing companies, usually involving a lunch or a dinner at one of London's smarter hotels. The company would put on a presentation, generally with slides, showing what a splendid company it was and why we ought to invest in the convertible issue they were about to launch. Mostly these were well prepared, slick and informative, if not totally objective, but there was the occasional flop. Consolidated Foods (later Sara Lee), the Chicago-based food

---

* Astonishingly, it was not until the 1990s that the UK Inland Revenue finally made a rather *sotto voce* statement that non-residents of the UK having their money managed in London would not be taxed in the UK. They were thirty years too late and the horse, having left its stable, was not likely to return soon. By then a colossal industry had been created in Jersey, Guernsey, the Isle of Man, Bermuda and the Bahamas to provide in a formal sense the management for the investments of non-residents who wanted to be advised by fund managers in London or Edinburgh. Billions of pounds of tax revenues have been lost to the UK's exchequer on the earnings from management fees which British fund managers were forced to cede to the offshore centres, to say nothing of the large amounts of invisible export earnings that should have been earned for the UK. Thanks to the myopic attitude of successive British Chancellors of the Exchequer and the Inland Revenue, the UK missed altogether an entire and very productive area of financial business that could and should have been encouraged to function from London rather than St Helier, St Peter's Port, Douglas, Hamilton and Nassau.

company, gave an excellent dinner with free-flowing wine at the Savoy Hotel, following which they showed a film of their operations. When the lights went up at the end of the film, about two-thirds of the audience had disappeared. Several others were asleep.

Korner and I saw a lot of Sandy Schwarz, a young partner of Bache, who had co-ordinated Bache's efforts in placing shares of the fund. On one of Schwarz's visits to London, Korner and I decided to invite Siegmund Warburg to join us for lunch so that Schwarz could meet the leader of our firm, of whom he had heard so much. It turned out to be a bad decision.

I already knew that Siegmund did not approve of the Convertible Bond Fund, despite its potential to make good profits for the bank. There were several reasons for this disapproval. First, he disliked anything that involved the ordinary public investor. This was a legitimate prejudice on his part, since retail business requires a different set of attitudes and practices from the more elitist banking business that he preferred, which is concerned with companies and institutional investors. Secondly, the Convertible Bond Fund was not his idea, and he had been sceptical, wrongly in the event, as to its likely success. Thirdly, there had been an article about the fund in *Fortune*, then the leading American business magazine, in which I was quoted, alongside a ghastly photograph of me that had been taken in the corridor outside the dining rooms at 30 Gresham Street. Eric Korner was also quoted in the article, and I somehow escaped overt censure for breaking the rules about speaking to the press through Korner's partnership in my crime.

It was clear that Siegmund was not in a happy mood when our lunch began, and he became increasingly irritable as it proceeded, despite Sandy Schwarz's affable conversation, which incorporated a diplomatic amount of flattery – something to which Siegmund was not usually immune. I cannot now remember exactly what caused his explosion. There is something about a row which can black out the memory of what actually provoked it. It may have been that Schwarz suggested we should make a further issue of shares in the fund, thereby increasing our fee, but also its profile. Whatever it was, Siegmund disagreed and I took Schwarz's side. This was serious disloyalty; it simply was not done to disagree with Sir Siegmund Warburg in front of outsiders. He went apoplectic and, stopping just short of yelling at me, stormed out of the room, beckoning an embarrassed Korner to join him and slamming the door loudly.

Schwarz and I were left to finish lunch alone. Much as I liked Sandy Schwarz, I did not enjoy the rest of the meal.

For some days after this, Siegmund cut me dead. His telephone calls stopped. Then one morning I got a message to go to his room. He was charm itself, and there was no mention of the incident. I was forgiven, it seemed, but I did not exactly forget.

In the year or so that followed, I applied myself energetically to analysis of the numerous convertible eurobonds from which we could select our portfolio, but this did not prevent some embarrassing mistakes. Chrysler convertibles, in which we had a large investment, proved a big disappointment, but worse than that, I made the almost unforgivable blunder of persuading Warburgs to manage small eurobond issues for two minor American companies, one a discount department store chain in California, and the other a company which sold correspondence courses in art and photography from an office in Connecticut. Both companies ran into financial difficulties, and we lost money for our clients. These were painful experiences, but as always there were lessons to be absorbed. I learnt that one should be wary of investing in companies in which the chief executive is too much of a salesman; the expectation he generates is almost always greater than the realisation. And one should recognise that the depth and quality of management in small companies is generally much less than in larger and richer ones.

The Convertible Bond Fund, in the end, did not survive, but we made in all about $1 million in management fees – quite a lot for the time. It did well for a while, but with a decline in the American stock market in 1970, interest in it waned and we had redemptions from shareholders. Several years later, it was merged with a convertible bond fund run by Capital Group, a highly regarded and globally oriented fund management group in Los Angeles, which I came to know and respect as a member of the board of the combined fund for a few years.

*

The success of the launch of the Convertible Bond Fund prompted an awareness in Warburgs that we might be able to offer our investment management services more widely outside the UK, and it was suggested that I might accompany one of our directors to Sweden, where he had developed a broad range of connections. I was thrilled to go on my first visit to Stockholm, but I was not prepared for the bedroom farce which was to follow.

On the first morning of our two-day visit, I joined my colleague in his room at the Grand Hotel and couldn't fail to notice the flirtatious attention he was paying to the pretty young chambermaid who brought our breakfast. I soon forgot it as we went about our day, calling on banks, paper companies and other Swedish companies, all of which were well disposed to Warburgs and to my companion personally. In the evening, he and I were to host a dinner party in a private room at the Grand for some twenty-five of the firm's closest business friends in Sweden, none of whom I had met previously.

I duly showed up at the appointed hour of 6.30 p.m. to receive our guests for drinks. They started arriving, but there was no sign of my colleague. After a while he telephoned me breathlessly to tell me he had been caught in an embarrassing situation with the chambermaid. She had lost her job and he had been ordered out of the hotel by the general manager and told never to return. I would have to host the dinner and make some excuse for his absence. I returned to the party and told our guests that my colleague had suffered an upset, thus lying the truth, as Siegmund might have put it.

The next day, we completed our programme of calls, but my colleague was uninterested in my account of the previous night's dinner, which I had somehow struggled through. He was totally preoccupied with a forthcoming visit to Stockholm that he was due to make with Siegmund Warburg a month later. They were both scheduled to stay at the Grand. How could he possibly explain to our founder that he was staying at another hotel? I suggested that he might say he wanted to save the firm money by going to a cheaper hotel, but that lacked credibility because Siegmund was not a penny pincher and in any case believed that directors of Warburgs should be seen staying only at the best hotels. I heard later that the hotel manager relented and allowed my colleague just one further visit to the Grand Hotel; thereafter he stayed at the Strand.

*

Another association formed largely thanks to the initiative of Eric Korner was with Securities Agency, which managed a number of investment trusts in London. Through the trusts, it had influential holdings in several major British industrial companies, such as United Newspapers, which owned the *Sunday Express* and the *Daily*

Express, and British Electric Traction. It also controlled a much smaller company, London and Rhodesian Mining and Land, later to change its name to Lonrho.

With origins dating back to 1890, Securities Agency had been developed by Harley Drayton, who had joined it as an office boy at the age of 14, and who died rather suddenly of cancer in 1966 at the age of 64. He was a smoker, as it seemed were all the members of the board of Securities Agency. Nobody thought much of the dangers of smoking then, and the warnings which were beginning to be heard were dismissed as alarmist. Tobacco shares sold on high multiples of earnings.

On Harley Drayton's death, Sir Robert Adeane, an entrepreneurial investor with an aristocratic style, was appointed Securities Agency's chairman. Adeane had a backgound in overseas railways, having been involved in such romantically named companies as the Ottoman to Smyrna Railway, the Buenos Ayres and Pacific Railway, and the Costa Rica Railway, of which he was chairman. His approach to business could hardly have been more different from that of the Warburg uncles, but there was mutual respect, and I found him entertaining and appreciated his buccaneering ways. I remember his comment at the time of the 1967 devaluation of sterling under the government of Harold Wilson: 'Bloody devaluation, I had to miss a whole day's shooting.'

Another senior executive of Securities Agency was Angus Ogilvy, whose brother Jamie was later to be a colleague in Mercury. Angus Ogilvy was mainly instrumental in 1961 in bringing in the swash-buckling Tiny Rowland as chief executive of Lonrho. Lonrho, under Rowland's leadership, was to be described by Prime Minister Edward Heath as the unacceptable face of capitalism. For a period, Warburgs was finanical adviser to Lonrho, but it ended the assignment when Rowland paid no attention to its advice. Henry Grunfeld used to remind us sometimes of an extract from *Advice to Bankers*, which was issued to American banks by the Secretary of the Treasury in 1863: 'If you have reasons to distrust the integrity of a customer, close his account. Never deal with a rascal under the impression that you can prevent him from cheating you.'

Compared to merchant banks of longer standing, Warburg's investment department was, as I mentioned earlier, under-represented in the lucrative investment trust market, and we would dearly have loved to acquire Securities Agency, which managed seventeen trusts with combined assets of about £100 million, equivalent to more than £1 billion in today's money. It was not for sale, but in 1966 Korner arranged the next best thing, a joint venture between Warburgs and Securities Agency, and who was to say what might happen down the road?

Together we formed a new company to invest opportunistically in small and medium-sized industrial or financial companies, and we called it Mersec, linking the Mercury Securities and Securities Agency names. Henry Grunfeld became chairman with Robert Adeane as his deputy. Our other representatives were Eric Korner, David Scholey and myself, and theirs were Angus Ogilvy, Geoffrey Lloyd MP and Martin Rich. I joined the board of Municipal Trust, one of their investment trusts with assets of £5 million, under the chairmanship of Angus Ogilvy, and Robert Adeane became a director of Selected Risk for several years before passing his seat on that board to David Stevens (in whose hands had been the day-to-day investment management responsibility at Securities Agency since 1968).

Mersec brought stakes in London and Edinburgh Insurance, and put together a rescue package for the travel company Sir Henry Lunn, but our two firms drifted apart and in 1971, when Securities Agency, which had by then changed its name to Drayton Group, itself became a merchant bank, we bought out its shares in Mersec and parted amicably. Drayton Group merged in 1984 with Montagu Investment Management and later, under the leadership of David Stevens, became part of Invesco MIM, today known as Amvescap. David Stevens, now Lord Stevens of Ludgate, is today chairman of United News and Media, the old United Newspapers, which still owned the *Express* newspapers in 1999.

*

We joked a lot in the investment division in the 1960s, but we took our jobs extremely seriously. We were deferential to the older generation, and although few of us might have admitted it, there was an element of fear in our dealings with such people as Siegmund Warburg, Henry Grunfeld and Frank Smith, who combined superior intellects with an aura of seniority and discipline, and who were quick to pounce on any errors in our written work, however unimportant they might seem to us. I believe that Frank Smith, as well as Henry Grunfeld, read copies of just about every document and letter that went out from the office other than routine ones, as well as every internal memorandum. They were demanding bosses, and we were respectful and compliant to an extent that seems scarcely believable in today's world of more egalitarian and informal management structures, where everyone calls everyone else by their first names.

There were times when friends in other City houses asked why I put up with the seemingly neurotic demands of a diverse crew of eccentric older men with foreign backgrounds, who obviously didn't understand the British way of life. (In reality, of course, they understood it only too well and took advantage of it by thinking differently and working harder.) After all, it was 1963, the year in which the Beatles made their first trip to America (in one of my better judgements I forecast they would be a flop there), and in which, in the immortal words of the poet Philip Larkin, sexual intercourse began. It was the age of permissiveness and the swinging sixties in London, which followed the grim days of rationing in the early 1950s. My contemporaries from Oxford were enjoying the new atmosphere, but there was nothing permissive about the lifestyle at Warburgs. We might have been a night club, but it was in the wrong end of town.

Such thoughts did cross my mind from time to time, but I knew that life at Warburgs was more exhilarating and more varied, and for someone who had spent five years in Canada, more international in scope than in other merchant banks. Those with experience of working in other firms noted the almost total absence of internal politics in Warburgs – we simply had no time for it. It was a continuous education in human psychology as well as in finance and investment, interspersed with much laughter. I am sure it gave us a better schooling in finance than any business school could have done.

There was another reason to stay with Warburgs, if the full truth be told. I believed I would make more money in the business environment created by a team of brilliant Jewish financiers, who had already shown their competitive edge over the more conventional and longer-established City firms. Warburgs had first obtained a quotation on the London Stock Exchange in 1954, reversing into a quoted shell company called the Central Wagon Company, later Mercury Securities. I had been granted options on Mercury Securities and was well aware that its shareholders had made some twenty times their money in its first seven years as a publicly owned company.

The uncles, whatever their demands on our time and our nerves, were instantly accessible and did not stand on hierarchical ceremony. By inviting you to their houses or flats in London for dinner or some other purpose, they brought you into their circle, and you felt you were almost part of an extended family. And it was difficult not to sympathise with Siegmund Warburg's determination to recreate, in London, a Warburg banking firm to carry on the traditions of the eighteenth-century Hamburg firm which had been plundered by the Nazis.

These rational considerations aside, the high-tension atmosphere in Warburgs was addictive, and one sensed that to work anywhere else in the City would be anti-climactic. In the early days, very few people left the firm. Remaining with one company through a working lifetime was considered admirable. Today such loyalty is considered to be a mark of someone with no imagination or ambition. A decade later, people did leave, and when they did, they were immediately treated, in the revisionist world of Warburgs, as non-persons whose contribution to the firm had been negligible. Geoffrey Elliott wrote humorously of the 'venom as chilling as though I had sold atomic secrets to the KGB', shown by the seniors in Warburgs when in 1981 he announced he was leaving the firm to join Morgan Stanley in New York.

In a Warburg-induced spirit of self-criticism, I have sometimes reflected in more recent times as to whether, by staying with the Warburg and Mercury Group for forty-two years, I was demonstrating a lack of imagination; ambition was not an issue because it was assumed that you had it if you worked at Warburgs. One of the uncles once noted that most people change either their wives or their jobs in their middle years, but it might be careless to do both. Having changed wives, I have been able to reassure myself that I was right to stay with the same employer. Despite John Wilmot, Earl of Rochester's couplet:

> Since 'tis nature's law to change
> Constancy alone is strange,

there is a lot to be said for staying in one firm; in the long run, the grass may well not always be greener on the other side of the fence. Indeed, it was noticeable, with only a few exceptions, how people who left flourishing careers with Warburgs and later Mercury faded into relative obscurity with their new employer.

In the 1960s you were not expected to leave, but nor did you expect to be dismissed. There was in any case little incentive to leave for a higher salary when income tax took away 80 per cent of the increase. The uncles did not sack anyone. Perhaps they thought that, as newcomers to the City, they would get a reputation for unBritish behaviour if they resorted to dismissals. They had a better idea – the drip-drip procedure. One executive whom they wanted to leave came in one Monday to find his desk moved to another room with more junior people; a week later, there was no copy of the *Financial Times* on his desk; the week after that, his desk was moved again; the next Monday, he had no telephone. To no one's surprise, he left.

CHAPTER 9

Some Wall Street Tycoons

Siegmund Warburg's indifference to the firm's investment activities did not extend to what we called 'nostro investments', those made for the bank's own account. He believed that some of us in the investment division should at least be clever enough to dream up investment ideas which would make money for the bank itself rather than thinking only about the clients. In this area, Siegmund was something of a gambler, and he was prepared to have a go once appropriate research had been done, but for whatever reason, perhaps fear of failure, the rest of us didn't produce many ideas and certainly not enough to redeem Cinderella's reputation as a costly and largely irrelevant appendage.

As fund managers in the investment division in the early days, we were required to manage 'stock accounts', which were one type of nostro activity. We were allocated small sums of the bank's money to run as dealing accounts in competition with each other. This was supposed to give us practice in managing money and to provide our superiors with some insight as to which of us was any good at it. It was an awful idea because it forced us into short-term speculation in risky low-quality shares rather than sensible long-term investments, and there was an inevitable temptation for us to pay attention to the stock accounts at the expense of our clients' portfolios. Bob Arnheim frequently came out on top, and although short-term dealing goes against the grain of everything I believe about investing, I usually managed to stay above the middle of the pack when our stock accounts were measured every quarter. This said more about the unsurprising inadequacies of a number of my colleagues in this type of investing than any budding talent for speculation on my part. Happily, the stock accounts did not survive – they made nobody happy and the firm no richer.

There were, however, some more substantial and interesting nostro investments which Warburgs made in the United States as a result of Siegmund's own networking and imaginative thinking.

Unaffected by the pro-European chauvinism of some other members of the firm, he had an appreciation of the opportunities for such investments in America, and because he knew I shared his attitude, I was lucky enough to be involved in most of them. One that had an unfortunate ending for Warburgs occurred in the late 1960s in a company which Siegmund created with much foresight, and then abandoned in a fit of vengeance directed at its chief executive. It was a costly mistake.

Warburgs had for many years owned a company in the US called American European Associates or, despite Siegmund's not too serious objections to the abbreviation, AEA. It had some $3–4 million of investments in American securities, managed in New York by another German Jewish refugee called Kurt Loewenberg. Both Loewenberg and his son Ralph, who worked with me on the American desk in Warburgs in London for a while in the 1960s before joining our small office in New York, were extremely knowledgeable investors who specialised in buying shares that no one else wanted, often in mundane industries such as railroads and coal.

Nowadays these are classified as value investments, the expectation or hope being that sooner or later their value will be recognised in the share price through take-over, improved management or simply greater awareness. In those days, they were more commonly referred to in Warburgs as special situations, an expression that was alternatively used by some of the uncles as a euphemism to explain to clients the stale investments they held as a result of unsuccessful speculations we had indulged in with their money. One of my roles was to keep in touch with Kurt Loewenberg, and later with Ralph, as to the always unconventional and generally profitable investments which they made for AEA.

Then Siegmund had a brilliant idea for AEA. He was bored with its portfolio of special situations, despite their good performance, and wanted to make a bigger splash in the United States. Encouraged by his close friend Dick Dilworth, a well-connected former managing partner of Kuhn Loeb with a patrician manner who was running the 'family office' of the Rockefeller family, and George Love, a retired chairman of Chrysler, he proposed turning AEA into the first substantial buy-out investment company* in the US.

---

* A buy-out occurs when a purchase is made of an entire business or division of a business. If it is financed with borrowings, it is called a leveraged buy-out (LBO).

A number of rich families in America and Europe were invited to invest through what were called participations – something close to limited partnership interests. The objective of the reborn AEA would be to take major stakes in companies or divisions of companies in the US that might be for sale, financing the purchases partly with the participants' money and partly with borrowed money. Siegmund described this as financial engineering; much later these transactions were known as leveraged buy-outs (LBOs). To provide industrial expertise, it was decided to invite as additional participants a handful of retired chief executives of major American corporations. The blue-blooded initial participants in AEA included the Rockefellers, the Mellons, the Harrimans, the Hannas of Cleveland and the Agnellis as family participants, and the former chief executives of IBM, EI du Pont de Nemours, General Electric and General Motors as individual participants. Siegmund also involved a small American investment banking firm, Laird, with which he had a short love affair.

So, in 1969, AEA opened for business in its new incarnation in an office in Rockefeller Center on the floor immediately below Warburgs' own fledgling office. The chief executive was Carl Hess, a Wall Street investment banker and former management consultant whom Siegmund, Dilworth and Love had recruited. Among the management team was Vincent Mai, a member of Warburgs' corporate finance division with a nose for investment values, who had chosen to move to New York a year or so after Warburgs opened its office there, and Jake Eberts, a young Canadian who later became a successful film producer. Jake first achieved fame with *Chariots of Fire* and *Gandhi*, and he was later involved in the production of *The Killing Fields*, *Local Hero*, *Driving Miss Daisy*, *Dances with Wolves* and *A River Runs Through It* – all in a different class to today's typical Hollywood product. He has written a book about his career in the film business with the memorable title of *My Indecision is Final*.

As luck would have it, AEA's first investment, The Leisure Group, a California-based retailer of sports goods run by two seemingly bright young business school graduates, was an immediate and utter disaster. Within a few weeks of our investment, the company got into serious difficulties and AEA's participants suffered a total write-off. At about the same time, it transpired that AEA had placed some money on deposit with Laird, which was soon to crumble under the weight of some unsuccessful investments of its own.

That was the final straw for Siegmund, who was furious. Laird, viewed by him a few months earlier as the epitome of creative banking, was now seen as a band of reckless adventurers with whom one should not do business, let alone place money on deposit. He sensed that he had backed a loser in Carl Hess, and the praise he had until then heaped upon him turned to condemnation of the most vitriolic kind. However, he was powerless to do anything about it, because the more forgiving Dilworth and Love were not prepared to contemplate firing Carl Hess on the evidence of just one investment. This, I think, was the cause of Siegmund's frustration – he had created something, but he was not in control of it; it made him physically ill.

Somehow his venom passed me by, although, as a director of AEA, I had visited The Leisure Group with Carl and had backed his investment judgement. But I was given the unpleasant task of negotiating our withdrawal from AEA. Siegmund simply wanted no more of it, and we beat an ignominious retreat. It was a decision based on emotion, and it turned out to be a serious misjudgement.

Thereafter, AEA was astonishingly successful. The shares we sold in 1973 at $1 per share were worth over $250 per share twenty-five years later. No wonder *Fortune* described it as 'The Richest Little Club in the World'. It was at the top of the league table of leveraged buy-out investment companies, and participations in AEA were eagerly sought after by university endowment funds and other institutional investors. Even the ubiquitous Henry Kissinger joined the club.

Carl Hess had the last laugh. In 1988, he brought in as chief executive Vincent Mai, who some years earlier had left Warburgs in New York to join Kuhn Loeb (which became part of Lehman Brothers). The following are extracts from a letter that Vincent wrote to me at the time:

> As a keen observer of life's ironies I thought you would be interested to know that I will be leaving Shearson Lehman in the spring of 1989 to become President of AEA. I will be taking over responsibility for running AEA from Carl. He is now 76 years old although he doesn't look a day older than when we first knew him.
>
> While AEA is today a very different operation from the entity you and

I knew, I could not help but think back to the early days when you and I used to discuss AEA's difficulties and potential. There is no doubt that AEA is yet another manifestation of Siegmund's uncanny vision, having started in the business long before LBOs became the vogue. While today's LBO craze, with massive leverage and other attendant excesses, has become rampant, AEA has stuck to its knitting as originally conceived by you and others and has done extraordinarily at it.

I think I can rightly say that you can take partial credit or criticism – depending on one's point of view – as a mid-wife of my pending move.

Under Vincent Mai's able leadership, AEA has continued to prosper, and Carl still plays an elder statesman role in his eighties; Vincent is chairman and chief executive, Carl is chairman emeritus. What a shame that Warburgs did not keep its founding shareholding – that we failed to take the long-term view, as we should have done. It would have made a wonderful golden coach for Cinderella, and perhaps Siegmund would not have been so keen to get rid of us ten years later.

*

A weekend in the early 1970s spent with a branch of the Mellon family near Pittsburgh provided some good theatre. It was arranged by an exceptionally charming colleague on the Warburgs board, Terence O'Neill, a member of one of Ireland's ancient families who as Captain O'Neill had been Prime Minister of Northern Ireland from 1963 to 1969, the most liberal-minded Ulster Unionist leader even to this day. He had tried hard to prevent his country tearing itself apart, and his failure to find a formula for peace left him profoundly pessimistic that a solution would ever materialise for the seemingly intractable Irish problem. He echoed a theme of my Irish mother who, having lived the first twenty years or so of her life near Dublin, believed there was an element of the Irish population which was addicted by tradition to fighting, whether with fists or bullets.

During his role as Prime Minister, Terence had courted a number of rich American families of Ulster extraction with a view to attracting investment in Northern Ireland. The Mellons were one of the most prominent, and he had struck up friendships with several members of the family. So one Saturday morning, Terence, David Mitchell, then head of Warburgs' New York office, and I set out from Pittsburgh in a large black limousine to stay with a branch of

Siegmund Warburg – self-proclaimed observer from outer space.

Eric Korner, uncle with a twinkle.

Henry Grunfeld in 1994, at the age of ninety – Siegmund's troubleshooter who ran Warburgs.

Facing page

ABOVE Warburgs' offices at 30 Gresham Street in 1966. This view is now obscured by the Guildhall Library.

BELOW Eric Roll – Mercury's first chairman – an indefatigable traveller who knows and remembers everyone.

RIGHT 'Get rid of it!' Siegmund gives me his instructions in 1979 at his house overlooking Lake Geneva.

Warburgs' chairman's committee in 1980: (from the left) Herman van der Wyck, Oscar Lewisohn, Henry Grunfeld, David Scholey, Eric Roll, Siegmund Warburg, Geoffrey Seligman, PSD.

Andrew Smithers,
guru, strategist
and columnist.

The 'gang of motorcar salesmen', 1986. From the left: Richard Bernays,
Stephen Zimmerman, PSD, Leonard Licht and David Price.

David Price, PSD and Stephen Zimmerman, June 1988.

The Prince of Wales opens Mercury's Youth Enterprise Centre in Brixton,
February 1989. From the left: Hugh Stevenson, the Prince of Wales, PSD,
Stephen Zimmerman.

David Price,
unflappable and
full of wisdom.

Cartoon of
David Price
by Paul Hyman
of Mercury.

the Mellon family some 50 miles distant. On arrival, we were greeted in a proprietorial manner by a very grand but obsequious English butler named Douglas, who enjoyed the opportunity of addressing Terence as 'my Lord' (he was by then Lord O'Neill of the Maine) and generally acted as if he were in charge of the household.

Our host and hostess joined us for the first time for lunch, which was notable for the generous availability of martinis and wine, and the interventions of Douglas in the conversation. While serving the carrots, he might, for example, correct our apparently rather uncertain hostess with 'No, madam. It wasn't Italy where you were on holiday in the summer. It was Spain.'

We toured the racing stables in the afternoon without our hosts, and in the evening we met in the drawing room for a cocktail party in Terence's honour, at which they contrived to appear only shortly before it was time to move on to dinner. Their absence didn't matter, however, because Douglas was well up to the task of introducing all twenty-five or so guests to Terence, David and me as he circulated with a tray of drinks.

After a small dinner party at the Rolling Rock Country Club, we returned to the Mellon house around 11 p.m. to be greeted again by Douglas, who suggested to the three of us that we might like a game of billiards and a glass of brandy. However, our somewhat tired host, anxious to indulge in both of these pleasures, was denied them. 'No, sir, not you', Douglas commanded him. 'You, sir, will go straight upstairs to bed.'

It was not a productive weekend from the business point of view; nor was it a consolation to know that the Mellons were getting even richer through their participation in AEA while Warburgs was not. But it was greatly entertaining.

*

A nostro investment with a far happier outcome, especially for me personally, was in Deltec, which had been started in Brazil in 1946 by Clarence Dauphinot, a charismatic Princeton-educated American, who once told me that his considerable curiosity and interest in the rest of the world originated from his stamp collecting as a boy. While working in the immediate post-war period as a foreign bond trader for Kidder Peabody, one of the leading investment banking firms in New York, Dauphinot noted the absence of any capital market in Brazil, despite a growing demand for money on the part of Brazilian companies and the existence in that country of plenty of money in individuals' savings accounts and stashed away under mattresses. With the help of, among others, Al Gordon, his boss at Kidder Peabody, Clarence Dauphinot formed Deltec with an initial capital of $2500, with a view to developing a market in securities in Brazil.

In the early days of Deltec, Dauphinot and a few associates used to drive around small towns and villages in Brazil in jeeps, selling at first pots and pans, shovels and Old Crow whiskey to pay the expenses, later progressing to selling securities to people who had never heard of them. They discovered in the process that, if they could get the headman of the town or village, perhaps the mayor, to buy the shares or bonds they had for sale, others would follow his example.

In 1958, Clarence Dauphinot met Siegmund Warburg on the introduction of Salim (Cy) Lewis, senior partner for many years of Bear Stearns, a major Wall Street investment house which was a founding shareholder in Deltec. By then Deltec had developed into a successful investment banking firm with offices in a number of Latin American countries, specialising in selling commercial paper (short-term debt obligations) of companies in the region to banks in the US, Canada and Europe. Clarence Dauphinot wanted new institutional shareholders for Deltec in Europe, and Siegmund agreed to help him find them. Siegmund had a high regard for Clarence and persuaded a group of prestigious banks, including Deutsche Bank, Banque de l'Indo-Chine, Banca Commerciale Italiana and Bank of London and South America to buy shares in Deltec. Warburgs made a nostro investment, and Ronnie Grierson joined the Deltec board as our representative.

In January 1964, by which time I had been with Warburgs in London for less than three months, I received a telephone call from Siegmund one weekend asking me to go round to his flat in Eaton Square. He took me for a long walk and asked me to attend a Deltec board meeting the following week in Nassau to act as an observer for our firm. Ronnie, it transpired, had upset Clarence Dauphinot, I believe through talking critically about Deltec to outsiders, and, after discussions between Dauphinot and Siegmund, had resigned from the board. He had been replaced by Rad Guard, an elegant non-executive director of Warburgs with a background in retailing and a considerable talent for golf and cricket, but no particular interest either in South America, other than through a directorship of Harrods Buenos Aires, or in investment matters. Siegmund said he thought I would enjoy following Deltec's affairs with a view to my succeeding Rad Guard as a director in due course.

He briefed me in great detail as to the various unusual characters on the Deltec board whom I would meet, one of whom was Cy Lewis. Lewis was a large bear of a man with a self-destructive lifestyle, who had a sign on his desk in the main trading room at Bear Stearns reading 'Angry Boss'. It was sometimes said that he was the man who gave meaning to the first part of his firm's name. Not normally, if ever, given to use of the written word, he relied on his voice, which was both deep and loud. He was also something of a bully.

After dropping out of Boston University in 1927, Lewis tried his hand as a shoe salesman before getting a job as a 'runner' (messenger) for Salomon Brothers – a job he described as 'a pain in the ass'. He joined Bear Stearns in 1933, becoming senior partner a year or so later. He was the antithesis to Siegmund in the way he conducted business. Reflecting the style of Bear Stearns in those days, Lewis was an aggressive short-term trader, a type Siegmund characterised as having a 'boersianer' or stock exchange mentality as far removed from his own concept of an elite *haute banque* as it is possible to imagine. Lewis and his partners seemed to regard shares as bits of paper to be bought and sold, but seldom kept.

Initially, Siegmund and Lewis got on well, and they had a common interest in contributing to Deltec's growth, but the clash of personality types almost guaranteed that this would not last, and the deterioration in their relationship, as it turned from guarded co-operation to mutual suspicion and finally to intense distrust, was sad to watch. It was to culminate some years after my first introduction to Deltec in a transaction concerning Triarch, my old employer in Toronto. I was still involved in Triarch's affairs, first as Warburgs' point of reference in succession to Ronnie Grierson, and secondly as chairman of T and L until it was sold at a full price to Slater Walker of Canada in 1975.

Deltec had acquired a controlling position in Triarch in 1967 with the encouragement of Siegmund and Tony Griffin, who both thought there should be new opportunities as well as useful diversification in an association between two investment banking firms, one with a thorough knowledge of Latin America and the other of Canada. In 1972, Deltec received an attractive offer for its holding in Triarch from the Canadian brewing company Labatts. The offer, however,

was only for Deltec's shareholding of some 60 per cent of Triarch
with nothing for the minority shareholders, which included Warburgs and some of the other original British shareholders in Triarch.

Siegmund insisted, understandably, that Deltec should not accept
the offer unless it was extended to all of Triarch's shareholders. He
conveyed his views in a series of telex messages, phrased in a
moralistic tone opportunistically assumed to suit the circumstances,
while Lewis railed against Siegmund on the telephone to anyone who
was prepared to listen. I'm ashamed to say that on one occasion I
did, and I was subjected to an attack on Siegmund in such venomous
expletive-sprinkled language that I had to remind Lewis in no
uncertain terms that he was talking about the man who paid my
salary, and with whom, moreover, I was in total agreement on this
matter.

The problem was eventually overcome through the diplomacy of
Clarence Dauphinot and Gus Levy, another member of the Deltec
board, who was then chairman of the New York Stock Exchange
and the dominant influence in Goldman Sachs. Levy was famous in
Wall Street as an arbitrageur and a pioneer in the trading of large
blocks of shares. I found him a rather cold person, but he was
effective as a peacemaker in the fight between Siegmund and Lewis.
As a memento, he gave me his tie of the prestigious New York Bond
Club (which I still have), mainly I think because he took a liking to
my wife Maureen.

After the battle for Triarch was over, Cy Lewis befriended me and
Maureen, and we often met him at his Park Avenue apartment,
where we were expected to consume industrial-sized cocktails. His
favourite was a stinger-on-the-rocks – a lethal mix of brandy and
crème de menthe with ice. It was through him that I first met Steve
Ross of Warner Communications, which was later both a client of
Warburgs and an investment opportunity.

One morning I arranged to play golf with Lewis after a Deltec
board meeting at Lyford Cay in the Bahamas. It was raining, so he
suggested we should have a drink in the bar until the rain stopped.
Some four hours later, during which time Cy had consumed at least a
dozen martinis, the rain was over and we went out on to the first tee.
Swaying gently, he struck a perfect drive down the middle of the
fairway.

I came to like this seemingly quite lonely and unhappy man. I was
influenced perhaps by his constant suggestions that I should work for

him and open an office for Bear Stearns in London, but it became increasingly difficult to listen to his unprintable comments on the man for whom I did work and for whom I had a much higher regard.

On one of his visits to London in the early 1970s, Lewis introduced me to Robert Maxwell, who had been taken on as a client by Bear Stearns, over drinks at Claridge's. Maxwell was all over me when he heard where I worked. He wanted a good relationship with Warburgs, but the firm would have nothing to do with him. In later years, Maxwell was briefly a client of Mercury's when his company British Printing Corporation acquired a company whose pension fund was managed by Mercury. Maxwell, however, chose to intervene in the investment policy of the pension fund, a practice we considered unacceptable, and we mutually agreed to sever the relationship.

Since those days, Deltec has survived all manner of vicissitudes and adventures, including the expropriation of its substantial assets in Argentina in the early 1970s. It made a speciality of acquiring control of old-line British companies operating in Latin America, such as Harrods Buenos Aires, Rio de Janeiro Flour Mills, City of São Paolo Land and Leach's Argentine Estates. The shares of these companies were neglected by all but a few contrary-minded investors in the London market, so that Deltec, recognising their value in a Latin American context, was able to acquire substantial holdings at favourable prices.

Thanks to Clarence Dauphinot's perseverance and wisdom, and his ability to survive and even thrive on crises, Deltec has prospered, and the initial capital of $2500 had by 1999 increased to nearly $200 million. I became a director of Deltec in 1967, and some twenty-five years later, initially at the suggestion of Arthur Byrnes, one of the two senior executives in Deltec in New York, I was appointed deputy chairman. On Clarence's death in 1995 – he was still managing the business the day before he died at the age of 81 – I was invited by the board to be its chairman. In 1999, it was an investment management business with the largest shareholding in the hands of the attractive, elegant and acutely intuitive Penelope Dauphinot, Clarence's widow. It has played an important part in my working life, mainly because of the variety of interesting people I have met among its clients, its shareholders and its management. It is yet again something which I owe in the first place to Siegmund Warburg.

CHAPTER 10

Heroes and Rogues

The satirist Mort Sahl caricatured the typical Wall Street banker as someone who comes out of an apartment block on Park Avenue in the morning puffing a huge cigar, is saluted by a doorman in a Ruritanian admiral's uniform, is shown into a limousine the length of a bus and goes downtown to 'start stealing'.

When asked why he chose banks, Willie Sutton, a notorious American bank robber, said it was because that's where the money is. It should be no surprise to find that Wall Street, just like the City of London, has its share of rogues and thieves. But I do not believe they are any more numerous there than in most other walks of life, and I have found that the vast majority of financial people in New York, London, Toronto and elsewhere are scrupulously honest and ethical. The titans of Wall Street I had the luck to meet in America may have been rough, tough and even ruthless at times, but they were not crooks. They behaved like gentlemen, they had charm, they took an interest in the young, and they were very rich. Barons they may have been, but never robber barons.

A person with the highest integrity, and one of the most unforgettable characters I have met, is Albert H. Gordon, better known as Al, an initial supporter of Deltec and still one of its directors and shareholders in 1999 at the age of 98. Al is a store of wisdom on life, health, wealth and behaviour, with unusual views on just about everything.

In 1931, at the age of 29, and having been a commercial paper salesman at Goldman Sachs, he was one of three people who invested in Kidder Peabody, an old-line Boston investment banking firm which became insolvent following the stock market crash of 1929. He rescued Kidder Peabody from its difficulties, and for the next fifty years and more led it from the front, worked tirelessly and applied his imaginative mind to its development into one of the best Wall Street houses.

In 1995, some years after Al had passed the mantle of leadership to a younger generation, Kidder Peabody was nearly ruined when some $350 million of profits turned out to be illusory. The firm was merged into Paine Webber, and it fell to Al, who had remained chairman emeritus, to sign, together with the chairman of Paine Webber, a morale-boosting letter to the employees of both firms. This was some sixty years after he had joined it to take charge.

He had a fearsome reputation in earlier years, but he always took a close personal interest in his employees, and treated them fairly. There were occasions when he had to dismiss people whom he liked, and he continued to pay them a salary out of his own pocket. A fitness fanatic who chides his friends on their unhealthy lifestyle, Al, in his more evangelistic moods, tells me I should take more exercise and eat fewer desserts. He is particularly vehement in his condemnation of smoking, and he claims that if he ever gets to heaven it will be because of his constant campaign against smoking. An employee of Kidder Peabody told of an occasion when Al visited his office looking for someone else. Noticing the employee's desk strewn with coffee cups and cigarettes, Al said tersely as he left the room, 'Boy, you sure have a lot of bad habits.'

In his seventies, Al took up competitive running, and he completed the London Marathon when he was 82. A week later, he joined me for an oxymoronically described fun run at Culzean Castle in Ayrshire to raise money for the National Trust of Scotland. His mere presence and the publicity it attracted increased the Trust's receipts considerably, to say nothing of Al's own generous contribution, which was followed with further gifts in subsequent years. Tom Wyman, a former president of Columbia Broadcasting System (CBS) and head of Warburgs' New York office at the beginning of the 1990s, told me that he once met Al when they both arrived at the same time at La Guardia airport in New York. Al greeted him with 'When's your appointment? I'd like to walk into the city with you.' The shortest distance by road to central Manhattan is 8 miles.

Al and Siegmund never got on very well with each other, but they shared some values and interests. Al believes in a low profile and an inconspicuous lifestyle, even to the extent of travelling economy class on transatlantic flights with just a haversack to sling over his shoulder for baggage. A great reader, he is a devotee of Trollope, who he says has broadened his horizons, and he has a fine collection of Trollope first editions. And Al, just like Siegmund, will allow no obstacle to stand in his way. He attributes this to an experience at school when, despite his mediocre batting, he hoped to get into the school baseball team. The coach asked him, 'Gordon, can you hit the ball?' Al said, 'I think so', to which the coach caustically replied, 'I want someone who knows he can.' Thereafter Al has always known that he can do it, whatever it is.

His Kidder Peabody chairman's reports were often enlivened by literary allusions which illustrated his independent and sometimes prophetically contrarian views of financial markets. Writing in 1987 during the euphoric period in the markets which preceded the notorious and spectacular crash in October that year, Al came up with a verse from a not too well-known British poet of the fifteenth century, John Skelton, who was court poet to Henry VII:

> Though you suppose all jeopardies are past
> And all is done you looked for before,
> Ware yet I rede [warn] of Fortune's double cast,
> For one false point she is wont to keep in store.
> And under the fell oft festered is the sore.
> That when you think all dangers for to pass,
> Ware of the lizard lurking in the grass.

Conversely, at a time when markets were gloomy and depressed, he quoted Euripides:

> How oft the darkest hour of ill
> Breaks brightest into dawn.

Al's son John, together with Arthur Byrnes, runs Deltec's New York office, and I am happy to say that Al has a room there today. His advice and experience are available to us, and his trenchant views enliven our discussions. I am one of many who admire him greatly for what he is and what he has done, although I can hardly match Eric Chu, who started Kidder Peabody's office in Hong Kong. Chu has named his two sons Albert and Gordon.

*

Needless to say, not everyone I met on Warburgs' business was a saint. In the late 1960s, Robert Vesco, plunderer of Bernie Cornfeld's notorious 'fund of funds' company, Investors Overseas Services, and now a refugee from United States justice living in Costa Rica or

Cuba, came to 30 Gresham Street to market eurobonds of one of his companies, which was still apparently legitimate at the time. His wrap-around dark glasses gave him a mafioso appearance, and we had little difficulty in declining to underwrite his bond issue.

At a dinner given by the chief executive of one of our client companies in the Chicago area and his British wife, I was introduced to an expensively dressed and glamorous lady purporting to be a baroness. I met her again in London and found her unpredictable, but was none the less shocked when I read in *Time* magazine that she had been arrested in connection with the theft of a 44-carat diamond ring at the Ritz Hotel in Paris. 'A very Ritzy diamond heist' was *Time's* headline. The victim had advertised a reward of $300,000, and the baroness showed up with the ring to claim the reward, unaware that the people who greeted her were policemen.

John Doyle was another fugitive from American and Canadian justice, who was accused of fraudulently taking $20 million from Canadian Javelin, a Canadian resources company. He came to London in the 1970s, but was banned from entry to Warburgs because of his reputation and some earlier unsatisfactory meetings with our New York colleagues in Kuhn Loeb. He invited me to breakfast at the Connaught Hotel. Curiosity got the better of me because I wanted to see what an alleged large-scale fraudster looked like, and I accepted. White-haired, overweight and in his sixties, Doyle was wearing a yellow shirt with a stiff white collar and some prominent mother-of-pearl cuff links. His main objective in meeting me seemed to be to complain about all the bankers in London and New York who refused to meet him. At last report, in the mid-1980s, Doyle was living in Panama with his fourth wife and their poodle, Chanel.

A more engaging rogue was Armand Hammer, whose Russian father emigrated to the US and became a pioneer in the American socialist party. Armand was born an American, and his name was taken from the Arm and Hammer emblem of his father's political party. Originally qualifying as a doctor, through his father's friendship he met Lenin in the 1920s and struck a deal with him under which he obtained mining concessions in the Soviet Union in exchange for allowing his American company, Allied Drug, to be used for KGB espionage.

In a fascinating 1997 biography, *The Secret Life of Armand Hammer*, Edward Jay Epstein exposed Hammer as a fraudulent and corrupt operator in the oil business, who posed as an art benefactor and philanthropist giving out in his own name to charities, including those of Prince Charles, millions which in reality came from the company he controlled, Occidental Petroleum. His much-publicised purchase for $5 million in 1980 of a Leonardo da Vinci Codex was, it transpired, financed by the company, but this did not prevent him from changing its name to the *Codex Hammer*. A habitual womaniser, his most bizarre accomplishment was to fool his wife into believing he had given up one of his mistresses by persuading the mistress to change her name and wear a blonde wig.

Hammer had the aura of a buccaneering businessman, as befitted someone who had successfully built up Occidental Petroleum from small beginnings. He was known to his subordinates as 'the doctor', and while he was recognised as a ruthless dictator, we did not think of him as a crook. Henry Grunfeld had been introduced to Hammer by Roy Thomson, the Canadian press lord who owned *The Times*, and on one of my visits to California in the early 1970s, he arranged for me to visit him.

Occidental was forming a syndicate of companies with a view to applying for some drilling concessions in the British sector of the North Sea, and Hammer wanted to find a Scottish partner to provide the right face for the bidding process. The Labour government under the Minister of Energy, Tony Benn, would be allocating the blocks of acreage in the North Sea among the many competing drilling syndicates, which included most of the world's leading oil companies. Oil companies are by nature risk-takers and find it hard to resist participation in any new prospective exploration area. This time they would be judged on a number of criteria, including their substance and experience and the degree of Scottishness in the composition of their syndicate partners.

Hammer instantly put me at my ease by calling me by my first name. He had a twinkle in his eye and an avuncular, if somewhat conspiratorial, manner, and I warmed to him. I told him that all Scottish companies, including the investment trusts managed in Edinburgh, Glasgow and Aberdeen, were already committed to other syndicates, having seen a great opportunity to associate themselves with powerful overseas oil companies at minimal cost and with the prospect of riches. But surely, said Hammer, Warburgs with its renowned ingenuity could come up with some imaginative solution?

His quest for a Scottish partner had come so late in the day that no one at Warburgs could think of an uncommitted Scottish company or institution of any type or size; there were none. Next best, however, what about Roy Thomson himself? Although a Canadian, he had started out in the UK at the age of 60 with the acquisition of the *Scotsman* newspaper and later a television licence in Scotland which he had described as 'a licence to print money'. So Hugh Stevenson, then a young lawyer in the corporate finance side of Warburgs, who was on the team which dealt with Thomson Corporation's affairs, and I, together with one of Occidental's top geologists, went round to see managing director Gordon Brunton and others at Thomson Corporation.

Charts were spread out on the table, names of geological formations such as the Devonian and the Jurassic were explained, and hopes of major discoveries were assessed. Brunton understandably felt that it was not appropriate for Thomson Corporation, as a public company engaged mainly in publishing and travel, to get involved in such a risky venture as oil exploration, but said that he would like to 'think it through with Roy'.

Roy Thomson, myopic and bumbling, and talking in a rich and unreconstructed Canadian accent, joined the meeting and immediately seemed excited at the prospect of joining the ranks of the oil tycoons. He believed in Hammer's flair for finding oil, he told us. He decided to participate in Occidental's bidding syndicate in his own name, but giving an option to Thomson Corporation to acquire the participation for a nominal sum if the drilling were successful. It was a master touch. Roy Thomson owned a majority of the shares of Thomson Corporation and, if the drilling results were such that the company elected to exercise the option, the value of the participation would be reflected in an enhanced share price, and his wealth, as well as that of Thomson Corporation, would be increased instantly and possibly substantially.

In the event, Occidental's syndicate was fabulously successful, discovering two major oil fields in the North Sea, the Piper and the Claymore. Thomson Corporation duly exercised its option, and for a nominal sum it acquired from Roy Thomson a 22 per cent interest in both fields. It was the foundation of the enormous fortune of the Thomson family, now the richest family in Canada with, according to *Forbes* magazine in 1998, assets of nearly $15 billion.

The value of Occidental, of course, also increased significantly, and the company paid us a fee for the introduction to Thomson Corporation, even though Hammer already knew Thomson and, indeed, it was Thomson who had introduced us to Hammer. It was while I was in Los Angeles to negotiate the fee that I received a telex from London containing a typographical error which caused me some amusement. I had sought guidance on the level of fee I might ask for following a preliminary meeting with Hammer in which I had sensed that Hammer would not be ungenerous because it simply had not occurred to him that Roy Thomson could be thought of as Scottish. He was happy to give us credit for the idea. There was also a possibility that Hammer might ask us to play a continuing role in advising on the bidding process. The message I received from London was that I should seek a fee at a certain level, but that I should indicate to Hammer that it could be higher, 'if we were to play a bugger role'.

I saw Armand Hammer on several subsequent occasions. I visited him at his home in Beverly Hills, an unpretentious house except for a few stunning pictures, and met his long-suffering wife, Frances. Henry Grunfeld and I once went for a drink with him in his suite at Claridge's very late one evening when he had flown in from Moscow. He had great energy and was fun to be with. We had no reason to regret our brief association with him or with Occidental, especially in the light of what it achieved for our clients the Thomsons, but it was as well that we did no further business with Occidental, as the nature of its business became increasingly controversial in part because of its activities in Libya. In 1988, Occidental was the operator of the Piper Alpha drilling rig that collapsed in the North Sea with the loss of 167 lives – the worst ever oil disaster. Hammer went on running the company until his death in 1990 at the age of 92.

*

Many of the Wall Street people I came to know were rich because they were partners in extremely profitable businesses, but some of them were also shrewd investors, and I was curious to discover their methods. These often amounted, I found, to no more than backing quite heavily a very small number of companies where they knew and believed in the top management, and holding their investment indefinitely, regardless of short-term fluctuations.

I had learnt quite early in my study of other investors that to attempt market timing judgements is futile and costly. I have yet to find anyone who is consistently correct in forecasting the markets' short-term movements. Even if someone is clever enough to sell a share at the right time, he almost never gets in again before it is too late. One might say that the odds of getting each separate part of a double trade right in a market dominated by professional investors are one in two, so the odds of getting both parts right are one in four. Moreover, I have found that a person who makes the first trade correctly is likely to congratulate himself on the view he took and keep the same pessimistic attitude for too long. It requires plenty of self-discipline to control one's emotions after the market has had a strong rise, and to resist the siren calls of those people who tell you to sell, but it is common sense to ignore them.

In the 1970s, Nick McAndrew and I were regular guests for lunch with Hubert Simon, who ran the London office of Loeb Rhoades, a leading American stockbroking firm. Hubert was another German Jewish refugee to London, who spoke English with a trace of a German accent and a faintly cockney overlay. He always gave us a good lunch, talking most of the time, and had a running battle with his butler George who, in an attempt to keep Hubert's consumption down, locked away the Bendicks chocolates after leaving just one for each of us on the table. Each time Nick and I would watch with much amusement as Hubert, too ashamed to ask George for it, looked frantically for the hidden key to get some more chocolates. He was a top bridge player and had made a great deal of money investing in the American stock market. No matter what the uncertainties in the outlook or the level of the market, Hubert was always bullish and thereby always right in the longer term. It was a lesson in the virtues of buying the best and holding on through thick and thin. But Hubert never got his extra chocolates, and George confided in me that he was not allowed any at home either.

CHAPTER 11

The Best Kept Secret

The main problem with Cinderella in the 1960s and early 1970s was that it didn't contribute to Warburgs' profits. It was what we called a cost centre, not that any serious effort was made to undertake what accountants call a full costing exercise to determine what its true losses were. There were some profits from 'nostro jobbing' (buying and selling securities for the short term), mostly contributed by John Difford, an expert trader in eurobonds. If these were stripped out, and in reality they were an extension of the eurobond issuing activity of Warburgs rather than the investment management business, it was losses we saw when we looked at the figures, and they were unremitting, year after year.

I first became aware of the possibilities for achieving profits in an investment business when I visited the Capital Group in Los Angeles in 1972, following the merger of our Convertible Bond Fund with theirs. I was impressed by their ability to make money from investment management alone, with no banking or corporate finance to provide diversification – a far cry from Cinderella's losses. But it was Leon Levy who finally showed me, almost a decade later, that investment management was not only more interesting than investment banking, corporate finance or stockbroking, which I had already discovered, but that, once certain conditions were met, it should also be more profitable, and more consistently so. Leon knew what he was talking about because he had built up Oppenheimer & Co. in New York as a successful firm in both stockbroking and investment management. He explained to me the unique economics (one might almost say magical economics) of investment management, obvious in hindsight, but widely ignored by bankers, stockbrokers and investment research analysts until quite recently. It was the best-kept secret in the financial business.

The theory is quite simple. Fund managers charge fees based on the market value of their clients' portfolios, which, if history is any guide, will increase over any reasonable period of time. Where a fund management organisation has a sufficient critical mass of funds under management to meet its costs, any increase in market values will bring additional revenues which flow through directly to profits because there is, or should be, no increase in costs. If, for example, the markets in which the clients' money is invested rise by 10 per cent over a period of, say, a year, the increase in profits might be anything from 25 to 50 per cent depending on the cost profile of the particular fund management operation. The markets do the work for you, and they do it while you are asleep, on holiday, at the theatre or at the races.

Of course, it does not always happen quite like that in practice; there are things which can upset the calculations. First, you have to produce reasonably good investment results for your clients to avoid loss of business. Secondly, costs do have a habit of increasing even without logical justification; an outstanding fund manager can demand, and today expects, to be paid more if the amount of funds he is looking after gets larger even when the increase has been caused by the markets and not through his own efforts. Thirdly, there is always the danger of the unexpected – an administrative mistake perhaps, an investment guideline breached, a wrong valuation given to a client, or even a loss of securities held for clients in a custodian bank. And, of course, stock markets decline in value some of the time, and there can be down years. History suggests, however, that they are the exception. The world's largest stock market, the American market, has lost ground in only two of the last twenty-five years.

These and other problems do indeed occur, but the general principles hold true. If a fund management company which is already established with an adequate level of funds under management provides good results for its clients, keeps its cost under control and has an efficient 'back office', the growth of profits should be excellent from the market effect alone. Any new business is a bonus, but it becomes less important as the organisation grows; at a certain point, the return from the market is likely to make a bigger difference to the size of funds under management than new business.

The theory worked beautifully for Mercury's shareholders during the eleven years it was a publicly quoted company from 1987 until its purchase by Merrill Lynch in 1998. Its profits grew at an average of about 20 per cent per annum, and those people who held the shares throughout, as many members of Mercury's management did, made some thirty times their original investment in capital gain and dividends. But it was irrelevant to Cinderella in those early days because we did not have the necessary amount of funds under management to take care of our costs. And, in any case, how many of us then really knew the secret? Did we realise that, once we got to break-even point, our profits were likely to take off?

In 1968, at the top of the market that year, our funds under management reached a new peak of £500 million, still too low to pay for our by then rather numerous fund managers and the long tail of people in the back office. Custody, settlements, registration, dividend payments and accounting were all essential functions of an efficent investment department, and they were labour intensive in those days when every transaction was booked manually. Our clients were mostly private individuals, who have smaller portfolios than institutions but create the same amount of paperwork, while our fees were too low. It was not viable for us to ask our clients for fees on a commercial scale because certain other merchant banks had become accustomed to charging very low rates to their founding families and friends – a practice they were later to extend to pension funds.

I was spending more and more time on Warburgs' American business and lived most of 1969 and 1970 and several periods thereafter in New York. When I was in London, I sat in the international division of which I was to become head in the late 1970s, and when Andrew Smithers organised an enjoyable annual cricket match between the investment division and the international division, in the earlier years at his family's ground in Knockholt and later at the Leigh-Pembertons' ground near Sittingbourne, both in Kent, I found myself playing for the international division against my former investment colleagues. Investment remained my main interest, however, and I kept in touch with the investment division's activities through membership of the board of Warburg Investment Management (WIM), under which title the division was incorporated as a subsidiary company of Warburgs in 1969.

The investment division had moved from Gresham Street to another unattractive building around the corner in Cheapside that year. It was called St Albans House, and happily was torn down two decades later, uncovering in the process some archaeologically interesting remains of Roman London. The hope was that incorporation of the division, together with the move to separate premises, would be seen externally as a further improvement in Cinderella's status, and would help in gaining new business. There was no substantive change, however, in the way it was viewed internally in the bank. To Siegmund and the uncles, WIM was useful only in that it provided a pool of clients with which the bank could place its new issues and underwritings, and the occasional recruit for corporate finance.

*

The first chairman of Warburg Investment Management was Eric Roll. Eric is an exceptional person of great warmth, who has a huge range of friends around the world and a near-perfect memory for their names and background, which is reciprocated by the affection they all have for him. As David Scholey once noted, if someone from London were to land on an iceberg in Antarctica, one of the penguins would be likely to ask how Eric Roll was.

Once described as a man of the intellectual left with his heart in the right place, Eric has had at least four successful careers, as an academic, a civil servant, a merchant banker and a best-selling author. His book *The History of Economic Thought*, written over thirty years ago, is still a must for all students of economics. An ardent europhile, Eric was involved in the UK's early negotiations to join the European Economic Community, and he was described by Professor J. K. Galbraith as the most accomplished negotiator in public affairs in the post-war period, ahead of Henry Kissinger. He joined the board of Warburgs at the same time as I did in 1967, having been persuaded by Siegmund to come to his firm rather than Schroders. Happily, he remains engaged in the business of Warburg Dillon Read today as an energetic and peripatetic nonagenarian.

Despite his encyclopaedic knowledge of economics, economies and economists, I suspect Eric would be the first to admit that he is not an investment specialist. He was, however, a good chairman, and was also about the only Warburgs director who took the trouble to walk the hundred or so yards to visit Cinderella in St Albans House. Most of the other Warburg seniors lived in a world of indifference to WIM – out of sight, out of mind, seemed to be their attitude.

The day-to-day management of the newly formed WIM was in the hands of the likeable and capable Nick McAndrew, who later took over the chairmanship from Eric, with Andrew Smithers as his deputy. Our erstwhile leader, Milo Cripps, had departed after some difficulties with the Tyndall group. Some time later, he started a

banking business, Cripps Warburg, with George Warburg, Siegmund's son, in which John Morgan, who had been with WIM in the
1960s, also worked for a while. Cripps Warburg failed after some
loans it had made went sour, to the dismay of Siegmund who had
allowed, if not actually encouraged, Warburgs to make a token
investment in it. Milo then left the City, and he has since done very
well in the antiquarian book field as owner and manager of
Quaritch. George, a cultured and charming person whose wife is
American, joined a regional bank in Waterbury, Connecticut, and
later retired there.

The gloomy view of WIM on the part of Siegmund and the uncles
masked a real, if almost imperceptible, improvement in the business
in the late 1960s and early 1970s. A promising young management
team was taking shape, and gradually but surely the book of business
was increasing. Our largest account when I arrived in 1963 was the
Tyndall unit trust group, but some serious pension fund money
started to come our way with appointments to the Hawker Siddeley
and British Rail pension funds in 1967 and 1968. We were a pioneer
in the new world of specialist pension fund management which came
into being around that time. Until then, pension funds were managed
either in-house or by insurance companies, and were invested mainly
in government bonds. The credit for our initial involvement in
managing pension funds goes largely to Andrew Smithers. It was he
who saw the opportunity, thought up the presentation material,
developed connections with the pension benefit consulting firms,
which then as now were the key to appointing investment managers,
and above all made the prescient intellectual case for investing in
equities.

Not everyone in Warburgs supported Andrew's efforts to talk to
the bank's corporate clients about our proposals for their pension
funds. There were those in corporate finance who thought that any
contact between their clients and members of WIM, with its racy
ideas for equity investment, might be counterproductive. Besides,
Mercury Securities, the quoted holding company of Warburgs,
owned a pension consulting firm, Metropolitan Pensions Association, which stood to make more money by introducing pension funds
to insurance companies than to the investment division of its sister
company. Nevertheless progress was made. Among the Warburgs
seniors, Geoffrey Seligman was a believer, and it was he who helped
to persuade Hawker Siddeley of the merits of appointing us. Others

to follow in 1969 were Ford Motor Company and the Post Office and, through David Scholey's efforts, another type of institutional client, the Co-operative Society, better known as the Co-op.

Our pension fund business continued to grow in the early part of the 1970s. John Morgan had achieved a good track record in equities for Tyndall, and we were able to use this in our approaches to potential pension fund clients. While our merchant bank competitors were content to provide investment advice to the pension funds of their own existing corporate clients, we were the only ones to have an organised marketing campaign aimed at companies that were not clients of our parent company. Andrew Smithers was joined in his marketing pitches by David Price, who turned out to have a special flair for salesmanship, and by David Rosier, who was an able deputy.

We lost the Tyndall account at the start of the new decade, and with it some £125 million, or about a quarter of the funds under our management, but in 1972 we started our first unit trust, The 30 Gresham Street Fund, shortly thereafter to be managed by Leonard Licht and Norman Bachop. Generally, WIM's investment results were good until the bear market of 1973 and 1974, which, in view of our strong commitment to equities, came as a major setback, and it was not until 1976 that we reached £1 billion in funds under management for the first time. In the next three years, the amount doubled.

*

Responsibility for North America was assumed by Rodney Donald, a friend of mine from Canada, who in addition to an outstanding skill in investment markets has a comprehensive understanding of American and Canadian history and politics, including a special knowledge of the American mafia and its background. He continues to play a part in Mercury's business today as a director of its Canadian subsidiary. Rodney formed part of an international investment section which was looked upon condescendingly by the majority in the investment division, who preferred to follow the UK market. It included Tim Gare and Manfred Adami, and was joined in the early 1970s by Consuelo Brooke, our first woman fund manager, and Andrew Dalton, both of whom were to play a major part in Mercury's growth some years later.

Another talented member of the international team was Christopher Purvis who, when applying from Oxford for a position in

Warburgs, had shown music and wine as his interests, which drew
the comment from an amused Siegmund, 'That sounds a bit
bohemian, doesn't it?' I was sorry when Christopher was persuaded
to leave Mercury in 1981 to represent Warburgs in Tokyo. Norman
Bachop transferred to WIM's American desk in 1977. Significantly in
terms of Cinderella's status within Warburgs, he was told that one of
his main responsibilities was to be helpful to the international section
of Warburgs' corporate finance side.

International investment for British residents was inhibited by
exchange control regulations until they were abolished in 1979 by
Geoffrey Howe, the first Chancellor of the Exchequer in Mrs
Thatcher's government. Until then, British residents who wanted to
make overseas investments were required to do so by buying
'investment dollars', which traded at a fluctuating premium to the
official dollar/sterling exchange rate, thus adding a further variable
element to the outcome of such investments. An alternative available
only to institutional investors who could obtain Bank of England
permission was to borrow dollars for overseas investment, and we
took full advantage of this alternative to the benefit of several clients.

These exchange control limitations made it more desirable for us
to get mandates to manage investments for institutions based outside
the UK. Nikko Warburg, another of Andrew Smithers' inventions,
was put together in partnership with Nikko Securities to manage
money from Japan. It was run by Andrew Dalton and attracted some
$40 million from a dozen or more Japanese companies.

In 1971, we acquired a banking business with six people from
Barclays Bank in Jersey, which was to play an important role in
Mercury's offshore funds business. The following year, Richard
Bernays, who had joined us from the advertising world, took the lead
in organising a new offshore fund in Jersey, The Common Market
Trust, for which we raised £25 million to invest in continental
European shares. This was followed by the Transatlantic Market
Trust, which began with £10 million to invest in North America.
Both were later combined in Mercury International Investment
Trust, whose assets had grown to more than $4 billion by 1998,
when it was wound up on tax considerations.

In 1975, inspired by some studies made by Chris Novakowski, a
Canadian consultant living in London, on the possibilities for
lowering investment risk through international diversification,
Andrew Smithers, by now our recognised guru, had the unlikely but

clairvoyant thought that we should try to persuade American pension funds to let us invest part of their assets in overseas markets. It made sense because there was always at least one stock market that was performing better than the New York market. We already managed some money in international markets for the Ford Foundation, and if a charitable foundation was far-sighted enough to see the merits of investing in foreign markets, why not the pension funds? So we set up a new company, Warburg Investment Management International (WIMI), which obtained permission from the Securities and Exchange Commission to solicit business in the US. Its first chairman was Andrew Smithers.

Andrew did some of the initial 'mission selling', explaining the concept of international diversification, while Norman Bachop, our resident songwriter, went one step better and put the case for it into verse, to the tune of 'Thoroughly Modern Millie':

> When your local market rates are quite deplorable
> Foreign markets then no longer are ignorable
> For the fact is . . .
> International diversification
> Lowers your volatility
> Raises your internal rate of return
> Improves your liquidity
> Invest just ten per cent
> Outside the US
> If New York markets fall
> Then your results may well impress
> With their relative success
> If domestic price inflation should increase
> Unanticipatedly
> And the currency should start to decline
> Even if belatedly
> Your foreign stocks
> Will counter shocks
> And stem that decline
> So split your fund
> And give some money
> To us at WIMI now
> We'll show you how.

WIMI opened an office in the Chrysler building in New York in 1976 under the direction of Burton Weiss, an American who came to us from Warburg Paribas Becker. He was joined by Richard Oldfield and their chain-smoking secretary Mrs Godfrey, who claimed that Winston Churchill had dangled her on his knee, and her cat, Tokay. Burt's experience as an institutional stock salesman with the old A.G. Becker gave him a perfect understanding of the requirements of the American pension funds, and through his marketing skills and the able assistance of Richard Oldfield and later Stephen Cohen, business started to come in towards the end of the decade after an agonisingly slow start. We can claim to have been among the first investment managers to promote American institutional investment in overseas securities, which was to reach torrential proportions in the 1980s and 1990s, but unfortunately there were others who captured more of the available business than we did.

We incorporated Mercury Fund Managers, also in 1976, to develop our fledgling activities in unit trusts, and to give that sector of our business its own identity. The 30 Gresham Street Fund became the Mercury General Fund and additional unit trusts were started. However, we were ambivalent about the unit trust business and reluctant to enter it enthusiastically. Did we really want to go into the retail end of investment management? Would it taint our slightly elitist private client business and would it damage our prospects with institutions? Were we prepared to advertise our unit trusts, despite our founder's strong dislike of any sort of advertising? To help us address these questions we turned to Fred Grant, a commonsense businessman who had successfully run Metropolitan Pensions Association. Gradually, Fred persuaded us that the unit trust business was something you were either in or you were not; there was no halfway house. It took us quite a few more years to decide that we should be in it wholeheartedly.

CHAPTER 12

Ping Pong and Poker

When asked shortly before his eightieth birthday whether he was Jewish, Spike Milligan replied, 'No, but I try.' I know what he meant. Having a Scottish father and an Irish mother has, I believe, given me a certain empathy with 'incomers' in our country, and I have liked almost all the Jews I have met. I admire them for their talent, their determination and their humour, and I believe as Robert Mayer, a Jewish banker, said in self-parody at his hundredth birthday party in London some years ago, that Jews are just like the rest of us, only more so.

My attitude was, however, put to the test in an incident in the early 1970s, which showed Siegmund in his most supportive mode. A young man working on the international side of Warburg Investment Management, threatened with dismissal because of some indiscretions, retaliated by accusing me in a conversation with Eric Korner of having a special relationship with an attractive lady stockbroker (unfortunately not true) and, more worryingly, of being anti-Semitic. Korner spoke to me in a direct way, and I sensed that he might have wondered, even if only momentarily, whether there could be a grain of truth in the charge. After all, which of us is entirely free of all prejudices? When Siegmund heard it, however, he was outraged that someone could doubt the motives of a director of Warburgs in such a manner. He demanded that the young man be sacked immediately.

Siegmund's attitude to Jews and Jewishness always intrigued me. He sometimes complained that we did not recruit enough Jews (there were comparatively few Jews among the younger generations at Warburgs, although fortunately we had some very talented ones in WIM). He undoubtedly felt a special bond with Jews, whether they were religious or not, and he might say about someone, 'He's a Jew, you know', as if to imply that this automatically meant he was someone with whom one could do business. At the same time, I'm sure he was tougher on the Jews in the firm than on the rest of us. Perhaps being a Jew entitles one to be more critical of other Jews.

One day I was in Siegmund's office when he was going through his itinerary for a visit to Israel the following week. He read out to me the names of some of those he would be visiting and, slapping his hand on to his forehead in a characteristic manner, said with mock exasperation, 'Oh, my God, all those terrible Jews.' Most of all, he disapproved of Jews who refused to acknowledge their Jewishness, and this was one reason why he, and the firm, would not countenance a relationship with Robert Maxwell.

He was expert in the game of 'who was who', which consisted of ascribing Jewish origins to people with anglicised names. He was particularly good at this when it came to identifying the roots of the famous London merchant banks, almost all of which, according to Siegmund, had Jewish roots. Geoffrey Elliott, a senior Warburgs' corporate finance director, tells of a conversation between Siegmund and Saul Steinberg, who was later to play a role in the Mercury story. 'Of course,' Siegmund told Steinberg, 'you realise the Hambros are Jewish.' 'I didn't know that', replied a surprised Steinberg. 'Well, the Hambros know', said Siegmund.

*

California has beautiful scenery, a marvellous climate, superb wines and friendly people, and in the 1960s it had strong economic growth and thereby opportunities for investments that I thought had been largely neglected by the London investment community. I persuaded Siegmund to let me fly there from New York in 1966 to prospect for new business for the bank, and to try to identify a few companies in which we might invest.

It was the first such visit by anyone from Warburgs, but it was not to be my last. I went back many times in the next few years, with congenial travelling companions such as Tony Constance, who combined English practicality with South African enthusiasm, having had part of his education there, Vincent Mai, who had French parents but coincidentally was also brought up in South Africa, and Steven Lash, an American who spent some time in Warburgs in London, and who is now a director of Christie's, the auction house, and a senior member of its management in New York. I fell in love with California, and it proved to be a happy hunting ground for us in more ways than one. We arranged eurobond issues for a number of companies based there. Many of them were less conservative than their opposite numbers on the east coast and seemed to be more adventurous and open to new financing ideas. It was the era of the American conglomerate – companies that believed they could apply their skills to the management of any business or, for that matter, any country. One of them, Litton Industries in Los Angeles, came near to closing a contract with the government of Greece to manage that country's entire economy.

So far as the Mercury story is concerned, however, a more significant connection was initiated in California which was to bear fruit some seven years later. We had only a few contacts there, but through Siegmund I had met Amnon Barness, an Israeli who was a friend of Siegmund's son-in-law, Dov Biegun, husband of his daughter Anna. Barness had moved to California and was doing well in various entrepreneurial activities. While registering disappointment with me that I did not respond to his hint that I should 'date' his moderately attractive secretary by inviting her to dinner, Barness nevertheless introduced me to some of his business friends, including Royce Diener, who was then a financial consultant.

Diener was interested in the possibilities offered by the eurocurrency markets, and some years later he published a new edition of his book *How to Finance a Growing Business*, in which he acknowledged the contributions of Gian Luca Salina and Michael Bentley, both Warburgs corporate finance colleagues, and me in educating him on those markets. When he was not writing, Royce was giving advice to companies, including a publicly quoted hospital company called American Medical International, of which he soon became chairman. American Medical was anxious to expand in England and, with help from Geoffrey Seligman, Warburgs arranged for it to purchase the Harley Street Clinic, which was owned by a commercially minded doctor with an entertaining conversational manner, Stanley Balfour-Lynn. Soon afterwards, American Medical opened another hospital in London, the Princess Grace, and I recall Royce stylishly escorting Princess Grace of Monaco at the crowded opening ceremony on an extremely hot afternoon in the summer of 1977.

It was Stanley Balfour-Lynn who asked me, one day in 1973, if we would interview a young man called Stephen Zimmerman, who was the son of a friend of his. It was a fortuitous but, in the long run, very productive introduction for us. Stephen was to play perhaps the most important role of anyone in the subsequent fortunes of Mercury. He was a member of the senior management triumvirate when Mercury's shares were floated in 1987, together with Leonard Licht and David Price, and he was still at the head of the firm with Carol Galley when Mercury was bought by Merrill Lynch in early 1998. All four of them made a major contribution to Mercury's development, but only Stephen was in a top position throughout its life as a public company.

*

In 1977, I joined the Chairman's Committee of Warburgs, which otherwise consisted of Henry Grunfeld, Eric Roll, Geoffrey Seligman, David Scholey, Oscar Lewisohn and Geoffrey Elliott. Siegmund liked to pretend he was not a member, but he attended and dominated the committee's weekly meetings. Warburg Investment Management was rarely on the agenda, perhaps because it was considered too terrible to waste time discussing, or too embarrassing, but reports started to reach the Chairman's Committee that it was showing adolescent and unacceptable signs of independence. Taking a cue from Rhodesia's Unilateral Declaration of Independence, and ignoring Siegmund's dislike of acronyms, Geoffrey Elliott and I joked to each other about WIM's UDI.

It was rumoured that WIM offered its guests gin and whisky before lunch, that its consumption of cigars was excessive, that ping pong was being played in the basement and that 'I must go upstairs to do a little research' was an alibi for a poker game. While these and other examples of UDI tendencies were viewed as serious breaches of discipline in the prevailing mood of the Chairman's Committee, they were in reality harmless. The Warburg work ethic was as deeply entrenched in WIM as it was in other parts of the bank. The ping pong and poker games were a side show of minor consequence and may even have been beneficial in team building. ('Unless you play ping pong properly, you can never be a leader of men', Osbert Sitwell claimed he had been told by his father.) However, it was decided that action would have to be taken to re-establish Gresham Street's control over St Albans House, and increasingly I became aware that my name was being mentioned.

In November 1977, I spent a week with Siegmund in Montreal and Toronto, and he shared with me his extreme unhappiness about WIM in a sort of replay of the conversations I had had with him

when I lived in Canada fifteen years earlier and he had told me he
wanted me to take charge of his unsatisfactory investment department. Once bitten twice shy, I was not sure I wanted the
responsibility this time; nor could I see any clear way in which I
could be inserted either above or alongside Nick McAndrew and
Andrew Smithers, who knew so much more about their business than
I did. But it was apparent that Siegmund was going to come up with
some plan and that I would be a part of it.

*

Siegmund was at his very best during that Canadian trip. Triarch had
long since been sold, but thanks to friends in Canada such as Tony
Griffin, Bill Wilder (previously head of Wood Gundy, which was
then the leading investment banking firm in Canada), and the
Desmarais and Thomson families, we had a wide range of contacts in
the Canadian business community, and had managed a number of
eurobond issues for Canadian provinces and companies. Warburgs'
reputation in Canada was on a pedestal, and there was much
curiosity on the part of our connections there to meet the banking
legend himself.

Siegmund entertained everyone we met with his always original
views of the world and his generally incorrect predictions as to where
it was headed. Although then 76 years old, he never flagged despite a
full programme of meetings, lunches and dinners. Aside from our
discussions on the problems of the investment division, the trip was
memorable to me for three main reasons.

First, Siegmund, hard as he tried, proved to be quite incapable of
using one of those disposable Gillette razors, which I bought for him
after he came down to breakfast one morning complaining of a small
cut he had inflicted on himself with his cut-throat. After a few tries
with it, he gave up. I reminded him this was in keeping neither with
his character nor with a note he had written me a little earlier saying,
'I always follow the advice of my boss, PSD.'

Next, I saw a perfect demonstration of the trouper who performs
to the highest standard even when the house is half empty. We had a
lunch appointment with D'Arcy McKeough, Minister of Finance of
the Province of Ontario and an old ally of our firm, who was
detained at a debate in the Parliament. We were left with two fairly
junior aides, whom Siegmund treated as if they were even more
important than the minister himself. He held them spellbound for

well over an hour, and when McKeough finally arrived in time for
coffee, Siegmund told him what interesting and intelligent aides he
had.

My third recollection is of Siegmund's first meeting with Conrad
Black, then an up-and-coming tycoon of 33 with a high-octane
intellect and the appearance of a caged tiger. He was at an early stage
of a career which was in due course to lead to control of the *Daily
Telegraph*. Black owned a large holding in Massey Ferguson, the
Canadian manufacturer of farm machinery. Massey was founded in
the middle of the nineteenth century and sold some tractors to
Napoleon III at the Paris Exhibition of 1867, but a hundred years
later it had fallen on hard times. Siegmund thought it would make an
attractive acquisition for Volkswagen or Daimler Benz.

Bill Wilder arranged for Siegmund to meet Black and they got on
well. Black made it clear that he did not want to sell Massey, whose
shares were selling at a depressed price, but some months later he
agreed to allow Victor Rice, whom he had installed as Massey's
president, to attend a lunch meeting in London with the head of
Daimler Benz, which Siegmund would host.

The London lunch was lengthy and the discussion amiable. There
was a 'constructive exchange of views' – a banker's euphemism
denoting that nothing much was achieved in advancing the real
purpose of the occasion, which was to see whether Daimler Benz
could acquire Massey Ferguson. Siegmund seemed preoccupied
during lunch, and I noticed that he was smiling from time to time as
if enjoying some private joke. When the guests had parted with the
usual professed agreement to keep in touch, which as often as not
means that neither side has the slightest intention of contacting the
other again, Siegmund called me to his room and with great
excitement asked me if I had noticed Victor Rice's cuffs. It was the
only thing that had interested him during the entire three-hour
meeting. Rice had his initials, VAR, inscribed on his cuffs in large
letters, so that your eyes were unavoidably directed to them
whenever you looked at him. Siegmund had been so mesmerised by
them that I never heard from him what he thought about the meeting
or what we should do next.

I was to see more of Victor Rice in later years. At one time, he
invited me to become chairman of Massey's UK operation, a position
for which I regarded myself as completely unsuited, as it involved
labour relations and heavy industry – matters about which I have

very little understanding. The proud son of an Essex chimney sweep, Rice was one of the great survivors in the manufacturing world. Twenty-two years later, he was still running the company which used to be Massey Ferguson, but not before its name was changed first to Varity Corporation (note the first three letters of the name) and more recently to Lucas Varity, and its headquarters were moved first to Buffalo in New York state and then to the UK. In 1999, however, Lucas Varity was acquired by the American company TRW. Rice finally left the company, but with a handsome financial settlement.

Siegmund and Conrad Black subsequently developed a close rapport and used to have 'little lunches' at the Ritz in Paris and elsewhere. Black has an amazing memory for historical facts and a vocabulary which reaches into unfrequented pages of the dictionary, and he shared Siegmund's interest in books. They had a lot to talk about and seemed to form an only slightly wary mutual admiration society. I was therefore amused to read the following description of Siegmund in Black's autobiography published in 1993, eleven years after Siegmund's death: 'he was, in our dealings, the most elegant, the most believable, the most subtle, as well as the most prestigious of all shoplifters'. Dan Colson, Black's extremely able and engaging right-hand man in London, tells me that this comment, given its author's proclivity for colourful prose, was highly complimentary.

*

I had two conversations with Siegmund immediately after we got back from our Canadian trip. He asked me to buy for him 'a few shares' in a company we had visited in Montreal, where the chairman, a long-standing friend of both Siegmund's and mine, had told us in confidence of a capital restructuring of his company which was likely to have a beneficial effect on the company's share price. I could not understand, and was reluctant to embarrass him by asking, why it did not occur to Siegmund that what he was asking me to do for him came close to insider dealing, and for what could be only a very small gain, certainly not one that would make any difference to his overall wealth. I came to the conclusion that it must have been a reversion to the customs of an earlier generation, when people in the City felt it was perfectly normal to take advantage of casually but deliberately imparted pieces of confidential information.

Our next conversation had rather more far-reaching consequences.

He had decided to establish a new Policy Committee of Warburg
Investment Management, under my chairmanship, to supervise its
business. I would be joined by Ronnie McIntosh, a genial and wise
ex-civil servant who had joined the Warburgs board as a non-
executive director, and Bob Boas, an extremely intelligent member of
the corporate finance division, and we were to meet regularly with
Nick McAndrew and Andrew Smithers.

It was a tricky assignment because Nick and Andrew could blind
us with science, telling us only what they chose to. But Siegmund's
intention was to provoke change, and he succeeded. Within a year,
Nick accepted a position to run Rothschilds' investment division.
Later he moved to Scotland, becoming chairman for several years of
Murray Johnstone, a successful Glasgow fund management company. It was later sold to United Asset Management, an American
company which makes a business of acquiring investment management businesses – it learnt the secret of fund management economics
early on. Nick now lives near Inverness, sits on the boards of several
Scottish companies, and fishes.

Siegmund saw his opening when Nick departed. He wasted no
time in appointing me chairman of WIM in Nick's place, thus
deliberately bypassing Andrew, who was understandably upset. By
then, however, Siegmund's patience had run out. Not for the first
time did he make a major decision on emotional considerations.
Warburg Investment Management had to go. My first duty as
chairman, he told me, was to 'get rid of it'.

CHAPTER 13

'Get Rid of It'

I suppose I should have been pleased to be appointed chairman of Warburg Investment Management, thereby being given, in name at least, the job which I thought Siegmund had promised me fifteen years earlier. However, it was hardly a vote of confidence to be told that, while I could have the chairmanship, the company had no future in Warburgs. Whereas Groucho Marx didn't want to belong to any club that would have him as a member, Siegmund was in effect saying he didn't mind my being chairman of Warburg Investment Management provided somebody else owned it.

Disposal did not make much commercial sense. For all its shortcomings, WIM was making progress. Andrew Smithers was providing intellectual stimulus in his new role as *de facto* chief executive, and Leonard Licht and Stephen Zimmerman, as the leaders of the two investment teams in the UK pension fund business, were putting together some impressive investment results. Moreover, there was even a glimmer of profitability, which was to become much brighter in the next few years.

Siegmund probably sensed my reluctance to go about getting rid of the business, so he took the lead in arranging for the two of us to visit Robert Fleming & Co., a merchant bank specialising in investment and one of the best at it. We were given lunch by Bill Merton, Flemings' chairman, and Joe Burnett-Stuart, his deputy and later his successor. On such occasions, Siegmund liked to behave in the traditional City manner. He remembered the form for lunchtime conversation which he had observed during his days as a trainee at Rothschilds in the 1920s, and when he learnt many years later that Evelyn de Rothschild, chairman of Rothschilds, and David Airlie, chairman of Schroders, had spent a weekend together without once discussing business, he had duly noted it, despite his astonishment. So, although eager to bring up the subject he was there to discuss, Siegmund refrained from doing so until he had had a sympathetic assent from Merton and Burnett-Stuart to his question, 'Do you mind if we talk shop?'

He then told them that Warburgs had been unable to make a go of its investment business, Warburg Investment Management, perhaps because we didn't have a stable of investment trusts to manage, as Flemings and other merchant banks had. 'I would like you to take my little investment department,' he said. 'You know how to do this type of business, and we don't. You can have it. All of it.' Our hosts were dumbfounded. They gave absolutely no reaction, either then or, to Siegmund's and my amazement, thereafter. Perhaps they didn't believe he was really trying to give it away, or more likely, they thought that there was no way they should take on a business in which the savvy Sir Siegmund Warburg and his clever partners had failed to make any profits.

Disappointed by Flemings' lack of response, Siegmund spoke to Ian Fraser, who had left Warburgs some years earlier to become the first Director-General of the Take-Over Panel, and then chairman of Lazards. Lazards, like Flemings, had a good reputation on the investment side. I believe that this time Siegmund asked Fraser if Lazards would like to buy WIM for £100,000, but they too were not interested.

No one in those days thought that fund management businesses had any value other than a rather low multiple of profits if there were any. The concept of attributing a value to the amount of funds under management did not then exist, certainly not in the UK. WIM, managing as it was then more than £1 billion of client assets, would today be given a value of 2 or 3 per cent of that, say around £25 million, even though it was barely making any profit. But to Siegmund, in 1979, its only value was negative, and apparently that was also the view of Flemings and Lazards.

Looking back, it is hard to comprehend Siegmund's extraordinary wish to give away Warburgs' investment business. It was in reaction to a complex set of emotions, but some of the reasons were easy to detect. No one likes losses or inadequate profits; he resented the loss of control evident in WIM's UDI; he had always thought of investment management as a second-class activity only slightly better than stockbroking; and he didn't like the large number of people we had to employ in it.

Siegmund hated it when private clients sometimes complained to him personally that their portfolios had not performed as well as they hoped. There was a famous story, which probably contained elements of both truth and hyperbole, of a conversation he had with a client of a certain age whom we can call Mrs Abrahams:

MRS ABRAHAMS: Sir Siegmund, you told me to invest in your new offshore fund ten years ago and I paid a price of $5 a share. Now the price is still only $5 – it's very disappointing.
WARBURG: But my dear young lady, if I'd known you were a *short-*term investor, I would never have put you into it.

There was another consideration. Despite his somewhat left-of-centre views on many issues and his disavowal of British establishment attitudes, Siegmund was a snob. We are all, I imagine, snobs about something. He was a banking snob. He wanted Warburgs to be elitist, to be *haute banque*, to give well-thought-out objective financial advice to top-class companies and governments in the manner of a highly regarded general practitioner who can call on the skills of specialists as required. The investment activity didn't fit into this image – it dealt with private individuals, who could be a frightful nuisance.

*

Fortunately, Siegmund's attention soon focused on other priorities, especially our joint investment with Paribas in Warburg Paribas Becker, which was providing plenty of headaches. As understudy to Geoffrey Seligman, I had been a director of Warburg Paribas Becker from the start of our association in 1974 and therefore, once again, spent a great deal of time in the United States in the succeeding years. (We sold our interest to Paribas in 1983.) My chairmanship of WIM was thus unavoidably rather part time at first.

With better results as the 1980s began, Siegmund came to accept that we were in the investment management business to stay. He seemed to have a renewed interest and talked to me about it almost every working day. As always, he was mainly curious about the people aspects. He thought that Andrew Smithers was too independent and argumentative to be in charge, and he instructed me to arrange things differently.

Andrew is a delightful person who was much liked by his colleagues, but he sometimes wore his undoubted intelligence on his sleeve. When one day at a Warburgs 9.15 meeting he was asked, in his capacity as in-house economics guru, for his opinion on a change in interest rates the previous day, Andrew started his reply with 'Well, now, how can I make it simple for you?' He once told me that he could argue either side of any debate with equal conviction and that he would always come out the winner – a facility he managed to demonstrate on several occasions. However, he is an inventive thinker with visionary instincts, who made a significant contribution in laying the foundations for Mercury's subsequent growth in the 1980s.

I had many conversations with him. He could usually convince me that whatever I said, or was about to say, was wrong, but we finally agreed in 1982 that he would move on to other areas. He spent time in the US and Japan, studying strategic aspects of Warburgs' business, and in the process he became very knowledgeable about those two countries. He went on to start a successful economics consulting business of his own, and he currently writes a weekly column in the *Evening Standard* on economic or political issues, which is usually provocative, original and funny.

Andrew had so dominated the management of WIM that it was not immediately clear who should take his place. We formed a committee of six from the next generation, consisting of Alan Baker, who was running the fixed-interest side, Richard Bernays, Leonard Licht, Richard Malnick, David Price and Stephen Zimmerman, with David as *primus inter pares*. It was not an ideal solution, nor was it intended to be any more than a temporary arrangement, but I believed it would give an insight as to which of the six had leadership aspirations and attributes.

*

It was a huge shock when Siegmund died in London just after his eightieth birthday in 1982. Somehow one expected him to go on for ever. I knew I would miss him greatly, and I wondered what the bank would be like without him. Henry Grunfeld moved swiftly and matter-of-factly to reassure everyone. He circulated a note to say that, in line with Siegmund's wishes, there would be no funeral service and no memorial service, and there should be no flowers. It was back to business, but for me it could never be quite the same.

There was in fact a 'memorial occasion' in the Guildhall several months later, with music from some of Siegmund's favourite composers, Bach, Handel and Mozart, and addresses by Henry

Grunfeld, Eric Roll and David Scholey. Eric ended his remarks with a very apt quotation from *Hamlet*:

> He was a man, take him for all in all,
> I shall not look upon his like again.

Eric and David were joint chairmen of Mercury Securities and of Warburgs by then, but David, some twenty-five years younger than Eric, was now the reigning successor to Siegmund, with Henry Grunfeld and Eric Roll as his counsellors. The next stage in Warburgs' development would depend largely on David's leadership and his ability to motivate the rest of us. Our loyalty was not in question.

Some while before he died, and on more than one occasion, Siegmund told me with conviction, and I am sure others too, that within five years of his death Warburgs would break several of his most cherished rules. We would, he said, change the name of the quoted company, Mercury Securities, to incorporate the Warburg name; we would produce glossy annual reports in place of the plain off-white ones we traditionally used (he actually used the word 'glazed'); we would have brochures with photographs of members of the firm, as all our competitors had; we would advertise; we would grow too big and have too many people; and worst of all, we would join the City establishment and inherit its complacency.

Siegmund's distrust of the City establisment had been confirmed during the well-chronicled British Aluminium take-over battle of 1958 – a defining moment in the history of Warburgs when it had taken on most of the establishment merchant banks, which joined together in tribal loyalty to oppose it. Warburgs won the struggle on behalf of its clients Reynolds Metals and Tube Investments, thanks largely to the brilliant tactics devised by Henry Grunfeld. Siegmund paid him the ultimate compliment by suggesting that, if he had been on the other side, Warburgs would have lost.

The successful outcome of the British Aluminium affair put Warburgs on the map, but it left Siegmund and others in the firm with mixed feelings about the City establishment. At various times, he described its members as anti-Semitic, cowardly, dilettantish and self-protective. He accused them of calling him a 'damn foreigner' behind his back. Was he too sensitive? Did he secretly want to be part of it? There is no way of knowing, but I do know that he believed that, if the bank joined the establishment, it would lose its non-conformist edge and decline into mediocrity.

*

It may seem incredible that we could defy Siegmund's wishes so soon and so completely, but he was to be proved right on all counts. The name of the quoted company Mercury Securities, after a period as Mercury International Group, was changed to S.G. Warburg Group in 1987. By then Warburg Investment Management had become Mercury Asset Management, so although the change in our parent's name ignored Siegmund's sensitivity over using the Warburg name in the publicly quoted company, for us in Mercury Asset Management it had the incidental benefit of allowing us to keep the Mercury name for ourselves.

Coloured annual reports were introduced very quickly after his death, and while I never saw it, I was told there was a brochure available in Warburgs' Tokyo office with photographs of some of the executives there. And it was in Warburg Investment Management, I am afraid, that we indulged in some popular advertising.

Of greater consequence, however, and fulfilling the remaining parts of Siegmund's prophecy, was the acquisition by S.G. Warburg Group (as it was to become) of three firms at the heart of the City establishment. In 1983, Warburgs increased to 29 per cent (the maximum amount then permitted) a small nostro investment that we had initiated some years earlier on Andrew Smithers' suggestion in his family-connected firm Akroyd and Smithers, which was one of the three serious jobbing firms (market-makers in shares and bonds) on the London Stock Exchange. It had started as a market-maker in Canadian shares in 1875 and was a dealing firm if ever there was one; it was said that they viewed the short term as now and the long term as lunchtime.

Then, in 1984, came the announcement of a proposal to acquire two leading stockbroking firms, Rowe and Pitman, with links to the royal family and founded in 1894, and Mullens and Co. Mullens held the position of government broker, which gave it privileged access to the Bank of England until the position was abolished in 1986, and could claim origins that went back to 1786. The acquisitions could not be completed until the deregulation of the London Stock Exchange in 1986 known as Big Bang, when, for the first time, banks were allowed to own more than 29 per cent of a member firm of the Stock Exchange. At the same time, the holding in Akroyd and Smithers would be increased to 100 per cent.

With this boldly conceived combination of a merchant bank, a market-maker and two stockbrokers, Warburgs aimed to take on the strong American investment banking houses which it now saw as its main competition. The *Financial Times* noted with tongue in cheek that we were forming a sort of Old Etonian Goldman Sachs. That was hardly accurate, although there was a fair number of Etonians in Rowe and Pitman, but no one could deny that we had joined the establishment. Moreover, we had become very large, the number of employees increasing from under a thousand in 1982 at the time of Siegmund's death, already too many for his liking, to more than five times that number by 1987.

Siegmund's distrust of the City establishment was one of a complicated set of attitudes he had towards Britain and the British. He admired its people for the spirit they showed in the war, and praised the 'wonderful English middle class'. However, he was often critical of British attitudes, sometimes vehemently so. He despised the Treasury and the London Stock Exchange and, like the other uncles, did not join any London clubs. In one of his autobiographical papers, he mentioned as people he admired in England in the pre-war period Maynard Keynes, Montagu Norman, Leo Amery and Violet Bonham Carter. They were all rebels to some extent, and he called them his mental godparents.

He was knighted during the premiership of Harold Wilson and was, I believe, quite proud of his knighthood, although justifying his acceptance of it on the grounds of the encouragement it would give to other refugees. Perhaps his relationship with the British came close to love-hate, but I leave the final word on it to the philosopher Sir Isaiah Berlin. He had been to lunch with us at Mercury in 1991, and had amused us tremendously with his conversation and his stories. In a thank-you letter, he wrote:

Dear Mr Stormonth Darling

Thank you ever so much for that delightful and informative lunch. I don't think that Siegmund would have disapproved of anything we said, although he might have thought we had been a little too frivolous and not paid enough attention to the great issues that are shaping our world. There really was a turnabout in his life in England – not as a result of

Tube Investments, but as its primary cause. He remained a deep
anglophile, but at a certain stage, perhaps as a result of his treatment by
the City, he gave up all hope of rescuing this country from its inevitable,
slow and dignified but still inevitable, decline. That he used to say to me
over and over again. I think that, wonderfully perceptive man as he was,
in this case he was genuinely mistaken.

Yours sincerely
Isaiah Berlin

*

In his mainly excellent book *The Warburgs*, Ron Chernow wrote of
Siegmund's life as a tragedy. He quoted Siegmund's doctor, Dr Carl
Heinz Goldman (whom incidentally Siegmund sent me to consult on
several occasions), as believing that he was a deeply unhappy and
lonely man, plagued by suspicion. According to Goldman, who
certainly knew Siegmund intimately, he did not get on with anybody
and thought most people were fools.

It was a grim assessment which did not seem to me to ring true. Is
it consistent with the receipt of almost a thousand letters of
condolence on his death? Siegmund himself said that 'Life is no more
than an interesting game' (compare Ernest Hemingway's 'Life is a
game to be won decently or lost courageously', which Siegmund
might have felt was too philosophical in its acceptance). I can think
of no one who appeared to find more interest in life, particularly in
his observation of people, and if there was sincerity in his game
analogy, as I believe there was, he can hardly have been entirely
unhappy.

Undoubtedly there was stress and pain, and disappointment and
melancholy, mostly self-inflicted. He believed, as some Russian
intellectuals seem to today, and as his favourite writer Thomas Mann
did, that the soul can never be discovered until there has been much
suffering. 'The greater the price paid in effort and sacrifice, the more
important is the resulting achievement in spiritual growth', he wrote.
One wonders if he did not, for whatever reason, impose too grinding
a sense of duty on himself.

Siegmund did not realise his ambitions for a Warburg bank in the
US and had only a minor role in the re-emergence of M.M. Warburg
in Hamburg, where his cousin Eric and Eric's son Max have restored
the Warburg banking name to its rightful position. By any reckoning,

however, he achieved a phenomenal success in the UK, and both he and the bank were widely respected. William Rees-Mogg wrote in *The Times* five years after Siegmund's death that he was undoubtedly the greatest banker of the post-war period in London – an assessment that few would dispute. It is not for me to pronounce on whether his life was happy or not, but I do know that he made numerous other people happy on many occasions.

*

It was not long before the predators appeared to see if Warburgs could be acquired following Siegmund's death – it was still two years before its four-way London-based merger with the two stockbroking firms and Akroyd & Smithers would be first announced in 1984. One approach came from Mark Millard, a senior managing director of Loeb Rhoades, 74 years old at the time. He asked me to lunch with him in New York within a few days of Siegmund's death to talk about it. Millard knew Warburgs extremely well, and he spotted the value in our share price.

Mark Millard had been a long-standing friend of Eric Korner and thus of Warburgs. He was born in Kiev, but spent his early days in Germany until the Nazi persecutions, and then lived in Hungary for five years. He left for the United States in 1938, when he was 30, joined Loeb Rhoades and became a partner in 1944. Mark was a person with considerable personal magnetism. He had a long face with dark, piercing eyes and a lugubrious expression, and he spoke slowly with a soft and melodious voice. He collected old books on architecture and was a keen amateur photographer with a flair for composition. He gave me a copy of a privately published collection of his photographs which, while technically accomplished, emphasised light and shadow but mainly shadow – I wonder what a psychoanalyst would make of that. He was full of ideas and very good company.

Mark had enormous experience of the oil and gas industry, and starting with nothing, he had made a lot of money in deals and investments. He and Eric Korner had the idea of forming an offshore fund, which they named Energy International, to invest in shares of energy companies (more of this later). As his assistant whom he involved in the affairs of the Energy Fund, Mark Millard had employed the urbane Claus von Bulow, who knew the oil industry well having worked with J.P. Getty. Von Bulow was to stand trial in

1982 for the attempted killing of his already incapacitated wife, the former Princess Sonny von Auersperg, allegedly by injecting her with insulin. I was startled to read of his indictment a few days after having breakfast with him at the Racquet and Tennis Club in New York. He was found guilty, but was later acquitted on appeal. He now lives in London, writes book reviews, and is an agreeable and amusing lunching companion.

Another rather more forceful overture came from John Gutfreund, then chairman of Salomon Brothers, someone who was to play a part in the Mercury story several years later when his firm fraudulently used our name in a US Treasury bond auction. Gutfreund was to pay a heavy price for that episode, being forced to resign in some ignominy. In 1982, however, Gutfreund was in full command of one of the most powerful Wall Street firms. He was bursting with self-confidence and was known as 'The King of Wall Street', a title that he said he hated. Gutfreund and his wife Susan, famous for her observation that it is very expensive being rich, were widely believed to be the inspiration for the Wall Street society couple in Tom Wolfe's *Bonfire of the Vanities*.

Gutfreund came to see David Scholey and one or two others, including me, at 30 Gresham Street. It was a pleasant enough meeting in which Gutfreund, puzzled perhaps that David responded to his approach with more politeness than enthusiasm, told us that we would all make much more money if Warburgs became part of Salomon – or, as he put it, would we 'prefer to be country gentlemen'?

But Warburgs was not for sale. It would march to its own tune, without Siegmund's inspiration, in the expectation that it could compete on a global basis with firms such as Salomon Brothers, Goldman Sachs and Morgan Stanley, and without being acquired by any of them. It was the start of a new era, not just for Warburgs but also for Warburg Investment Management, whose days as Cinderella were now numbered.

PART TWO

New Mercury

CHAPTER 14

Stirrings of Independence

Mr Five Times a Night was the name the press gave to Sir Ralph Halpern after details leaked of his affair in early 1987 with an attractive young model, Fiona Wright. While perhaps disappointing in comparison with the feats of Evel Knievel, the daredevil motorcycle jumper who, it is said, took advantage of the services of eight ladies within twenty-four hours, and the French novelist, Victor Hugo, who claimed nine in forty-eight hours, Halpern's accomplishment attracted some attention at the time.

Two years earlier, Halpern had had an impact on WIM, shortly to be known as Mercury Asset Management, of a quite different kind. Unconsciously, he was to bring about a turning point in the relationship between Warburgs and its increasingly precocious offspring. The name Warburg Investment Management was changed first to Mercury Warburg Investment Management and then to Mercury Asset Management in 1986. 'Asset management' was considered a slightly more trendy designation than the synonymous alternatives 'investment management', 'fund management' and 'money management'. The new name had already been adopted for the company internally in 1985, and, for the sake of simplicity, I shall refer to Cinderella henceforth as just Mercury. I always preferred this usage to the more often used MAM.

Halpern, in 1985, was chairman of Burtons, known in my youth as Montague Burton, or the Fifty Shilling Tailor, a title they had long since shed. That year Burtons decided to make a bid for another department store, Debenhams, and it so happened that Mercury owned, for its clients, 14 per cent of Debenhams shares as well as 4 per cent of Burtons. Warburgs were Burtons' advisers and, as often occurs where publicly quoted companies are concerned, the take-over became a contested one when House of Fraser stepped into the fray as a rival bidder for Debenhams. There were indications that Halpern, and possibly some members of Warburgs too, expected that

Burtons could at least count on the shares of Debenhams controlled by Mercury in what was likely to be a closely fought take-over battle.

It was evident to Mercury, however, that as a fiduciary its first duty was to its own clients, mostly pension funds, and that its loyalty to them had to rank ahead of its relationship with the corporate finance side of Warburgs and its client Burtons. So it was that when Mercury had a favourable opportunity to sell its Debenhams shares in the stock market, which was by then pricing the shares above the formal bid level, it took advantage of it. The buyer of our shares was Burtons' competitor for Debenhams, House of Fraser. It was reported that Halpern, while recognising Mercury's right to act as it had, was furious and was considering sacking Warburgs as his advisers.*

It was the first time that an investment management subsidiary or division of a merchant bank had acted in a take-over fight in defiance of its parent's interest. A few minutes after Mercury's sale of its Debenhams shares was announced, David Scholey came into my room, looking angry. He was, however, the accomplished professional, and he realised that what we were doing was, in our judgement, right for our clients. He refrained from saying anything critical, but his unspoken feelings were clear to me.

Our action was applauded in some sections of the financial press next day. 'Chinese walls' (a set of arrangements which separate the activities of the different divisions of a merchant bank where conflicts might occur, which can perhaps better be described as information barriers) were now seen to be working, at least in Warburgs. It was not long before it dawned on our own corporate finance colleagues that what we had done was in their long-term interests too. The ground rules were now there for all to see: a corporate client engaging Warburgs to act for it in a take-over bid would be doing so for the latter's skills, and not because it expected Warburgs to deliver any shares of a target company owned by clients of Mercury.

*

Big Bang in 1986 was a momentous event in the history of the City of London. It was the culmination of years of negotiation between

---

* His fears that Burtons would lose the bid proved unnecessary; they won it anyway, although by a narrow margin, and successfully completed the acquisition of Debenhams. Ironically, twelve years later in 1998, Debenhams was de-merged from Burtons, which changed its name to Arcadia. The chief executive of Arcadia said he could envisage 'no scenario where the value of the two companies would be greater together'.

the Conservative government of Mrs Thatcher and the London Stock Exchange, aimed at ending the restrictive practices of the Stock Exchange, especially its limitations on membership and the fixed level of commissions it charged on Stock Exchange transactions.

With Big Bang came a stricter system of accountability and new rules of behaviour for all members of the financial community. It was both deregulation and regulation at the same time, and it heralded the end of the clubby and protected old Stock Exchange. A new world of more open competition lay ahead, with the main threat to the London merchant banks likely to come from the American investment banking firms such as Morgan Stanley, Goldman Sachs, Merrill Lynch and Lehman Brothers. They could now join the London Stock Exchange and engage in domestic British investment banking on equal terms with British firms, but with the advantage that they also had direct access to the much larger US capital market.

Warburgs' response to Big Bang of bringing together a merchant bank with two stockbroking firms and one leading market-maker in shares and bonds was as adventurous as anyone's. The planning in 1984 and 1985 for the new combination, which would shortly be called S.G. Warburg Group, was elaborate and intensive. However, in aiming to reinvent itself as a global investment banking firm incorporating banking, corporate finance and stockbroking, Warburgs chose its merger partners almost entirely to meet that objective. No thought was given to whether the new combination would have any benefits for the investment management division. Mercury was also largely ignored in Warburgs' new marketing literature, which was produced to accompany Big Bang, and in briefings to the press. We were still Cinderella in the eyes of our investment banking colleagues.

Warburgs might have considered acquiring Phillips and Drew instead of Rowe and Pitman. Phillips and Drew was a stockbroking firm which had diversified into investment management for pension funds and had built up its funds under management to an amount not much less than that of Mercury. It was a major competitor of ours with a fine reputation. The acquisition of Phillips and Drew would have provided the stockbroking arm that Warburgs wanted, and would at the same time have created a formidable force in investment management. When I raised the matter I was told they were 'not our kind of people', and were not in the same class as

Rowe and Pitman. Besides, our colleagues in Akroyd and Smithers, of which Warburgs by then owned 29 per cent with a commitment to increase to 100 per cent, were adamant that the brokerage partners they wanted were Rowe and Pitman.

It was not lost on the members of Mercury that little if any consideration was being given to what was good for their business. This was a misguided policy on Warburgs' part, to say the least, because the first half of the 1980s was something of a golden period for Mercury. Thanks to investment performance well above the average of our competitors, Mercury's pension fund business was growing rapidly. Total funds under management rose from around £4 billion in 1983 to £11 billion in 1985. We were breaking out of the pack of some six or seven investment management houses, and were soon to be the largest. The main problem I was hearing was that our management was overstretched, and we did not have enough fund managers to handle the new business that was coming in.

Our unit trust business was also now moving forward under the leadership of Richard Bernays and, from 1984, James Dawnay, with a greater conviction that we needed to be in it as a diversification from the pension fund business. Advertisements for Mercury aimed at unit trust investors began to appear in newspapers and underground railway stations and on the radio. Some of us objected to an early advertising theme, promoted by Saatchi and Saatchi and favoured by Richard, which depicted Mercury as 'the fox in the City', but we agreed, in my case reluctantly, to various sporting images of no particular relevance to our business. Advertising was an area in which we could only improve over time, and we did.*

Our efforts to gain business in the US were proving more of a struggle. Following a promising start to the decade when WIMI's funds under management reached $500 million – it seemed a great achievement at the time – we were introduced by Jim Wolfensohn, a good friend of both Siegmund Warburg and David Scholey, and today chairman of the World Bank, to Aetna Life and Casualty, a vast insurance company from Hartford, Connecticut, with an active investment management arm. Aetna wanted to acquire a London

---

* Richard and James, incidentally, were both keen fishermen. There was an occasion when both were out of the office on the same day. An examination of Richard's desk diary showed that he was 'in conference with Dawnay'. James's diary, however, was more specific. It read 'Fishing with Bernays'.

merchant bank or, failing that, to enter into a joint venture with the investment division of one. So we formed Aetna Warburg Investment Management. The idea was that Aetna's sales people would talk to their many American corporate pension fund clients, and Aetna Warburg would thereby gain lots of mandates to manage some of those pension funds' money in the international markets. One of Aetna's more visionary salesmen used the analogy of a giant vacuum cleaner that would scoop up money from all their clients.

In the event, we got not a single new account through Aetna. Their clients did not want to hear from Aetna's representatives about Mercury's capabilities in managing money in overseas markets; they needed to hear about them direct from Mercury. So the joint venture made little difference to our business, although Burt Weiss of WIMI and I enjoyed attending one of Aetna's sales conferences in Puerto Rico and learnt a few salesmen's tricks and heard a few late night stories.

Mercifully we were rescued from the joint venture when Aetna had a chance to buy into another London merchant bank, Samuel Montagu, only a year after the partnership started. Thanks to the foresight of Michael Gore, Warburgs' resourceful and careful chief financial officer, who drafted the original agreement, and the negotiating skills of Burt, Aetna, which had already paid us on coming into the joint company, now had to pay us again to secure a divorce, which was thereby achieved on amicable terms. WIMI, on its own again, was, however, about to enter a period of decline. Poor investment results and then Burt's unexpected resignation in 1983 led to an outflow of accounts. Richard Malnick, a good fund manager with a passion for everything American, as chairman in succession to Burt, and David Scott, as chief investment officer, bravely held the fort, with coaching from Rodger Smith of Greenwich Associates.

Greenwich is a management consultancy company based in Greenwich, Connecticut, specialising in the banking, investment banking and investment management industries. It was founded by the visionary Charley Ellis twenty-seven years ago, and is still led and inspired by him today.* It conducts polls of your clients and then,

* When I retired as Mercury's chairman in 1992, Charley Ellis kindly invited me to join Greenwich's small but intellectually high-powered board. I have learnt much from this association, not least that Americans are often more analytical and more dedicated to the success of their businesses than many of us in the UK. Perhaps this explains why executives with American experience are increasingly in demand in Europe nowadays.

for a fee, tells you what they really think of you and what you ought to do about it. Rodger's advice was constructive, but the information he had to pass on to us was hardly encouraging. It was not until Bob Michaelson joined us in 1984 to take charge of WIMI that it started to recover.

Despite these disappointments in America, Mercury was beginning to look like a real business at last, with the potential to stand on its own feet. We were now a positive contributor to Warburgs' results, our profits reaching £3 million in 1983 and £10 million by 1985. Relationships between Warburgs and Mercury, however, had been strained by the Burtons affair, and by Warburgs' perceived self-oriented approach to Big Bang. Mercury's top management was feeling its oats, and for the first time there were real stirrings of independence in the air.

*

Another overseas adventure was in Japan. Andrew Dalton had already been in Tokyo as Warburgs' first representative there, and during that time he had seen the possibilities for persuading Japanese institutions to invest some of their money outside Japan. He was back in London in 1985 when Mercury opened its own representative office in Tokyo with Stephen Cohen in charge, and he returned there to succeed Stephen in 1987.

I visited Tokyo two or three times during the 1980s. With Andrew's coaching, I learnt never to ask a question at a meeting that courted a negative response, because a Japanese businessman will never actually say 'no'. Indeed, I discovered that it is sometimes better not to talk about business at all. In a meeting with a senior official of Dai-ichi Mutual Life Insurance Company, a good client of Mercury, I managed with the aid of endless cups of green tea to sustain a conversation for what seemed like thirty minutes, but in reality was probably only five, on the subject of cherry blossoms. It remained a mystery to me how one actually ever did any business with the Japanese, but it seemed to present little difficulty in different periods to Andrew Smithers, Andrew Dalton, Stephen Cohen and Cliff Shaw. Christopher Purvis, as a former Mercury person who went on to represent Warburgs in Tokyo, was helpful in their efforts.

On the assumption, I suppose, that 'once a Japanese visitor, always a Japanese expert', I found myself being asked from time to time to host dinners in London for Japanese visitors who were clients of

Warburgs or Mercury. Following a signing ceremony for a loan that Warburgs had arranged for a Japanese shipping company, some of us took a party of six shipping executives to dinner in a private room at Tiger Lee, a Chinese restaurant originally recommended to me by David Li, the well-connected chief executive of Bank of East Asia in Hong Kong.

The Japanese, I was told, would enjoy Chinese food and some rice wine. They had been travelling and were probably victims of jet lag too. After dinner, it was up to me to propose a toast to our guests, for which I had carefully prepared a speech expressing all the right sentiments, such as 'honour to be associated with . . .' and 'looking forward to further opportunities to work with your fine company' ('work with' was preferred to 'be of service to' in Warburg-speak, the latter expression being considered too obsequious). But I saw to my horror that all six of our visitors were asleep and slumped over the table at different angles. So much for our stimulating conversation.

In the absence from London of others more appropriate to the task, I was commandeered one day in the 1970s to take the chair at a large lunch at the Savoy Hotel for Akio Morita, chairman of Sony, at which he introduced the first Walkman cassette player. We were each given a blue and, by current standards, rather heavy Walkman, viewed at the time as a nearly miraculous invention that would transform people's lives, as indeed it has. The one I received from Mr Morita works as well today as any new model; only the styling and weight have changed in twenty-five years.

A more challenging situation was provoked by the septuagenarian and very eminent chairman of a major Japanese financial institution which Mercury wanted to convert into a client. At Andrew Dalton's request, I hosted a dinner at the Capital Hotel in Knightsbridge for him and his colleagues. There were five of them and five of us at a long thin table, and we sat opposite each other rather like two rugby football teams preparing for a scrum. Andrew had briefed me on the right things to say during the early formal part of the dinner, and he had also warned me that, at the appropriate time, Mr Watanabe, our guest of honour and very much the senior person present, would through his body language and the use of his interpreter indicate that he wanted the mode to shift from formal to informal. From then on, apparently, we were to let our hair down and everyone would be very funny.

Sure enough, when both Mr Watanabe and I had uttered our well-rehearsed platitudes of good will, he relaxed visibly, started to smile and look rather more human and, with a few nudges and winks, launched his opening salvo to indicate that we should now start the entertainment part of the evening. His interpreter then said to me, 'Mr Darling, Mr Watanabe like to know, in detail, how English gentleman make love to English lady?' I had little difficulty in getting my revenge on Andrew for landing me in this situation, and replied that this was something that Mr Dalton was better qualified to answer than I was. Time has gone by and, unfortunately perhaps, I can no longer remember what Andrew said.

*

The reputation of a business is rather like virginity: it can only be lost once. We came close to losing ours in 1986 in a less than glorious episode which concerned one of England's most venerable and cherished companies. 'Reputation dented' was the verdict of *The Times* on Mercury's behaviour.

Josiah Wedgwood and Sons had opened for business in Etruria in the Potteries in 1769. Josiah Wedgwood I, its founder, was the grandfather of Charles Darwin, author of *The Origin of Species*. He achieved fame as the favourite earthenware designer of Empress Catherine the Great of Russia, who in 1773 commissioned from him a dinner service for fifty people, nearly a thousand pieces in all, for use at her eponymously named summer palace at Tsarskoe Selo near St Petersburg. Wedgwood sold them to her at below his cost – an early example of an intelligently planned loss leader.

Josiah Wedgwood and Sons became a limited liability company in 1895, but its shares continued to be owned by members of the Wedgwood family until about the 1960s, when an unofficial market in them developed in London. In 1967, under the leadership of Sir Arthur Bryan, the first chairman to come from outside the family, Wedgwood made an initial placing of its shares with the public. Mercury first acquired a position in Wedgwood in Milo Cripps' day in the 1960s. This was later sold, and subsequently Mercury reinvested in the 1980s, until by 1986 our clients owned about 24 per cent of Wedgwood. This investment, unusually large for Mercury in percentage terms, was initiated by Leonard Licht, one of London's most talented and famous fund managers, who was the leading architect of Mercury's excellent investment record in the British market in the late 1970s and 1980s.

Leonard has an encyclopaedic knowledge of British companies, an instinctive feel for value and the courage of his convictions. He used to make an impression on prospective new pension fund clients, who were expecting a learned dissertation on Mercury's investment methodology, by telling them that he just liked to buy shares 'which go up'. He was greatly liked and respected by a number of our more important clients, one of which, British Rail, thought he walked on water. Something of a prima donna and a reluctant team player, Leonard had a healthy disrespect for many of his colleagues and could often be offhand, occasionally unconsciously mimicking Siegmund's habit of throwing his telephone. But he has great charm and a delightful sense of humour, and no one could dispute his ability to pick winning investments. This was especially true in those days when intelligent sleuthing could uncover shares which were undervalued in the market through the absence of adequate generally available information or the reliable interpretation thereof.

Leonard aimed to buy companies with good brand names, where he believed the franchise had not been fully exploited. Wedgwood came into this category, but it had been a disappointment to him. Its business was hurt in turn by overseas competitors with new products and lower costs, by currency fluctuations and by changes in the buying public's taste. So it was that when a predator came along, albeit one with a very different style and background to Wedgwood, Leonard was ready to listen.

London International Group (LIG) was primarily a manufacturer of condoms under the label Durex, and had previously been rather more descriptively called London Rubber. It had been a corporate client of Warburgs, and there was an occasion when Eric Korner was given the opportunity to sell some of its shares to his clients. Uncertain how to describe the nature of London Rubber's business, and after much agitated consultation with colleagues, he told the clients, truthfully if economically so, that it made rubber gloves.

LIG's chairman, Alan Woltz, was an ambitious American from New Jersey, and the company had already acquired Royal Worcester Spode, third in terms of sales in the china business in the UK. Royal Doulton and Wedgwood, about the same size as each other, ranked ahead of Royal Worcester Spode, with Wedgwood the best name of the three. If Woltz could add Wedgwood to Royal Worcester Spode, his company would be perceived first and foremost as the country's leading manufacturer of china, even though condoms would still produce the largest share of its sales and profits.

Leonard had been upset by a rights issue that Wedgwood had sprung on the market in October 1985, which had depressed its share price, and he was receptive when Woltz offered to buy Mercury's shares as a first step in a take-over bid. LIG needed Mercury's commitment to sell as an encouragement to proceed with a bid, and Leonard agreed that Mercury would sell it a 9.9 per cent holding of Wedgwood as well as our remaining 14 per cent in the absence of another bid.

Arthur Bryan reacted with fury. 'We do not want Woltz', he protested publicly. In private, he contacted Eric Roll to complain of Mercury's atrocious behaviour. He accused us of betrayal and said, rather inaccurately in view of the long period during which we had been Wedgwood shareholders, that we were 'quick buck artists'. It was fashionable in those days to accuse fund managers of sacrificing the interests of British industry by their short-termist mentality, but on this occasion at least we were hardly guilty. On television, Anthony Hilton, a respected financial journalist, accused Mercury of 'an astonishing lack of loyalty', which he said was out of keeping with the responsibility we had for the health of British industry.

'Warburgs puts Wedgwood into play' was one of the newspaper headlines when our sale was announced. I felt there was some legitimacy in this characterisation, and was concerned that we were about to lose our reputation as respectable fund managers; we were in danger of being regarded instead as wheelers and dealers. I was cross with Leonard, but he reminded me that we must always do our best for our clients. When Eric Roll spoke to me, I was sympathetic to his suggestion that I should telephone Arthur Bryan, and I accepted the latter's invitation to visit Wedgwood's factory at Stoke-on-Trent with a colleague.

Arthur Bryan is one of the UK's great salesmen, and I found him genial and, considering the circumstances, friendly. There was no doubt that he dominated the company. He had joined it as a trainee in 1947 and knew every aspect of its business. He was, and is, an inveterate traveller and had been knighted for his services to British exports. I emphasised our duty to our clients, but on a personal level I was able to understand some of his unhappiness.

In the event, a white knight appeared in the shape of Waterford, the Irish crystal glass manufacturer. Waterford Wedgwood, the resultant merged company, was later the object of a further take-over by a financial group led by Morgan Stanley and including the Irish tycoon, Tony O'Reilly, chairman of H.J. Heinz. Many management changes followed in Wedgwood, but Arthur Bryan continues an involvement today as a consultant appointed by the Morgan Stanley group. (In contrast, Woltz was eased out of LIG in the early 1990s when the company nearly went bust. After a flirtation with such products as Butterfly Syrup cough mixture, it has reverted to its core business in condoms and latex gloves, and now classifies itself not entirely inaccurately, I suppose, as a health care company.)*

The relationship between Warburgs and Mercury deteriorated further as a result of the Wedgwood incident, but there was a happy consolation for us. A little while later, through Bear Stearns and other American investment banking firms, Mercury launched a closed-end investment fund in the US named The United Kingdom Fund. Mrs Thatcher had just been re-elected Prime Minister, and there was, almost for the first time, some interest on the part of American retail investors in investing in British shares. I approached Arthur Bryan to see if he would consider joining the board of the new fund, and I was delighted when he accepted. Ironically, Leonard Licht was the initial fund manager of The United Kingdom Fund. Arthur also became a director of a sister fund, The Europe Fund, which Richard Bernays launched for us in 1990, and since then he has been a diligent and supportive member of both boards, who has not missed a meeting.

---

* LIG was taken over in 1999 by Seton Scholl.

CHAPTER 15

Project Mercury

One day in 1985, Stephen Zimmerman and Leonard Licht told me that, if we wanted to be sure to keep the top management together in Mercury, it would be essential for some proportion of Mercury's share capital to be floated on the Stock Exchange, or perhaps for Mercury to be sold to a third party. Only in this way could they and other members of Mercury's management obtain a direct equity participation in their business. They reminded me, unnecessarily, that there were plenty of attractive alternative employment opportunities available to them in the market place. I was aware that Stephen and Leonard, as well as others in our top team, had had seductive offers both from overseas firms wanting to set up in investment management in London, and from other City houses which had fallen behind and needed to reinvigorate their investment businesses.

There were other reasons for their unhappiness with the prevailing situation. The creation of a monolithic financial conglomerate in the form of S.G. Warburg Group gave rise to the potential for conflicts of interest, which could bother some of our pension fund clients. How could we convince our investment clients that we would never favour a Warburg corporate client to their possible disadvantage? And what was to stop Mercury from giving into the temptation to allocate too large a proportion of the brokerage commissions which it generated to Warburg Securities, the arm of Warburgs that comprised the three Stock Exchange firms Akroyd and Smithers, Rowe and Pitman, and Mullens?

We had answers to these questions, of course. We could call in our defence the example of the Burtons/Debenhams take-over, where we had so clearly demonstrated our independence from Warburgs' corporate side, and we took a series of steps to reinforce it. We instituted a self-denying ordinance on the amount of commissions we would give to Warburg Securities, although we did not want to be too strict on ourselves if Warburg Securities turned out to be the best investment research house, as indeed it did a few years later. Mercury would also be physically separate. In the arrangements for the new conglomerate, it was decided that the old Warburgs would move to Finsbury Square to share offices with the three Stock Exchange firms, while Mercury would remain on its own at 33 King William Street. There would be no cross-directorships between us and Warburg Securities or the corporate finance or banking divisions. And, finally, we had in place a resolute system of Chinese walls to prevent leakage of information from one division of the Warburg group to another.

There was, however, a lingering, but in our case unjustified, suspicion that there were occasions when people managed somehow to transgress or simply ignore the largely invisible Chinese walls. Some of our investment management competitors, such as Henderson, ran advertisements proclaiming independence from any associated stockbroking or corporate finance activities, thus implying that firms such as Mercury were not independent and that our clients might suffer thereby. While most of our existing clients seemed to be convinced of our genuine independence, our competitors' advertising made it more difficult for us to get this message across convincingly when trying to attract new accounts.

In time we could probably have overcome the various false perceptions over our independence, but of greater significance was a feeling of general disillusionment on the part of the chief people in Mercury as to the Warburg merger. Not only were they disappointed that it had been designed without any attention to Mercury's interests, but they also had doubts that such a large merger, involving four different corporate cultures, would be successful.

The seniors in Mercury held options tied to the share price of Warburgs, but their efforts would now have less impact on the enlarged group's profits, and hence its share price. With their new self-confidence in the prospects for Mercury, they could foresee a situation in which Mercury's profits might increase while those of the rest of the group declined. This could mean a lower price for Warburgs shares, despite an improved achievement in Mercury. Understandably, they wanted their incentives to be tied to the future of Mercury and not the now more remote Warburgs.

In money terms, some of the offers that had been made to Mercury's senior management were exceedingly generous, and even if we could provide them with options on Mercury shares instead of those they held on Warburgs, Mercury's results would have to be extraordinarily good for them to earn as much as they could outside our firm. The proposals which Stephen and Leonard put forward were thus not lacking in loyalty to Mercury or to Warburgs. Moreover, they made commercial sense. It is common knowledge in the business world that people work more effectively for their shareholders when they have a meaningful stake in their own immediate activity. They may not work much harder, but they really care about the profits and the value of the business. They even start remembering to turn out the lights when they leave the office, and they save the paper clips.

Mercury's profits were now approaching 20 per cent of Warburgs' profits. So it was with the conviction that a flotation of Mercury which provided its executives with direct financial incentives was absolutely necessary that I knew I must speak to David Scholey. David was now sole chairman of Warburgs on his own, as Eric Roll had moved on to the less executive and more titular position of president. I was sure that the only way forward was to float part of Mercury, and that it was a matter of some urgency. I could see no other way to avoid departures of the best people in Mercury, and thereby damage to Warburgs' results. Project Mercury, in my eyes, had nothing to do with the launch of the first American in space in 1961, but everything to do with the launch of Mercury on the Stock Exchange as soon as possible.

*

I have always been impressed by the qualities of the stage trouper who manages to go on performing to his best ability no matter from what distractions or what distress he may be suffering. In his autobiography, *A Minstrel in France*, written in 1919, the Scottish comedian Sir Harry Lauder wrote movingly about such an experience. His greatly loved son, a captain in the Argyll and Sutherland Highlanders, was killed in France in the First World War. Within a very short time, Lauder was back on stage in a music hall in London to sing and make his audience laugh. One of his songs included the words:

> When we gather round the old fireside
> And the fond mother kisses her son . . .

Such was his emotion that Lauder was unable to sing these two lines.

The orchestra played on, and he recovered and sang the rest of the song, only to break down when he was back in the wings with the audience still applauding. 'You never know what you can do until you have to find out' was his comment in the autobiography.

It was one of Siegmund Warburg's tenets that a banker should be prepared to keep a number of balls in the air at any time, and should be able to switch his concentration totally from one transaction to another immediately and without hesitation, however disturbing or absorbing the earlier matter might be.

Among David Scholey's many admirable qualities is this sort of resilience – the mark of a trouper or a good banker. I have seen him leave an unpleasant and lengthy negotiation of great importance for the future of the firm and for himself, and within moments greet a visitor of little significance with the utmost diplomacy and attention. The visitor's impression would have been that David had nothing else whatever on his mind other than a wish to hear his views, which David did with all the appearance of great interest. He has that rare but striking ability to give undivided attention to the person he is talking to under all circumstances.

David is one of the most amusing after-dinner speakers I have heard, and regularly does an excellent stand-up comic routine at Warburgs' annual tea party for its pensioners, not least because he remembers everyone's name and can instantly recapture from his memory an occasion twenty years or so earlier, when, for example, he might have played darts with one of the now retired messengers. He is the master of the improvised one-liner. When one of our younger German colleagues once remarked at a management meeting, 'The trouble with you English is you're incapable of being direct', David snapped back instantly, 'You're wrong.'

In contrast to Siegmund, David made no pretence of avoiding a dialogue with the press, who appreciated his openness and humour, and it was no surprise that they responded by giving him fulsome reviews and profiles. Through a combination of flattery and charm, he deftly side-stepped the most awkward and probing grillings from well-informed journalists, with such comments as 'You do ask *the* most intelligent questions', before answering one that had not been asked. David was soon regarded as London's most powerful investment banker, which he certainly was, but he could just as easily have reached the top as a diplomat, a politician or, for that matter, an entertainer. As it was, he was deservedly nominated Banker of the

Year in 1986 by the influential American magazine *Institutional Investor*, with John Reed of Citibank as his runner-up.

If my own relationship with David had had its off days over the thirty-five or so years we had then known each other, I admired him for the leadership he had shown in the days after Siegmund's death, and later in implementing the merger of the four firms at Big Bang. Now, however, I was in an awkward position as the conveyor of news which I knew he would not welcome. At the very least, separation of Mercury would be time consuming, controversial and divisive. I could well imagine he would tell me dismissively that there was no way that any part of Warburgs was going to be sold off, either on the Stock Exchange or to a third party. He would probably say that I was being bullied by Mercury's already unduly independent and troublesome management team, and you know what you do with bullies – you stand up to them.

I also knew that David could be obstinate and sometimes quite fierce when responding to ideas that he found unattractive. These characteristics seemed to be more noticeable when he was with his right-hand man and subsequent successor as chief executive, Simon Cairns, also a pleasant and entertaining companion on his own. Together, they sometimes seemed to be engaged in an 'I can be tougher than you' act, which prompted one of our colleagues to call them 'a pair of piranha fish'.

So it was not without some trepidation that I first broached the subject of a Mercury flotation with David. 'That's very interesting', he said, in a characteristic manner that conveyed absolutely nothing as to his true reaction. 'We should talk about it sometime.' There was no indication when, if at all, any further discussion would take place. I suspected that it was to be a slow dance as far as he was concerned.

David was almost invariably late for meetings, which in part was a consequence of the concentrated attention he devoted to his previous meeting and in part had become a habit. It was offset by an almost miraculous ability to catch aeroplane flights at the very last minute, thereby upstaging those of his more anxious colleagues who had checked in much earlier. This was made possible only by the disciplinary reminders to depart for the airport delivered by his formidably intelligent and delightful secretary, Edith Randall, and by the driving skills of Jack Phillips, one of the most enterprising chauffeurs of all time, as well as one of the nicest people.

We did, however, eventually manage to get together for some

further talks, not, I sensed, without some reluctance on David's part and usually at well-spaced intervals and with Simon Cairns present. While they did not seem to like the idea of flotation much, at least David and Simon did not reject it outright, and they brought the matter to the Warburgs board. Here there were sharply divided views. There were those like John Stancliffe and Hugh Stevenson who understood both the strategic logic of a spin-off of Mercury as well as the pragmatic necessity. Others were neutral or open-minded, but there was a small minority from Warburgs' corporate finance side who were vehemently opposed to any form of separation, for reasons I can only guess at. I spoke individually over the following months to most of the non-executive members of the board and found them without exception to be understanding. Henry Grunfeld took the trouble to meet Stephen Zimmerman and Leonard Licht to hear their views, and, ever the wise pragmatist, he lent his influential support to the idea.

And so it was decided in early 1986 that Warburgs would make preparations to float part of the share capital of Mercury, probably 25 per cent, on the Stock Exchange. There were some on the corporate side who still had such an entrenched disdain for the investment business that they doubted, or at least purported to doubt, whether there would be any takers for Mercury's shares at anything more than a nominal price. This view, which I suppose was based on anticipatory *schadenfreude*, I found romantically naive.

*

If plans for the flotation preoccupied us in 1986, another important item on the agenda was the integration of the investment management arm of Rowe and Pitman, which their leader Jamie Ogilvy had named Rowan, and that of Mullens, into the newly named Mercury Asset Management. Although appreciably smaller than Phillips and Drew in investment management, together the two firms brought us more than £1 billion of funds under management, some high-quality clients, including more than 100 charities managed by Mullens, and several excellent fund managers. Merging three diverse firms, however, each with its differences in size, style, clientele and ways of doing business, was not going to be without its problems.

We had got to know each other over a series of breakfasts, which took place at our three offices in alternation. Rowe and Pitman's breakfasts were decidedly better than Mercury's, while Mullens' were altogether in a different class – they served fresh orange juice and home-made marmalade. Our team for these occasions consisted of David Price, Stephen Zimmerman, Richard Bernays and myself. Jamie Ogilvy led Rowan's with David Boyle, James d'Albiac and Richard Southby, while Richard Marriott and David Gascoigne represented Mullens.

There were two main areas of difficulty. Several of the fund managers in Rowan were partners in Rowe and Pitman, and as such had been accustomed to an annual income at least twice as large as their peers in Mercury. In future, they would have to receive the Mercury rate for the job, which came as a shock to some of them. One morning I was greeted by three irate former Rowe and Pitman partners threatening a lawsuit against Mercury. I explained as politely as I could that, if we were to continue to pay them the incomes they had been getting, we would have to do the same for all our more numerous fund managers, thereby doubling our salary bills and ruining our business. They had sold out their partnership interests to Warburgs and had to accept our right to decide on such matters. Eventually common sense prevailed, and two of the three were to become valuable long-term contributors to Mercury's subsequent growth.

The other problem was more technical, but equally thorny. Whereas Mercury generally charged its clients fees based on the value of their portfolios, our new partners, especially Mullens, as stock-brokers, charged most of their clients commissions on each purchase or sale instead of fees. In our view, while this was acceptable in the case of some private clients who preferred to be charged commissions for reasons having to do with capital gains tax, it gave an incentive to the fund manager, conscious or unconscious, to create undesirable turnover in the portfolio. Mercury had itself charged commissions in the past, but we did not see it as the way forward and nor did most of our clients.

In the case of Mullens' clients, there was an additional aspect. They charged commissions only, but made so few switches in the portfolios of their clients, most of which were charities, that the income they received fell some way short of paying the costs of managing the portfolios. Mullens' income as government broker had in effect been subsidising its investment management activity.

Our decision that, with very few exceptions, clients of the enlarged Mercury would in future have to pay fees was greeted with alarm by some Mullens partners. Robin Peppiatt, a highly likeable and respected stockbroker with a nose for horses as well as shares, an old friend of mine and no mean in-swing bowler in his younger days, got upset with me about it at a meeting of David Scholey's new Chairman's Committee in Warburgs. We would lose all Mullens' investment clients, he said, if we charged them fees. They had been clients of Mullens in some cases for generations, and it would be disastrous to make a change now. Luckily his fears proved unfounded and the loss of clients was minimal.

Mullens' list of charities, which emanated from its historical connection with the Bank of England, was indeed impressive. It ranged from the Imperial Cancer Research Fund, the Army Benevolent Fund, Chelsea Royal Hospital (the Chelsea Pensioners) and its naval equivalent, Greenwich Hospital, to less familiar names such as the Soho Working Girls Club and the London Society of Ragamuffins Benevolent Fund. When Warburgs acquired Mullens for £12 million at the time of Big Bang, the purchase was justified by our masters on the basis of Mullens' expertise in the gilt market (UK government bonds), although some cynics thought that Warburgs had been pushed into the purchase by the Bank of England, which had taken away Mullens' main source of income by eliminating its age-old role as government broker. Both these views failed to take account of the real franchise in Mullens, which was its business managing money for charities. Only Richard Marriott at Mullens, and some of us at Mercury, were aware of its potential.

Thanks to Richard Marriott's powers of persuasion, the majority of Mullens' charities agreed to pay fees. Since then their portfolios have been very well managed by Chris Littlejohns and others, and Mercury's business has grown with the addition of such charities as Guide Dogs for the Blind. In 1999, the management of money for charities constituted an important sector of Mercury's business.

There were also some differences of style to be overcome. Should we, for example, abandon our long-standing policy of not offering wine at lunch? I felt our policy made sense not only from the point of view of anyone who wanted to work in the afternoon, but also for the message of sobriety and seriousness which it sent to our clients. To me wine is one of the essentials of life, but not of lunch. Our Rowe and Pitman colleagues, on the other hand, reasoned that some of their clients would be horrified not to be offered a glass of wine or two at lunch, and might even take their business to a firm with a more epicurean attitude. Were our clients really so different to theirs, I wondered? We finally agreed that wine could be served if a director hosting a lunch particularly requested it.

It is the seemingly unimportant matters such as this which can sometimes damage relationships, but the compromise we reached kept people of both viewpoints relatively happy. Moreover, it gave John Rodwell and me some opportunities to indulge an interest in tasting new wines. We had some enjoyable if brief gatherings at Corney and Barrow, only in the evenings of course, sampling and discovering some excellent wines from Spain, Italy and the new world, which came within the tight budget we set, but were more delicious than all but the most expensive French wines. (Our host, Adam Brett-Smith, said that we tasted his fine wines at breakneck Mercury speed.) Despite this indulgence, lunchtime abstinence continued to prevail most of the time.

*

Our three firms finally got together under one roof in 1986, at 33 King William Street, to which Warburgs and Mercury had moved two years earlier. That the integration went fairly smoothly was due mainly to the leadership of three people. David Rosier was by then in charge of Mercury's private clients division, which was the destination of most of Rowan's clients and all of Mullens'. David is an energetic and enthusiastic person who has proved to be a strong leader, much admired by those who work for him. I had noticed, during our move to King William Street in 1984, that he, as well as John Rodwell, then in charge of administrative departments, each with a military background and accustomed to practise what used to be called 'man management', spent much of the weekend of the move in the new office making sure that everything would be in order on Monday morning for everyone else to function efficiently. Many others came in too, but only to see that their own desks had been set up correctly. It is surprising that management techniques involving consideration for colleagues are emphasised in the army, but taught in only a limited way in commercial firms.

Jamie Ogilvy, younger brother of Angus, is another person with exceptional charm. His family is descended from an ancient line of highland chieftains from the same part of the county of Angus as that from which my own family traces its roots. When he first arrived at

33 King William Street, he was horrified by our excessive preoccupation with work. Richard Bernays, the one of our seniors who knew Jamie best, took him out to lunch and told him, 'Don't look so miserable Jamie, we're not *that* bad.' I sometimes felt that Jamie believed, as did Field Marshal Viscount Herbert Charles Onslow Plumer, hero of the Matabele relief force in 1896 and of Ypres in the First World War, that all would be well with the world if every one of its institutions were controlled and led by Old Etonians. Now Jamie was thrust into the part of the Warburg group in which there were only a few of them, but he gave us staunch support in the sometimes fragile process of putting our firms together.

Always with good humour, Jamie teased us for some of our more idiosyncratic ways, but he nevertheless became an early convert to the use of graphology in recruitment. He is someone who needs to be the boss, and he managed to arrange a plush office for himself which was larger than that of anyone else in the building. I was not surprised that, when our merger had been more or less happily completed, he accepted a position as chief executive, and later chairman, of Foreign and Colonial, a well-regarded medium-sized investment management group which has held on to its historical name despite its politically dated connotations. He achieved notable success there, but I was sorry to lose his companionship and his laughter at Mercury.

I was lucky enough to be included in recent years in Jamie's annual Christmas lunch at Foreign and Colonial, when he entertained some twenty-five of his friends from the City and elsewhere, almost all Old Etonians. These lunches, which have ended now with his retirement as chairman of Foreign and Colonial at the end of 1998, achieved distinction for their excellent food and wine, and notoriety for Jamie's speeches, in which he insults to their considerable amusement each of his guests in turn. In my case, he has told the assembled company that I made too much money at Mercury, that I was in the wrong regiment in the army, that I might have been a decent chap if I had gone to the right school, and that my ancestors in Scotland were his ancestors' serfs and it still shows.

Richard Marriott, the senior Mullens person to join Mercury, was a former officer in the Greenjackets and then the Artists' Rifles, which is the Territorial Army affiliate of the SAS. He had played various roles within Mullens before taking charge of their investment side, and he had a reputation as something of a dilettante. We found, however, that he always applied himself with vigour to any task that had to be done. His diplomacy and self-effacing manner made him an ideal person to maintain relationships with the many charities. Richard is noted for the brevity of his speeches, which are different from Jamie Ogilvy's in every respect. At his sixtieth birthday, he said, 'I intend to make exactly the same speech I made at my wedding. Thank you all very much for coming', and sat down to some appreciative applause. He has restored an old family house in Yorkshire, where Mercury sponsored a performance of the *Marriage of Figaro* by Pavilion Opera in 1993, and in 1999 was Lord-Lieutenant of the East Riding of Yorkshire.

There were some people from our two new merger partner firms who found it hard to accept our larger size and more regimented lifestyle. Initially, we formed a division under the name Mercury Rowan Mullens to keep the businesses of Rowan and Mullens in a separate compartment from Mercury's own private clients business, and there was a transitory period when Jamie Ogilvy wanted it to have its own independence from Mercury. Mercury's objective, however, was to create a 'one-firm firm', and the achievement of full integration sooner than any of us might have expected was due in large measure to David Rosier's efforts and the support he received sometimes separately, because they did not always see eye to eye with each other, from Jamie Ogilvy and Richard Marriott.

Several years later, some of the former Mullens partners joined with Richard Marriott in arranging for Mercury to keep and display their library of books on economics and banking, which today adorn the bookshelves of Mercury's boardroom at 33 King William Street. It was a gesture which suggested that, whatever their initial reservations about us might have been, they came to accept that Mercury was a reliable guardian of their clients and their traditions.

CHAPTER 16

Enter Saul Steinberg

A funny thing happened on the way to Mercury's flotation. Saul Steinberg, seen by some as 'a bad boy of Wall Street', announced one day in 1985 that he had purchased, through Reliance Insurance which he controlled, 14.9 per cent of S.G. Warburg Group. One of his objectives, it was rumoured, was to persuade Warburgs' management to spin off Mercury to Warburgs' shareholders, or to sell it.

As a young man fifteen years earlier, Steinberg had borrowed $25,000 to start a company called Leasco, which leased IBM computers. It was a convenient arrangement for IBM customers because of the perennial obsolescence of computers, and Leasco was a considerable success. Steinberg then used Leasco's highly rated shares to acquire Reliance and, at the age of 29, he tweaked the noses of the American banking community by bidding for Chemical Bank through Reliance/Leasco. He was seen off by the Wall Street establishment on that occasion, but became a much-feared green-mailer – a term which describes someone who buys stakes in companies that he considers undervalued, and then makes a nuisance of himself by threatening to gain a controlling position until he is bought out at a premium either by the company itself or by someone else. Shortly before his investment in Warburgs, Steinberg had engaged in a notoriously rewarding greenmailing exercise with Walt Disney Corporation.

Short and chubby, Saul Steinberg had a reputation for being brash and conspicuously opulent. He owned his own Boeing 727 jet aircraft. He and his wife Gayfryd led a flamboyant social life in New York and entertained lavishly at their 34-room apartment on Fifth Avenue. Steinberg's second wife had accused him in divorce proceedings of a cocaine habit – a charge she later withdrew. There was, however, another side to Steinberg. He was a major benefactor of the Metropolitan Museum and had built a remarkable art collection, including Dutch, Flemish and Italian old masters as well

as modern pictures. He was an anglophile and an admirer of
Churchill. He had a brilliant mind, read everything and was known
as a shrewd observer of investment values.

Saul Steinberg was the last sort of person Warburgs wanted as a
major shareholder, just as it was embarking on its goal to become a
new force in international merchant banking. Despite Reliance's
protestations that it planned to be a long-term investor in Warburgs,
no one in the firm, except perhaps some of us who believed in a
separation of Mercury and felt his intervention might speed up that
process, viewed his purchase with any degree of charity. Steinberg
had obviously spotted the hidden value to Warburgs in its ownership
of Mercury, which could be realised if Mercury were to be sold, spun
off to Warburgs' shareholders or floated on the Stock Exchange.
David Scholey sensed all sorts of trouble and feared that Steinberg
might increase Reliance's holding to 25 per cent. He went on record
to describe Steinberg's purchase as 'unhelpful'.

Reliance did not buy more shares, but, true to expectation, it was
not long before Steinberg was calling for a 'valorisation' (realisation
of the true value) of Warburgs' holding in Mercury through a sale or
spin-off to Warburgs' shareholders. He was able to point out that
Mercury was carried at nil value in Warburgs' balance sheet, while
analysts were already prepared to assign a value to it of at least £100
million.

A few months after Reliance's purchases, Steinberg came to see me
in connection with the sale of a new issue of shares in Reliance. I
found him pleasant, well informed and amusing. Naturally, he
brought up the question of a spin-off of Mercury. The decision to
float had been taken before Steinberg made his investment in
Warburgs, but it had not been announced and I could not pass on
inside information to him. He would not have left our meeting,
however, with any impression that we in Mercury had any strong
disagreement with his views, or that nothing was being done.

A year later, in December 1986, we learnt that Reliance's holding
in Warburgs had been bought at an appreciably higher price than
Reliance had paid by the Canadian National Railway (CNR) pension
fund – a purchase that *Investors Chronicle* described as altruistic.
The fund was managed then and now by Tullio Cedraschi, whom I
had met on a number of occasions in Canada. He had been to lunch
with Rodney Ward and me at 30 Gresham Street, when he told us of
his ambition to buy a 'strategic' (i.e. long-term and substantial) stake

in a London merchant bank. When presented with the opportunity of acquiring Reliance's 14.9 per cent shareholding in Warburgs by Barry McFadzean, a former Warburgs director by then working as a financial consultant, he responded with alacrity. The CNR pension fund was greeted as a white knight by David Scholey, and Tullio soon joined the Warburgs board.

During 1986, the share price of Warburgs had improved steadily, at least partly on rumours of a spin-off of Mercury. Despite his investment background, however, Tullio's decision to buy Steinberg's holding appeared to have been based more on his feeling for the overall mystique of merchant banking than on anything to do with the prospective flotation of Mercury. He proved to be an analytical and pleasant, if somewhat maverick, director of Warburgs over the next few years, but to my surprise and disappointment, he was to sell the shares of Mercury which his pension fund received at the time of the flotation in April 1987 soon thereafter.

As to Steinberg, Reliance's original investment, costing around £65 million, had increased in value to £100 million – not a bad gain for a year's mild but constructively aimed greenmailing.

*

The course that we had embarked on more than a year earlier was now irreversible, but it was not until late in 1986 that it was formally announced that Mercury would be separately floated. The intention was to sell 25 per cent of Mercury's shares by way of a rights issue to S.G. Warburg Group's shareholders, at the same time obtaining a quotation for them on the Stock Exchange.

Before that could happen, we had to put together a board fit for a publicly quoted company, and that meant persuading one or two distinguished outsiders to risk their reputation and become non-executive directors. The seniors in Mercury had asked me to remain as chairman. As a Warburgs man for thirty years, I was by habit and instinct loyal to Warburgs, but I would now have to put Mercury's financial interest first and Warburgs' second. I would be allowed to remain on the S.G. Warburg Group board, while giving up my position as a director of its merchant banking subsidiary, the old S.G. Warburg & Co. My own financial incentives would in future be tied to the results of Mercury. It was a time of mixed emotions for me, but also one of some excitement and anticipation.

I would be a novice in my assigned role as chairman of a public company, and there were times when I suffered from the impostor syndrome, which means you ask yourself, 'What's an ordinary bloke like me doing in a job like this?' Sometimes I found myself wondering whether Warburgs was, after all, the meritocracy I had always thought it was, because, if so, what was I doing on such a lofty perch? I also occasionally reflected on one of Siegmund's favourite aphorisms, which Henry Grunfeld once told me he particularly liked: 'To get to know oneself is the first step to an inferiority complex.' But I knew I was surrounded by wonderfully capable colleagues. David Price would be deputy chairman and Stephen Zimmerman vice-chairman. Richard Bernays, Andrew Dalton, James Dawnay, Carol Galley, Leonard Licht, Bob Michaelson, Jamie Ogilvy and David Rosier would be the other executive directors of the quoted Mercury. They were young and had no experience of sitting on a public company board, but it was a strong team.

S.G. Warburg Group, as the continuing 75 per cent shareholder, was obviously entitled to representation on the board. Very sensibly, in terms of Mercury's need to be seen as independent, they agreed to just one seat, which went to Hugh Stevenson. Hugh was doing tremendous work on the separation agreements and the flotation documents, and he had acquired an in-depth knowledge of Mercury's business. Both Hugh and I would be members of David Scholey's Chairman's Committee in Warburgs.

For our first independent director we were looking for someone a bit older, a well-known figure in the business world who had been demonstrably successful as chairman of a public company. I wanted someone I could talk to, who would not hesitate to tell me bluntly when I was going wrong. I sought help from Denis Greenhill (Lord Greenhill of Harrow), a former head of the diplomatic service, who was a non-executive director of Warburgs. Denis was on various prestigious boards, including British Petroleum, the BBC and the Wellcome Foundation, whose commercial arm, Wellcome plc, was in the news because of its recently available treatments to alleviate the symptoms of AIDS. I asked Denis if he thought it conceivable that Alfred Shepperd, the well-regarded chairman of Wellcome plc (later Glaxo Wellcome) might be receptive to an invitation. Denis had a word with Alfred Shepperd and soon afterwards Denis, Hugh Stevenson and I called on him at Wellcome's imposing, if old-fashioned, offices on the Euston Road.

It was rather like visiting royalty. After several layers of security, we got through first to the office of Mr Shepperd's secretary, a granddaughter of the famous pre-war Yorkshire cricketer Wilfred Rhodes, and finally to the great man's cavernous room. He belied his reputation as a domineering autocrat; he was politeness itself, listened patiently to our story, told us warmly that he would reflect on our invitation and accepted it a few days later. Shep, who has a financial background, was a stalwart member of Mercury's board for the next eight years and chaired the audit comittee with diligence. He took a great interest in Mercury's people and its business, and was an invaluable colleague and wise counsellor to me on many occasions.

A short while after Shep's acceptance, Henry Grunfeld invited me to lunch with Jocelyn Hambro, formerly chairman of Hambros Bank and at the time chairman of J.O. Hambro and Company, a breakaway investment banking firm that he started with his son Rupert and other members of his family. Jocelyn Hambro, then 70, said to Henry Grunfeld, then 83, 'Well, what we've got to watch now, Henry, is not to get AIDS.' I resisted the temptation to tell him that, if such an event were to occur, I might be able to obtain treatment for them on favourable terms.

*

The next approach to a potential non-executive director arose from a conversation between David Scholey and myself. We agreed that I would invite the one and only Leon Levy, the person who had introduced me to the magical economics of investment management as a business. I had first met Leon many years earlier in London through Jake Eberts, the film producer who had been with AEA ('The Richest Little Club in the World'), in New York. I saw him again after he had visited Siegmund Warburg at the latter's house in Blonay on Lake Geneva in 1981. Leon had been amused by Siegmund's telling him that one of New York's most famous bankers was 'not a banker'. Siegmund's idea of a banker, Leon and I had surmised, was someone who was more than a mere banking technician: someone who read books or went to the theatre, who studied history or human nature, and preferably did not ski or play golf.

Leon himself is a philosopher economist who trained in psychology and found support from Siegmund for his view that events are not predictable, but people are. He has the air of an absent-minded professor, and in many ways that is what he is. He is reported to

have left his wife Shelby White behind on many occasions at parties
and receptions. He once hailed a cab in New York, opened the door
for a lady colleague to get in on the nearside, walked round to the
other side, opened that door and, hastily retreating, said, 'Oh, I'm so
sorry. I didn't know this cab was taken.'

At his seventieth birthday party on a boat in the Hudson River,
Shelby welcomed the guests and expressed her relief that Leon had
found the boat. Thereafter his adoring friends one by one told their
favourite stories on the same theme. One referred to an encounter
with Mick Jagger, to whom Leon is alleged to have said, 'I'm sorry,
Mr Jagger, I didn't get the name of the company you're with?'
Another concerned a conversation with Andy Rooney, a New York
television personality, whom Leon greeted with, 'I'm so glad to meet
you Mr Rooney. As a kid, I saw all of your movies.' True or false,
such stories about Leon are legion, and he puts up with the resultant
teasing with the utmost good humour.

The absent-mindedness camouflages an exceptional mind and a
remarkable insight, usually correct, into the future direction of the
American economy and financial markets. Having sold their stockbroking business, Oppenheimer and Co., in 1982, Leon and his
equally astute partner Jack Nash started a private investment
partnership, Odyssey Partners, which did extremely well for its
investors with average annual returns above 30 per cent, until Leon
and Jack decided to call it a day in 1997. It was, Leon has noted, 'a
journey fraught with opportunity and peril'.

Leon had unusual ideas for running an investment business. He
liked to employ young analysts because he thought anyone who had
been brought up in the atmosphere of the 1930s might have an
unduly pessimistic view. He insisted that his analysts invested their
own money in the ideas they suggested for Odyssey. As to ethics, his
guideline was that no one should do anything his mother would not
be pleased to read about in the *New York Times*.

He and Shelby have one of the finest collections of Greek, Roman
and Etruscan antiquities in the world, which was shown at the
Metropolitan Museum in New York in 1990. 'Ecstasy is fleeting but
antiquities are for ever', Leon wrote in my copy of the book *Glories
of the Past*, which illustrates the collection. Leon's love of ancient
history has also prompted him to finance an archaeological dig at
Ashkelon in Israel, which has uncovered a gorgeous golden calf. In
addition to that, he is an extremely generous person, having given

away vast sums not only in the US, but also to education and medical research in the UK.

When Leon came to see Siegmund in Blonay in 1981, it was to pursue a proposal to invest in Trans World Corporation, a conglomerate which owned Trans World Airlines and a number of other companies, including Hilton International (hotels), Canteen Corporation (food) and Century 21 (real estate brokerage). Leon believed that the sum of the parts of Trans World was worth at least twice the prevailing share price of the whole, and that Trans World would accordingly benefit from 'disaggregation', i.e. selling parts of the business or distributing them to shareholders. In November of that year, we made a nostro investment in Hepplewhite Partnership, which was set up by Leon to promulgate his idea and to persuade the management of Trans World to spin off some of its subsidiaries. The management was not listening, however, and a proxy fight (a voting contest) ensued. Hepplewhite, with just over 1 per cent of the shares, was outvoted in a fairly close fight, and the partnership was wound up with just a small profit. Ironically, Trans World came to realise the merits of Leon's ideas and in the next few years gradually carried out the programme he had suggested, to the considerable advantage of Trans World's shareholders.

Happily, Leon Levy agreed to come on Mercury's board when I asked him. He had already joined the board of Mercury Selected Trust, the old Selected Risk which Eric Korner had started in 1962, and now he was 'honoured', he said. He appeared to be genuinely pleased to be associated once more with a company founded by Siegmund Warburg, whom he greatly admired. At the same time, he made a prediction that Mercury would have a brighter future than Warburgs.

*

It is no easy matter to change a division into a stand-alone business. Most of the administrative functions of Mercury were shared with the other divisions of Warburgs. It was accepted that Warburgs would continue to provide Mercury with internal services, such as personnel, finance and information technology, until we could assume them ourselves, but the basis on which they would do so had to be agreed. Discussion of who should bear what proportion of such expenses could easily become heated.

There were concerns on the part of Warburgs' banking division that it might lose a major part of its deposits if Mercury were to become independent. The investment division had traditionally placed its clients' cash on deposit with Warburgs as a Bank of England authorised bank. It was a well-established and symbiotic arrangement that worked well: Mercury's clients were paid the finest possible rates of interest, while Warburgs had a stable deposit base which enabled it to conduct a wider banking business. The bankers in Warburgs were now worried that an independent Mercury might switch its deposit business to another bank. It was an important issue that had to be argued out and settled. That friction was largely avoided in our separation discussions, and agreements were reached amicably, was mainly due to the common sense of Hugh Stevenson, who led the negotiation for Warburgs, and David Price, John Parsloe and Nick Stewart, who constituted Mercury's team.

There were some other gaps to be filled. We needed a good chief financial officer. I had hoped that Simon Leathes, deputy to Michael Gore, Warburgs' chief financial officer, might join us. I knew that Simon was a good accountant with a sense for business reality because we had worked together on Warburgs' negotiation to buy 50 per cent of Potter Partners in Australia in 1985 and 1986, and I had seen him in action under pressure. He came close to accepting our offer, but in the end we were outbid by Warburgs, and Simon decided to stay there. Later we recruited David Causer from Bankers Trust, who responded ably to the challenge of building a finance division in Mercury and became in due course a key member of its board. I used to tease David whenever I saw him drive his racy sports car into the office garage. I assumed his choice of car must have been some sort of compensation for the prudence he was required to demonstrate for the rest of the day.

Richard Bernays nobly assumed the overall supervisory role for all administrative functions, effectively the position that in the US is described as chief operating officer. For compliance we had a ready-made expert in John Parsloe, one of the first compliance officers in London who was prepared, when necessary, to adopt an adversarial position towards his own colleagues. Initially I was one of those who feared that excessive compliance regulations and manuals would not only kill enterprise in Mercury, but also increase our expenses unreasonably. I soon came to see that a strong compliance code, in which companies and individuals have to comply strictly with

regulatory procedures and ethical standards, was a desirable protection in an increasingly suspicious and litigious business environment.
John later moved on to a more creative area of Mercury's business,
but I regard him, as well as John Mayo, a former senior partner of
the law firm Linklaters who became head of compliance at
Warburgs, as being among the leading designers of the City's current
strong compliance system. John Parsloe has other talents, not least an
ability to show up for work with trousers of one colour and a coat of
another. 'Well, you see, it was very early when I left home this
morning', he would tell me. 'It was still dark.'

On 5 March 1987, we signed a protocol of independence with
Warburgs, which recognised Mercury's commitment to act at all
times in the interests of its own clients. It was a document of critical
importance to Mercury's independence and thereby the future of its
business. It was to play a role in the collapse of the merger talks
between Morgan Stanley and Warburgs in 1995.

CHAPTER 17

His Lordship's Telephone

As 1987 began, there was renewed argument about the name we should have as a publicly quoted company. I believed, not least perhaps because I had some pride of authorship, that Mercury Asset Management was a good name providing an adequate differentiation from Warburgs. We were to be allowed to continue to use the Warburg name overseas, which was helpful because it meant much in countries such as the USA and Japan where Mercury meant practically nothing.

There were those such as Leonard Licht who thought we might be confused with Mercury Communications, then emerging as a competitor to British Telecom in the telephone market. There was also a Mercury dispatch rider service, a Mercury hotel company and even a Mercury escort service. Leonard believed it would be difficult for us to establish a separate identity to Mercury Communications against the background of the latter's all-pervasive advertising, and that we should adopt some more neutral name. I felt, to the contrary, that we could be an unintentional but not unconscious beneficiary in our retail business of the other Mercury's advertisements. Besides, Mercury is the god of commerce, which gave us an appropriate deity to look up to. So why rock the boat with some new name that left out Mercury?

Another worry was that we would inevitably be called MAM, an abbreviation that was thought undignified and undesirable. My brother Robin kept reminding me that MAM was the acronym which had been used by Music Agency and Management, a publicly quoted company of the 1960s which had the rights to the songs of the pop singer Engelbert Humperdinck, alias Arnold Dorsey. Humperdinck, who as a reformed character is currently enjoying a new lease of life as a singer in his sixties, was an active exponent of the sex, drugs and rock and roll culture of the 1960s – hardly an association we wanted for our clean and respectable investment management company. Fortunately, few remembered Humperdinck's company, so we kept the Mercury Asset Management name. But we did come to be popularly known as MAM just as surely as if a copywriter had sent out a message, 'Don't call me Mercury, don't call me Madam, call me MAM.'

Leonard Licht's fear of name confusion proved to be justified in one instance the following year. I received the following letter from the Earl of Selkirk:

Dear Mr Stormonth Darling

You may not be the correct person to write to in regard to telephones, in which case perhaps you would pass this letter on to a member of your staff who is suitable.

At my house in Dorset I have three telephone points and I wish to introduce intercommunication in what the Post Office sometimes calls a Keymaster.

I would be grateful if whoever is responsible could tell me whether this is the sort of job that Mercury could do.

Yours truly
Selkirk

I wrote back:

Dear Lord Selkirk

Thank you for your letter of 30th November. I think you may be confusing us with Mercury Communications which is a subsidiary of Cable & Wireless plc. Their address is Mercury House, Theobalds Road, London, WCI.

We are investment managers and do not know very much about telephones!

Yours sincerely
Peter Stormonth Darling

I should, of course, have sent him some literature on our unit trusts – an omission I immediately regretted.

Such matters of public perception were much on our minds, and we also had to learn how to deal with an increasingly inquisitive press, to which none of us had previously had much exposure. In the summer of 1985, I gave an interview to the *Observer*, then a leading

Sunday newspaper, and I cringe with embarrassment today at the rubbish I talked. A year later, in June 1986, Stella Shamoon, a sharp and probing financial journalist who now writes an excellent investment column in *The Times*, approached us with a proposal to do a major feature on Mercury, also in the *Observer*. Her inferred threat was that she was going to write a piece anyway, so we might as well co-operate with her to ensure at least that the facts were correct. I trusted Stella, and although she was always seeking an angle, she wrote about us fairly and informatively. Her article was headed 'Warburgs' Investment Powerhouse', and it contained a black and white picture of Richard Bernays, Leonard Licht, David Price, Stephen Zimmerman and myself looking rather like a gang of disreputable second-hand car dealers.

*

A number of us were addicted to the Warburgs style and were determined to keep it in Mercury as much as possible. In business school terminology, we were faced with an Ethos Preservation Challenge. We decided that the senior management group would operate as much as possible as a collegial partnership. We would continue the Warburgs practice of having a daily summary of mail and internal memoranda for circulation to all executives. There would be no name plate outside 33 King William Street. The meeting rooms would be functional with unlined yellow writing pads and sharpened pencils. There should be two Mercury people at every meeting with clients, and so on.

The challenge was to pass on to a younger generation the values which those of us who had been around in the old days had inherited from Siegmund Warburg, Henry Grunfeld, Eric Roll and others. The growth of Mercury's business in the first half of the 1980s resulted in our recruiting a number of university graduates – men and women in roughly equal numbers. We looked for those attributes that we believed might make them good fund managers, such as intelligence, curiosity, scepticism, contrarianism, intuition and a desire to get rich, but where we found these qualities, they were not always accompanied by humility or even good manners. It was an eye-opening and painful experience for me to hear a trainee fund manager, about 25 years old, ask the head of a well-known American company who was in London to talk about his firm, 'What makes you think I would want to buy your shares any more than all the others that get thrown at me every day?'

We had no difficulty in continuing to use graphology in recruitment because all of us, including our new merger partners, were firm believers in it. We had seen how well it worked in practice, first with Theodora Dreifuss in Zurich and later with Renata Propper in New York. Their analyses would each typically take them the best part of a day to complete for each subject, and would attest to such characteristics as honesty, loyalty, financial acumen, conceptual thinking, intelligence, memory, ego, ambition, leadership, stability and capacity to cope with stress. I am told that sexual deviation can be easily determined too, but we were not expected to be interested in that. Our graphologists asked only for details of the writer's sex, age and nationality. They were not much concerned with legibility or tidiness, but looked more for certain repetitious movements in the handwriting.

There were those among our competitors who ridiculed our use of graphology, and still do today. They might say, 'You can't get a job at Warburgs if the old lady in Switzerland doesn't like your handwriting.' It was true that, if Mrs Dreifuss expressed a very negative view, we ignored it at our peril. We once took on someone for a senior appointment in Mercury despite her warnings that he was an empire-builder and a highly nervous person who would let us down. Our interviews with him had led us to a different conclusion. We were keen to hire him, so I spoke to Mrs Dreifuss to see if she was quite sure that she ought to be so negative. She asked for another sample of his writing – it was possible he had been using the wrong sort of pen, she said. Her analysis was the same the second time, and she told me I would regret it if I did not follow her strongly held opinion. We did not, and she was right. Within three months he wanted to expand prematurely his section's activity in the US and the Far East. Within six, he had a nervous breakdown.

There were many such stories. I often found it educational and useful to look back years later at her, and subsquently at Renata Propper's, original analyses. If one of our colleagues was being particularly difficult, I could turn to the graphological test for an explanation, and it was usually there. It was remarkable to see just how revealing those tests were in the light of a few years' experience of their subjects.

I never asked to see my own analysis, which must have been on file somewhere at Warburgs, preferring to remain ignorant as to whether all of the weaknesses that I had tried to hide over the years had been rumbled. Out of curiosity, I did, however, have my writing analysed by two outside graphologists, Renna Nezos, who although Greek, founded the British Academy of Graphology in London, and Sheila Kurtz, an American whose consultancy firm was imaginatively called A New Slant. Both had written books on graphology, the former's a scholarly and discursive volume with an emphasis on Jungian psychology, and the latter's an easier read for the lay person. Their analyses of my writing, although made six years apart, were similar, and I found I could readily accept most of their detailed comments. Where I was reluctant to go along with some of the less desirable characteristics that they ascribed to me, I was assured by friends that those were pretty accurate too.

*

While hoping to preserve many aspects of the old Warburgs style, we also needed to establish our own identity and develop some ways of our own. One area for this was that of status. Even with generous financial rewards, people like to have a grand title on their visiting card, and with this in mind, we created nine wholly owned subsidiaries of Mercury, each with its own board. Allowing for overlap, this enabled us to have no fewer than eight chairmen, three deputy chairmen and more than seventy directors. Of course, while this structure had some clear benefits, we had to guard against the reciprocal danger that it would result in too many meetings, often a substitute for action. ('Bored with work?', goes the irreverent refrain. 'Try holding a meeting; feel important; catch up on your sleep; meet other people; write notes; bore your colleagues; put off decisions until the next meeting, etc.')*

I was told that we needed a proper logo to advance the branding of our various investment services and funds. Branding is supposed to promote client loyalty and cross-selling – the theory is that, if a client buys one of your products, he will soon buy another. While I could grasp the idea as it applied to consumer products of companies like Gillette, Nestlé or Dunhill, it seemed in those days an alien concept for a merchant bank or an investment management company, which

* My friends at Scottish and Southern Energy have come to terms with this problem in an original way. Arriving for a meeting in their conference room in Havant, one is greeted with a sign reading provocatively 'Is Your Meeting Really Necessary?'

I preferred to believe should market itself through reputation, service and performance. Branding has, of course, become fashionable in recent times. The director of tourism at Stratford-upon-Avon recently declared that Shakespeare was 'a great brand', and even the British government has tried to brand our country 'Cool Britannia'.

I was instinctively distrustful of logos, but agreed that we should have a small emblem with our name on some golf balls that we were planning to give out at a tournament that we had agreed to sponsor. My instructions were taken too literally. Mercury's name was written on the golf balls in such tiny letters that it required a magnifying glass to read it. It was just as well, perhaps, because the logo turned out to be the same as that of the Boy Scouts, except that it was upside down – not that it made much difference on a golf ball. We have come a long way since then. As a compulsive collector of Mercuriana, I have in my possession a letter opener, a T-shirt, a sweater, a sports bag, golf balls, a golf umbrella, some excellent golf tees, which, although wooden, seldom break, a baseball cap and even a stick of candy, each showing Mercury's logo at various stages of its development. With the prospect of name changes under Merrill Lynch's ownership, these may become collectors' items, but I hope not quite yet.

Warburgs had its own chef and butlers, as they liked to be called, to emphasise that they were in private employment and not mere waiters at the Savoy. (One silver-haired Warburgs butler in earlier days was so elegantly dressed that he was sometimes mistaken by guests as a senior director of the bank, and greeted as such.) We went a different route and appointed a catering company to provide a staff canteen and do the directors' lunches. John Rodwell, who had the role of caterer-in-chief, and I took great trouble to see that those lunches had the right touch – simple, healthy nursery food served without ostentation, with a wine cellar adequately stocked but seldom accessed. There would be small menu cards on the table omitting any modern restaurant-speak descriptions, such as 'sun-ripened tomatoes and basil on a bed of fresh baby lettuce with an aubergine ormolu garnished with crushed coriander'. Instead, the menu might read simply:

Tomato Salad
Sole
Poached Pears
Coffee

Sometimes our chef excelled himself, and one guest went so far as to say that the food was so good he had forgotten all about sex. We were pleased some years later when our excellent team of kitchen staff and butlers led by Franco Cassaccio, which John and I had so carefully coached, won the prize for Directors' Dining Room of the Year in competition with a thousand others.

One or two of our health-conscious seniors used to have specially prepared lunches brought in for them. It used to remind me of an occasion in the 1970s when Charles Douro, then with Deltec and now chairman of Sun Life and Provincial, and I had lunch with Walter Salomon, the eccentric head of a small merchant bank, Rea Brothers, and yet another German Jewish refugee who had a successful career in the City. He was served a magnificent lobster salad with a glass of Corton Charlemagne, while Charles and I were given some slightly tired cod and vegetables with a fairly boring white table wine. Salomon was under doctor's orders, he explained, and the chef's choice of menu for that day would not suit him at all. He hoped we would understand if he ate and drank only what his doctor ordered. Some ten years later, by which time I knew him better, I congratulated Walter Salomon on the knighthood he was awarded. 'Well,' he said in his Germanic accent, 'I always thought I was a sir, so it makes no difference.'

*

Since 1984, Warburgs and Mercury had shared the office building at 33 King William Street, but it was agreed that Warburgs would move, section by section in stages, to join its new Stock Exchange partners in Finsbury Avenue. The last Warburg person would not be moving until after our flotation in April 1987, but we needed to plan a new office layout before then. The members of Warburgs' Chairman's Committee used to occupy individual rooms alongside each other on the sixth floor of 33 King William Street – a sort of executive suite. We decided to alter that floor to encompass only reception rooms and dining rooms. Mercury's seniors would sit in open-plan rooms with colleagues of varying seniority and in different sections of our business.

We had virtually no pictures to decorate our walls because, when it came to their final departure, some person at Warburgs – I like to think at not too senior a level – meanly ordered that all pictures and decorations be removed to their new offices in Finsbury Avenue. We were left with one water-colour of King William Street because we were the ones still in that location, and some not completely unattractive Graham Sutherland prints of busy bees, which had been around a long time and to which that person at Warburgs thought his colleagues should no longer be subjected. They took most of the good furniture and all the silver. When Warburgs was sold to Swiss Bank Corporation in 1995 and Mercury consequently became fully independent, Michael Jodrell and Richard Marriott tried to recapture for Mercury a portion of the Rowe and Pitman and Mullens silver. Mercury was, after all, just as deserving an inheritor of it as Swiss Bank Corporation. Their attempts ran into initial objections from David Scholey and others, but were eventually successful in part.

We were shorn of our library, which, despite an agreement to the contrary, was removed in its entirety to Finsbury Avenue with the exception of one out-of-date Michelin guide. We were fortunate soon afterwards to recruit Sara Meyer from the *Financial Times*, and she built from scratch a research library far better than the one we lost.

We established a small art committee under the leadership of Michael Jodrell, incidentally in a class of his own as a private client fund manager, with Norman Bachop, Richard Bernays and John Rodwell. We gave them an allowance and held a beauty parade of several corporate art consultants, following which we appointed Sally Lescher to advise us. She looks at auctions and galleries, and alerts Michael Jodrell to any suitable possibilities for purchase. Both she and Michael have a fine eye for a picture, and over the succeeding years they have built up an attractive collection of more than a hundred twentieth-century British paintings from Laura Knight, L.S. Lowry, Alberto Morocco, John Nash and Lucien Pissarro to Diana Armfield, Ken Howard and Peter Kuhfeld among contemporary artists. It decorates the reception rooms and corridors of the sixth floor of 33 King William Street, so that it can be seen by visitors.

One visitor who liked the pictures was David Scholey. When I heard him some years after our float admire a Frank Short watercolour landscape on three separate occasions in the manner of Queen Mary, I knew we had to give it to him. This we did with an inscription expressing the very genuine thanks of all his friends at Mercury for the help he had given us over many years, to which he sent a charmingly worded reply.

*

As Mercury's April flotation came closer, we had to agree the difficult question of the price at which Mercury shares would be offered to Warburgs' shareholders. My discussions with David Scholey and his right-hand man Simon Cairns on this important matter were not as acrimonious as I feared they might be. In Mercury we wanted a low price, whereas Warburgs, as sellers, wanted a high one, although it could also be reasoned that, as they would continue to own 75 per cent of Mercury, they might want the issue to get off to a good start in the market place. It was not at all unhelpful to our cause that members of Warburgs' financial staff had for some years masochistically categorised Mercury's earnings as 'low quality' at internal board meetings. The basis for this assessment was a fear that clients of Mercury could remove their funds from us at any time. It was a fear that was usually unjustified because clients are surprisingly loyal to the fund manager whom they have chosen, unless investment performance is consistently bad over an extended period of time. The reality is that profits from corporate finance are the more volatile and less predictable because they are only as good as the last completed transaction.

Part of Mercury's objective in keeping the price low was to see that the options which were about to be granted to about ninety members of its management (the total number of employees was under 500 at the time) were priced to provide an attractive incentive. Nothing would have been more depressing for our management than to be given options at the issue price only to see that price fall following the float, thus putting their options 'out of the money'. In addition, the dozen or so of us in Mercury who had until then owned incentive 'warrants' in Warburgs, had agreed, in order to achieve separation of all aspects of our remuneration, to exercise those warrants and to reinvest the after-tax proceeds in shares of Mercury at the issue price. As a sign of good faith, we also agreed to hold the Mercury shares for at least three years (some of us held them much longer).

All sorts of arguments and statistics were produced to justify this price and that price, and eventually we agreed in early March 1987 on a price of 225 pence per share (90 pence per share as subsequently adjusted). This represented a price/earnings multiple of just over eleven times forecast earnings, not out of line with the shares of other quoted institutional fund management companies at the time. It put a value on Mercury of £158 million. It was agreed between us that, of the proceeds of the sale of 25 per cent, amounting to £39 million, £17 million would go to Warburgs while the other £22 million would be paid into Mercury. If the issue were successful, Warburgs would be creating in their balance sheet, more or less out of thin air, an asset worth about £118 million (75 per cent of £158 million) and likely to increase in value beyond that. Saul Steinberg would have been proud of us.

CHAPTER 18

Serious Money?

When dealings started in Mercury shares on 7 April 1987, they rose from the issue price of 225 pence to 341 pence. This was embarrassing because it looked as if the price we had agreed was too low. The shares fluctuated for a while thereafter in a narrow range, but there were some people who accused us of 'stealing' Mercury from Warburgs. That criticism was killed stone dead, however, at the time of the devastating market crash of October 1987, when our shares retreated to their issue price and briefly sold at a price below it.

The newspapers made less mileage out of the price than from their discovery, when Mercury's first annual report came out in July, that six directors of the company had received an income of more than £1 million in the year that ended 31 March 1987. I was the only one to be named because it is a requirement that the remuneration of the chairman of a public company is shown in the annual report, whereas in the case of directors the amounts paid are shown but without linkage to names. I thus served as the lightning conductor for my five colleagues, as the *Evening Standard*'s front-page headline on 7 July trumpeted, 'Mercury's Million Pound Men'.*

The six of us were among the first to cross the £1 million barrier for annual income in a public company. (There were, of course, other examples in private businesses that remained unreported.) I narrowly missed being the first named person on my own because the income of Christopher Heath of Barings, who easily beat me with his £2.5 million to my £1.05 million, was published on the same day. Christopher had built up a prosperous business in securities in Japan and south-east Asia which had been sold to Barings, and his income resulted largely from an earn-out arrangement arising from that sale.

---

* I could have wished for the French situation. An offer document from a French public company in 1997 included the following statement: 'No details have been given of directors' remuneration, because this would indirectly entail the disclosure of the remuneration of certain individuals'!

In both his case and mine, there were non-recurring factors, but the press referred simply to the amounts we were 'paid'. 'But, Mr Darling, you did receive over £1 million last year? You would agree, wouldn't you, that that's a serious amount of money?'

Some of the newspapers pursued me for lifestyle interviews. Christopher Heath gave one or two, and was photographed with his racehorses. I decided that I was not available – it would have been out of keeping with Warburgs' and now Mercury's style. One evening, however, I was sitting in my office quite late when I took a call from a journalist whom I did not know from one of the tabloids. He seemed decent, and out of curiosity I decided to see what he wanted to talk about. Secretly I was hoping he might point out that I was being paid more than the Prime Minister, so that I could quote to him Babe Ruth's answer to a similar question many years earlier. When he had just broken the record for home runs in one season and was being well rewarded for doing so, Babe Ruth was asked if he realised that he had earned more than the President of the United States. 'Well,' he replied, 'I had a better year.'

I warned the journalist that I doubted whether he would find my lifestyle anything other than bourgeois and boring. Part of the ensuing conversation went roughly as follows:

JOURNALIST: Can you tell me, Mr Darling, you have a chauffeur I presume, but what car do you drive?
PSD: No, I don't have a chauffeur. I have a seven-year-old BMW. Often I come to work on the Tube.
JOURNALIST: Do you have a holiday home abroad?
PSD: No.
JOURNALIST: Do you have a yacht?
PSD: No.
JOURNALIST: Can you tell me what clubs you belong to?
PSD: Well, I belong to the Clamp Club.
JOURNALIST: Where's that?
PSD: It rescues your car for you if it's been clamped.

There was no lifestyle article in his newspaper. I did give an interview to *Yomiuri Shinbun*, with a readership estimated at 15 million. Happily it only appeared in Japanese.

Soon we were joined in the million pound club by Lord Hanson and Mercury's old adversary from Burtons, Sir Ralph Halpern, but I continued to appear, incorrectly, in the top ten in some league tables for three more years. Such publicity is to be avoided if possible. Your friends regard you as fair game for their favourite charity. The best response to this is to set up a charitable trust with some friendly trustees and specific objectives for donations, so you can say that any particular charity does not fall 'within the categories my trustees would be likely to support'. Forgotten relations show up with hard-luck stories and find it unforgivable if you don't immediately restore them to the financial position they feel is their inalienable right.

Some years later, I was even subjected to a blackmail attempt over some innocuous stolen letters I had written, combined with threats to inform my business colleagues that I consorted with 'high class tarts'. The City of London Police came to my rescue expeditiously, and strapped with a hidden recording device, I arranged to meet a man at an open-air restaurant surrounded by plain-clothes detectives posing as customers. When the 'drop' had been completed, the police moved swiftly to arrest, and the blackmailer was subsequently sentenced at the Old Bailey to two years' imprisonment.

My new fame did at least enhance my social standing. At a wedding, I met one of the country's best-known lady social columnists, who greeted me with 'Peter, I hear you're the richest man in England!' It was reported in one of the Sunday supplements that I had been at some glitzy and fashionable ball on an evening when I was out of the country. My brother, sharper than me in both intellect and dress, informed me that someone in Scotland who had previously tended to ignore him had suddenly shown a fervent interest in speaking to him, but had turned away promptly when he found he was talking to the wrong brother. Belinda Pinckney, wife of my Canadian co-adventurer, Jeremy, who had seen me rather poorly dressed at a dinner in Edinburgh, wrote to me: 'I was just wondering whether, in the light of recent revelations, it was time for you to order a new dinner jacket.'

One year later, my income was reported at £165,000, a reduction of 85 per cent and surely a record decline for the chairman of a growing and successful public company. A colleague reassured me with the information that he had ordered some Salvation Army collection boxes. But any hopes I had that the reduction, widely ignored by the press of course, would put a stop to the unwanted publicity were soon dashed. The problem was that, once you were in the league tables, it seemed to be impossible to drop out of them.

In July 1989, together with David Scholey, I was mentioned in a Labour Party pamphlet, 'File on Fairness, Number 5' in a section entitled 'Increases in Take Out Pay for Top Directors'. Releasing the report, Gordon Brown, then no more than an opposition Treasury spokesman, commented that the UK's boardrooms had become an 'I'm all right, Sir Jack, society'. Shortly after that, at a City lunch aimed at developing a constructive dialogue with the Labour Party's economics specialists, a Labour peer whom I knew and liked referred openly to my 'unconscionable salary'. That was not quite the end of it. The *Observer* magazine in December 1989, just in time for the family to raise its expectations for Christmas presents, ran a feature article with colour illustrations on 'Britain's 50 Highest Paid'. Nearly three years after the original one-off payment, I was still shown as holding down one of the country's five highest-paid jobs. Professional sportsmen, couturiers, pop stars and other entertainers apparently did not rate. There I was in a rogues' gallery of photographs with Christopher Heath, Lord Hanson, Sir Ralph Halpern and Tiny Rowland, all smiling except me. The only person missing, it seemed, was Robert Maxwell, but he too was included in the last list I appeared in, in 1991.

It is a pity that such matters get so much attention in the British press, and what a contrast to the US. The great cynic Oscar Wilde observed that the only thing worse than being talked about is not being talked about. I learnt that a low profile, or none at all, was preferable.

*

The stock market crash of 1987, coinciding as it did with the first hurricane in the UK for 200 years, was a shattering event. Within forty-eight hours about 25 per cent of market values were destroyed. However, the power stations were still producing electricity, factories were working, the shops were open, and even in the City and Wall Street most people still had their jobs. It did not seem quite like Armageddon. I was telephoned by the *New York Times*, which wanted to know what the UK's largest fund management company thought about it. In an item on 20 October 1987, the day after the crash, under the heading 'Foreign Views of US Stocks', I was quoted as saying, 'I don't believe we've come to the end of the world.'

In a democracy there is always someone out there to take issue with you. A few days later, I received a letter from Eliot Janeway, a former adviser to President Lyndon Johnson and a vigorous critic of American post-war economic policies under all presidents from Roosevelt to Reagan, including Johnson. His pessimistic views gained him the label Calamity Janeway, and were reflected in the title of his final book, *The Economics of Chaos* (1989). Janeway's letter read as follows:

Dear Peter:

Greetings across the years.

This note is prompted by the quote attributed to you in the *New York Times* column which I enclose. I'm afraid that I feel prompted to enter a dissenting opinion. I do think that we have indeed come to the end of the world as it was when it was dominated by the Reagan euphoria. Specifically, I fear that we have suffered not the correction it is easy to welcome, but rather a decisive and dismaying reversal of direction, and that we are in for very much lower levels of stock prices once the present gap-closing rally runs its course.

Cordially,
Eliot

I replied:

Dear Eliot,

What a pleasure and surprise to hear from you.

I was astonished that anyone, least of all as eminent a commentator as you, should take any note of my throw-away line to the *New York Times* reporter. (What I actually said to him was that we were not going to allow a minor adjustment on Wall Street to affect our golf game.)

I am happy to see from your photograph that you look exactly the same as you did on morning television ten years ago preaching the forthcoming calamity.

If you find yourself in London, it would be good to see you again.

Best regards.
Yours sincerely
Peter

Eliot Janeway died in 1993. His constant and extreme bearishness served as a reminder in good times that markets do correct, and a reassurance in bad times that surely things could not be quite as catastrophic as he forecast.

The 1987 crash, fortunately, proved to be quite short-lived, but it spared Mercury from further consideration of a merger opportunity which, while imaginative and intriguing in concept, would not have worked well in practice. Peter Wilmot-Sitwell, formerly senior partner of Rowe and Pitman and at the time chairman of Warburg Securities, and a polished performer in the field of corporate mergers and acquisitions, was close to the management of Christie's, the long-established auction house. Peter thought that a merger between Christie's and Mercury could be interesting because there appeared to be a lack of correlation between their business cycle and ours. Christie's would tend to do well during inflationary times, when the tangible assets it sold at auction would be increasing in value, while Mercury's funds under management would rise in disinflationary periods, which are generally favourable for financial markets. Both Christie's and Mercury were quoted companies, and there might be sensible diversification for the shareholders of both companies if we were brought together.

Peter arranged for me to meet Guy Hannen and Joe Floyd at Christie's offices in King Street, next to the auction rooms, and later Peter and I had dinner with Charlie Allsopp, who, as Lord Hindlip, is Christie's chairman today. There was talk of arranging for 'your people to get to know our people', but the crash intervened, the share prices of both companies dropped sharply, and our minds reverted to more immediate concerns. The idea looked good on paper, but the nature of Christie's business and the mentality required for it is so different from Mercury's that I doubt if their management and ours would have got on well with each other for long.

*

We survived our first year as a public company despite the crash, and we ended it with an increase in funds under management from £21 billion to £23 billion and higher profits than we had forecast at the time of the float. We made progress in taking over administrative activities from Warburgs. We began to expand overseas with joint ventures in Australia, Germany and Spain, and opened a full, as opposed to a representative, office in the Isle of Man, whose government had been an important client for many years.

Not everything was roses, however, and I had sleepless nights over some custody problems which we had in Australia, and less surprisingly in Spain, where trading activity in securities had run ahead of the capacity of the local markets to process transactions. It was no fun to be told that about £5 million of transactions for our clients in Spain could not be 'reconciled', and that our bankers there could not trace that amount of securities belonging to our clients. As the records of the Spanish bank which was our custodian were in such disarray, the bank could claim that it was not sure whether the losses were its fault or ours. We talked to lawyers, and teams of our people spent endless frustrating hours in Madrid. There were times when the losses looked even larger, and others when the picture seemed brighter.

J.D. Rockefeller once said that all the money he made was inadequate compensation for the sleepless nights he had had. I knew how he felt. I was afraid that the Spanish problems could be the tip of an iceberg and that we could have even bigger difficulties elsewhere. Taking into account executive time, lost interest and actual losses of securities, these custody problems probably cost us about £10 million over two or three years. That takes no account of stress and worry – a chairman can never forget that, whoever might actually have made the mistakes, the buck stops with him.

In 1988, we persuaded another first-class businessman to join our board as our third independent and non-executive director. Jon Foulds, later to become chairman of the Halifax Building Society and to oversee its successful flotation in 1997, had a thirty-year career with 3i Group, private equity specialists, ending up as its chief executive. Well dressed and good looking, with a resemblance to Peter O'Toole, Jon was a tremendous addition to our board. His experience at 3i Group, apart from its immediate relevance to our own private equity activities, gave him an uncanny knack for detecting weaknesses in our business, and he pursued these with penetratingly direct questions, always delivered in a charming manner. When he resigned from Mercury's board in 1997 because of his increased commitment to the Halifax, he wrote to me that he had been 'proud to have been part of Siegmund's legacy'. We in turn had been very fortunate to have him on our board.

CHAPTER 19

Mercury Rising

The next few years seemed to pass remarkably quickly. We became accustomed to life as a publicly quoted company with a chance to control our own financial destiny. It had an electric effect on motivation and perhaps caused a commensurate increase in the stress level. Day-to-day management of the business was the responsibility of David Price and Stephen Zimmerman. We were fortunate to have two such capable people in their early forties, each with quite different attributes. I saw my own role as that of a conductor of an extremely good orchestra (or was it a jazz band?), although in truth I sometimes found I was more of a nanny or in-house psychotherapist. My main job as chairman was to appoint the right people, and then motivate them to do their best.

David is unflappable, an approachable and understanding listener with great patience, the sort you go to for a balanced view. He is an imaginative strategic thinker, a good negotiator and an outstanding marketer – in short, an all-rounder of the highest quality – and his leading role in the building of Mercury was always carried out calmly and with consideration and loyalty towards his colleagues. In addition, he has a well-developed sense of humour and a ready laugh. He is the only person I know who, having sat through an entire morning during an away day at Chewton Glen, a country house hotel in Hampshire, dressed in an open-necked shirt, actually put *on* a tie to play golf in the afternoon.

Stephen has the rare gift of being able to manage successfully both a business and a portfolio of investments. The qualities needed for these two disparate functions are, for the most part, contradictory. A business leader must be positive, a fund manager sceptical, but Stephen was able to move from one mode to the other. He is always well informed and has an uncanny intuition that seems to tell him reliably what other people are doing and what is on their minds. It is the same sort of feel that Siegmund and Henry Grunfeld had. He senses trouble ahead in the business and does not run away from it when it arrives. At the same time, he has a flair for investment that has been tempered for ever with a caution resulting from his experiences in the severe bear market of 1973–4, which came at the beginning of his career.

He has an engaging personality, and I always enjoyed talking to him – with the possible exception of a discussion which I came to anticipate with some amusement each year just before the annual salary and bonus review. Sometimes accompanied by Leonard Licht, he would tell me of all the fabulous job offers with ridiculously generous financial packages that were available to his senior colleagues at those particular times. He was careful not to mention himself, but the unspoken hint was ever present. Of course, I always caved in to his not so well disguised whitemail because he was of incomparable value to the business and there was no way we could afford to lose him. I knew that I had come to rely on him more than anyone to tell me what was going on, and what we needed to do. It is impossible for me to overestimate his contribution to Mercury during my period as chairman.

There were others whom I came to depend on too in the following years. Pat Chisholm at first and later Satvinder Maan, two superlative senior secretaries, somehow kept me from too much personal disorganisation. John Rodwell, in charge at different times of all administrative departments, as well as catering, sponsorships and charities, made sure that no detail was overlooked. Fire practices under his direction were carried out with all the efficiency and discipline of a military exercise performed by the Grenadier Guards. It was John who could arrange special services for senior executives – a bodyguard for one who was receiving telephone threats, a shooting lesson in the office garage for another who needed to remove a predatory crow from his garden. Kevin Batts in the reception area made sure that I had a regular supply of liquorice allsorts. (Once he rang me nervously from the lobby to say, 'I'm sorry to trouble you, sir, but there's a man here who says he's come to shoot the chairman.' Someone had omitted to advise him that I was expecting a press photographer that day.) Wilby Andian, a member of the cleaning staff who was originally from St Vincent in the West Indies, was always up to the minute with an informed, if somewhat partially pro-England, interpretation of the latest cricket news.

*

At this point, I must issue a health warning. The next three sections of this chapter describe various aspects of the development of Mercury's business in our first few years as a public company. They may be rather boring for any readers with no particular interest in business, and I suggest that they might skip to the final section of the chapter.

All parts of Mercury's business continued to grow in those years. Funds under management more than doubled in the six years from flotation, reaching £50 billion in 1993. Profits trebled, and we were reported to be the tenth most profitable UK quoted company in terms of return on capital. Our share price rose, at times substantially. A profile of Mercury in 1992 would have made the flotation offer document of 1987 look archival.

Our largest business, managing pension funds in the UK, continued to be our main profit-earner, with Carol Galley succeeding Stephen Zimmerman as its new leader. We were now managing about 8 per cent of the pension fund money in the UK, ahead of Phillips and Drew, BZW, Schroders, Prudential and NatWest. Leonard Licht was in charge of Mercury Specialist Management, a subdivision of the UK pension fund activity that was set up to run higher-risk portfolios invested only in equities. It started in 1983 and had an excellent record of investment performance for most of the 1980s.

The retail side, which by then incorporated private clients, charities and unit trusts, was transformed under the leadership of David Rosier, with Michael Jodrell and more recently Alex Roe as his deputy and Nick Coats running the growing international private client business. The fixed interest division, managed by Charles Jackson, who was helped by the talents of the inimitable Nick Ritchie, had perhaps the strongest growth of all. Nick looks remarkably like the comedian Tommy Cooper, and gets away with his invariably crumpled appearance because of his skills as a trader in bonds and his delightful laid-back manner. Peter Olsberg, with a wealth of knowledge of property, was running a successful activity in property investment for those institutional clients who wanted it as a diversification from securities. His team was to be voted 'Property Manager of the Year' in 1996. Gary Lowe was recruited from Fidelity in 1992 as head of the American desk.

We had spent some £25 million on information systems over the previous two or three years, having switched from an obsolete Sperry

Rand computer, larger than a king-sized refrigerator, to an IBM system. This put us in the forefront among fund managers in terms of systems, and we were lucky enough by then to have an excellent back-office staff led by Gordon Lindsay, a breezy and capable Scot known as the Doc for his qualification as a doctor of chemistry, David Batten, who brought with him valuable experience with Citibank, and Keith Hoffman. They were worthy successors to earlier expert administrators in the support areas, such as Graham Wood, who went on to take charge of personnel in Warburgs and later in Mercury, and Derek Ferguson, who moved to Jersey where, together with Frank Le Feuvre, he headed up a first-class operation for us.

*

Perhaps the most active area of expansion, at least during our first few years as a public company, was overseas. At the time of our float in 1987, we had just two overseas marketing offices in New York and Tokyo, offices in Jersey and the Isle of Man which existed largely to administer offshore funds, and a registered name-plate office in Bermuda. Our business overall, reflecting the background of several of our senior colleagues, was too anglocentric, and it was a major preoccupation of mine that we should find more international source money to manage. Suddenly, in 1988 and 1989, we seemed to be opening up all over the place. From a handful of employees overseas at flotation, we had nearly 200 three years later.

In Australia, we purchased a 50 per cent interest in the asset management arm of Potter Partners. Two years earlier, I had been involved, together with David Brooke of Rowe and Pitman, and Simon Leathes, in Warburgs' negotiations to buy 50 per cent of Potter Partners, which was one of the leading Australian investment banking firms, with its headquarters in Melbourne. Laurie Cox had masterminded the negotiations for Potters in that transaction, and now he was doing so again in the discussions with Mercury. Laurie is someone who plays it hard in business, and is then all sweetness and light in the evening. The pattern mirrors the Australian sporting tradition: you play hardball on the field and drink a beer with your opposite number afterwards. He had exhausted me in the first transaction, but afterwards claimed that I had got the better of him then (he used a more colourful and less printable term) and that he was determined it would not happen again.

I duly opted out of the Potters/Mercury negotiations, which were handled for us with skill and patience by Ian Barby, an able former barrister who had joined us some years earlier from Deltec. Arriving in Potters' Melbourne office for one negotiating session after a twenty-hour flight from London, Ian was greeted by a straight-faced Laurie Cox with 'If you can't put any more money on the table, Barby, you can take the return flight to London this evening.' A full year after the talks began, with almost daily conversations or fax messages between Laurie and Ian, a deal was struck. Laurie then became our partner and a good friend, and our Australian joint venture progressed well. In November 1995, Mercury purchased the other 50 per cent from Potters, and Mercury Asset Management Australia became a wholly owned subsidiary.

We opened a marketing office in Hong Kong, where we had a long-standing but not very profitable relationship with the Hong Kong government to manage a portfolio in fixed-interest securities. Warburgs had at that time a small joint-venture merchant banking operation in Hong Kong with Bank of East Asia, called East Asia Warburg, which was capably managed by John Walker-Haworth, later Director-General of the Take Over Panel. According to Jacques Attali in his book *A Man of Influence*, Siegmund Warburg had 'allowed' me, during the last few months of his life, when I was still head of the international division in Warburgs, to set up East Asia Warburg. I did not recognise this description when I first saw it in print some five years after the event. The leading light in Bank of East Asia, then and now, is David Li, a dynamic, peripatetic and very entertaining person with a partly British and partly Chinese upbringing and an honorary doctorate from Cambridge. I once caught David having two separate breakfast meetings at the Mandarin Hotel in Hong Kong on the same day; my own breakfast at 7.30 a.m. overlapped with both his first one, which had started at 7 a.m., and his second one at 8 a.m.

There was some possibility that we might enter into a joint venture with Bank of East Asia in investment management. Andrew Dalton and I had discussions with David in London to this end, and Ian Barby and Nick Stewart went to Hong Kong for further meetings. This time, however, he chose another partner, so we concentrated on building up our own operation in Hong Kong under the wing of John Gatehouse, who had previously worked there with Hong Kong and Shanghai Banking Corporation. John, charming and conscientious, and well tuned into the Hong Kong business community, developed a number of good clients, both institutional and retail, in at least one case with help from David Li.

We started another marketing office in Singapore under Digby Armstrong, having been given a mandate to manage some money for the Singapore government. At a dinner party at Digby's house there one evening, I noticed to my amazement that one of the guests sitting opposite me, apparently bored by the conversation of the ladies on each side of him, pulled out his mobile telephone and calmly dialled his stockbroker in New York. It was 1990 and early days for mobile telephones, which made it the more surprising. He was a grandson of Chiang Kai-shek, and he died of a heart attack at the age of 46.

A more comical interlude was our attempt to get started in India. Through a contact at Warburgs, we had met Ashok Birla, a member of one of India's powerful industrial families and grandson of its founder. Ashok wanted to start some mutual funds in India under the name of Birla Mercury. He was a lively fellow who, on one visit to London, told me that he was off to Paris for a few days of 'monkey business'. But despite the best efforts of Richard Bernays and John Rodwell, who travelled to Bombay to move things along, our exuberant prospective partner seemed quite incapable of persuading the Indian bureaucracy to give us the necessary permission to launch a mutual fund. Our competitors apparently had much less trouble. It took us a while to realise that we had backed the wrong Birla – a member of the family certainly, but one with a controversial background. It was probably as well that we avoided an activity in India; it would have been a burdensome distraction with little reward. Ashok Birla was to die in an air crash some years later.

We expanded our activities in Japan through the formation of a unit trust company in which, later on, a brilliantly perceptive Japanese economist, Tadashi Nakamae, became our partner. He has foreseen with unflinching accuracy the Japanese recession and stock market collapse of the 1990s. David Price, Andrew Dalton, Stephen Cohen and Cliff Shaw nursed our operations in Tokyo through some slow initial years, but our investment there has paid off handsomely in recent times. By 1999, Mercury was managing $17 billion of funds from Japan.

*

Stephen Zimmerman, a gifted personality who was at the top during all of Mercury's time as a publicly quoted company. Posing with another golfer.

David Rosier,
energetic leader
of private clients
division.

Leonard Licht
– brilliant share
picker.

Andrew Dalton – talented investor, orientalist and Scottish landlord.

Cartoon of Andrew Dalton by Paul Hyman.

ABOVE Leon Levy – investment genius, mentor, philanthropist and collector of antiquities.

Facing page

ABOVE Hugh Stevenson succeeds PSD
as chairman of Mercury, September 1992.

BELOW Brian Lara, sporting his Mercury
outfit, with Ian Botham and Sir Garfield
Sobers, in 1993.

ABOVE AND RIGHT
Herb Allison (above)
and David Komansky
(right) exchange
funny hats with
Carol Galley and
Hugh Stevenson,
following Merrill
Lynch's acquisition
of Mercury in
February 1998.

Facing page

ABOVE Warburgs
and Mercury donate
a new library to
Templeton College,
Oxford. From the
left: David Scholey,
PSD, Hugh
Stevenson.

BELOW Hugh
Stevenson, Carol
Galley and Stephen
Zimmerman, 1996.

PSD's assistant,
Satvinder Maan (right),
with her niece Mandeep
Virdi in New York,
May 1998.

Mercury's office building,
33 King William Street
(watercolour by Paula McColl).

In 1990, we purchased from Warburgs its 50 per cent holding in Bank S.G. Warburg Soditic, with offices in Geneva and Zurich, for £22 million. This was the old Banque de Gestion Financière, a typical small Swiss private bank which Warburgs had owned since the early 1960s. When I first visited it in 1965, its office, from which it was soon to move, was on an upper floor of a building in central Zurich, thus qualifying it as a *banque d'étage*, a designation with slightly derogatory implications. It kept its records in an attic reached by a wooden chicken ladder that you pulled down from the ceiling, with alternate steps for each foot. Like many Swiss banks, it was really an investment management operation for well-off individuals, and it was more appropriate that it should belong to Mercury than to Warburgs.

The other 50 per cent was owned by Maurice Dwek and his partners. A brilliant financier, Maurice had founded Soditic, an investment banking firm in Geneva, in 1971, and had courageously and successfully challenged the cartel of the three major Swiss banks in the Swiss-franc bond issue business in Switzerland. In 1994, Mercury bought the 50 per cent of the bank owned by Maurice and his partners for £48 million, thus completing the acquisition of 100 per cent of Bank S.G. Warburg Soditic. The higher price reflected the growth of the bank's business over the four years from our purchase of the first 50 per cent, as well as some appreciation in the Swiss franc. Maurice remained the bank's chairman. He was also a substantial and supportive Mercury shareholder throughout its life as a public company.

When Warburgs and Mercury went their separate ways in 1995, Mercury lost the right to use the Warburg name in the Swiss bank, and the next year it was decided to sell it for £110 million to the Swiss bank affiliate of the Republic Bank of New York group, controlled by Edmond Safra. Oscar Lewisohn, who had been an invaluable guide to Mercury for some years on the intricacies of Swiss banking, joined the board of Republic's enlarged Swiss bank, which also took on our bank's management.

There seemed to be less we could usefully do in continental Europe and the Middle East. In Spain, we had a short-lived joint venture with Banco Santander. It was memorable for me mainly for a lunch which Emilio Botin, its major shareholder, gave for some of us in Madrid. It lasted until 6 p.m. and was followed by a hair-raising drive to the airport by his chauffeur to catch the last flight to London.

This was not the only travel adventure to test my nerves while I was trying to do my duty as chairman in visiting our overseas offices and clients. I went with David Rosier and Richard Oldfield for a whistle-stop tour of Oman, Abu Dhabi and Kuwait in 1991. The Arab boycott of the 1970s was now a thing of the past, and many, but not quite all, Arab institutions were happy to consider us as investment managers despite our Jewish roots. Our visit got off to an unsettling start when we called on the British Ambassador in Oman. We had read in our briefing papers that his previous position had been as head of the Africa desk at the Foreign Office, and we were thus taken aback when, in response to a conversational question about South Africa, he answered that he really had no particular knowledge of that country. Our next question, also prompted by our briefing notes, seemed to be just as wide of the mark, and we hastily changed tack and told the Ambassador something about our own objectives in Oman. It later transpired that the assistant preparing the biographical briefings had mistaken Amman, the capital of Jordan, for Oman.

We flew on to Abu Dhabi, arriving shortly before midnight to discover on arrival that I had been wrongly advised by the travel agent in London and did not have the appropriate entry visa. I was bustled off into a small room not far removed in appearance from a prison cell and occupied by other 'illegal immigrants' of mixed backgrounds, where I was subjected to some fairly disagreeable abuse by an official who seemed to have a good grounding in racist insults. It was a character-building three hours before I was rescued through the string-pulling efforts of David and Richard.

Abu Dhabi, a small fishing village until the discovery of oil some thirty-five years ago, is a country of wall-to-wall palaces, but after a foreshortened and sleepless night I was not in the best mood to appreciate it. We had a full day of meetings, including lunch in one of the palaces, and returned to the airport in the evening only to find that I now needed to fill out a large batch of forms to get out of the country. I expressed some exasperation to my two colleagues, which drew an all too accurate comment from an investment banker from a rival firm who witnessed the scene. He said to one of them, 'I don't think your chairman is temperamentally suited to Middle Eastern travel.'

*

Jet lag has been described as an elitist disorder, but it is no respecter of persons in its capacity to influence behaviour and judgement adversely. Andrew Smithers recently pointed out that International Monetary Fund officials from Washington appear to have made good decisions when flying south, but bad ones when they have crossed time zones. It affects people in different degrees. There are some who are quite untouched by it. Unfortunately, I am not one of those.

Shortly after Mercury's flotation, I read of a miracle cure for jet lag using aromas. I met and was impressed by Daniele Ryman, the aromatherapist who developed the two remedies 'Awake' and 'Sleep', and I became a believer. I invested in her business and passed on the word to colleagues and friends. Her products were at various times distributed in British Airways, Lufthansa, Virgin and other airlines. Later Daniele paid me the compliment of naming a new aroma compound after me. 'Darling', which is supposed to induce romantic feelings and has been a good seller, is 'a seductive blend of ylang-ylang, vanilla and cedarwood'. Office use is not recommended in the light of modern-day strictures relating to sexual harassment. I am, however, encouraged to know that Carol Galley is today, like me, an occasional user of Daniele's anti-stress spray.

Daniele's jet lag remedies were not, however, powerful enough to restore my equilibrium when it was more than usually disturbed one Sunday at the beginning of August 1990. I arrived at Heathrow airport at 6 a.m. from Hong Kong and bought a copy of the *Sunday Times* to read on the way home, and there was the main headline staring at me: 'British merchant bank revives Nazi gas chamber firm'. It was reported that Mercury Asset Management, 75 per cent owned by Warburgs, had bought a stake in I.G. Farben, which, during the Second World War, had made Zyklon B gas and operated a slave labour camp in which as many as 25,000 people may have died.

I knew nothing about Mercury's investment when I arrived at Heathrow, but I rapidly discovered that Paul Marshall, a fund manager in our European team, had bought no less than 10 per cent of the shares of Farben for our clients. Paul is an intelligent and politically sensitive person, but he was too young to have had any knowledge of Farben's wartime activities. He told me that a group of investors had been put together with a view to pursuing some claims on Farben properties in East Germany which had been expropriated many years ago, and he thought the shares were an interesting investment.

At the end of the Second World War, the Allied High Commission decreed that I.G. Farben should be liquidated and its operations transferred to its original founder companies, Bayer, BASF, Hoechst and three smaller companies. All members of the management board of Farben were put on trial in Nuremberg, and those found guilty were sentenced. In the 1950s, Farben voluntarily paid compensation to the Jewish Claims Conference for forced labour during the war, as did many other well-known German companies. For more than forty years thereafter, Farben was in the hands of liquidators, who were unable to complete the liquidation because of claims on assets in East Germany that had been expropriated by the Soviet Union. The funds left in the company were invested by the liquidators. As a company in liquidation, it had not been free to change its name. The manufacturing activities of the old Farben had been returned to the three main founder and successor companies, Bayer, BASF and Hoechst.

While Farben thus no longer bore any resemblance to the heinous wartime company, Mercury had nevertheless, through its inadvertent action, caused unhappiness to some members of the Jewish community in the UK, especially older people with memories of the war. Eric Moonman, who was senior vice-president of the Board of Deputies of British Jews and had been a Labour MP, spoke of his 'shock and concern' that Farben was being revived and exploited in this manner. Sir Monty Finniston, a former chairman of British Steel, suggested that we should have invested our money elsewhere.

During the course of that Sunday, I noticed to my astonishment that the *Sunday Times* had actually changed the headline I had seen in its early edition, substituting the word 'Jewish' for 'British' in the later edition, which was the one most people read. Someone in the editorial staff had decided to give the story a nasty tweak.

Damage limitation was indicated. The concerns of the Jewish community were understandable, but we in our turn were upset by the tone and sensationalism of the *Sunday Times* article. I spoke to Henry Grunfeld who, as a victim himself of Nazi persecution, might well have been very angry at Mercury's actions, but instead I found him, as I had come to expect with the old troubleshooter, understanding and objective. With his help, I drafted a letter which appeared in the *Sunday Times* a week later, expressing our dismay at the manner of their reporting and setting out the facts that the newspaper had not bothered to research or include.

Alongside my letter was another from a woman in North London, criticising the newspaper for categorising banks such as Warburgs as Jewish and thereby fuelling anti-Semitism. 'I cannot recall', she noted, 'the Midland Bank ever being referred to as a Church of England institution.'

The *Sunday Times* made one further attempt to run the story, but it had no legs and soon fizzled out. According to a concluding article in the *Jewish Chronicle*, the *Sunday Times* claimed that it had not intended to cause any offence. The latter's spokesman said, 'There is no history, not a trace, of anti-Semitism in the *Sunday Times*.' Why then, one wondered, had it chosen to change its original headline?

CHAPTER 20

North America

I considered it a personal failure that, in my time as chairman, we never succeeded in acquiring or establishing a genuine business in the United States, the world's largest investment market. Bob Michaelson and I tried hard to find a suitable fund management business that we could acquire in the US which might complement the activities of Warburg Investment Management International (WIMI), and we had discussions with several. Almost without exception, however, we felt that their 'chemistry' was likely to prove very different to our own. Moreover, if you buy an American fund management business, you are almost certain to be putting large sums of money into the pockets of its managers because they invariably own either actual shares or incentive shares which become valuable on an acquisition. Thus, while the managers will usually agree to 'sign on' for three or five more years, they are sure to be less hungry than they were. Mentally at least, part of them will have 'gone to the beach'.

We saw a good example of this. Bob, David Causer, Mercury's finance director, and I went to visit a fund management business in Houston, Texas, which was for sale. We had two days of detailed discussions, exchanging information about our respective businesses. At the end of the second day, I was to have a concluding session alone with their chairman, who would make around $50 million on a sale. I went to his office on the 54th floor, where he had a swivel chair from which he could command a magnificent view of all of greater Houston and beyond. I asked him how he saw his own future if we were to buy the business and sign him up for five years as chief executive. After one drink he told me that his ambition was to be a merchant banker; he could handle the business that we would be buying in two or three days a week. After two drinks he told me, as he surveyed the world outside from his swivel chair, that his real aim was to become governor of the state; our investment business need take up no more than one day a week. We returned home wiser, but without an acquisition.

After its abortive joint venture with Aetna, and a subsequent three-year period of decline, WIMI was restored to health by Bob Michaelson in the mid-1980s. It achieved outstanding investment performance in 1985 and 1986, especially in the Japanese market, and by October 1987 had gathered over forty pension fund clients in the US and Canada with mandates to invest in the rest of the world. These were described in the trade as EAFE portfolios (Europe, Australia and the Far East). Sadly, costly mistakes were made during the market crash of 1987, and we missed much of the rally that followed. Our resultant performance was terrible, it did not recover and we lost almost all those accounts in the next few years.

WIMI's funds under management thus peaked at about $1.5 billion in 1987, and did not reach that figure again until 1990. By then it was in a new area of business in fixed-income management, and it acquired some good accounts. Thereafter, Richard Oldfield returned to WIMI and tried valiantly to restore our reputation in managing EAFE accounts, but it was too late – the damage had been done. Fortunately, however, Steve Golann in New York successfully marketed the exceptional talents of Consuelo Brooke in managing European small company portfolios, and by 1998 WIMI's funds exceeded $5 billion. It had been a roller-coaster ride since Andrew Smithers' pioneering initiative almost twenty-five years earlier. His concept of persuading American pension funds to invest some of their assets in overseas markets was right, but our implementation had been inadequate, and there were competitors who took advantage of it more successfully than we did.

A happier outcome was achieved with our launch in 1990 of The Europe Fund in the US as a sister fund to The United Kingdom Fund, which began its life three years earlier. The amount raised was $109 million, which came mainly from American retail investors, with some demand from Japan. The issue was led by Merrill Lynch, with Nomura Securities and Warburgs' American subsidiary, S.G. Warburg Securities, as co-managing underwriters.

We already had in place a high-class board for The United Kingdom Fund under the chairmanship of Tony Solomon, a former president and chief executive of the Federal Reserve Board of New York, who steered it with adroitness and good humour through various tribulations. Tony has had a varied and interesting career. He tells of the time when, during the Second World War, at a very early age, he was a regional governor in Iran as part of the Allied Mission administering that country. A propagandist on Radio Moscow asked its listeners, 'How do you feel being governed by a kid of 23 whose name is Solomon?' The board's most senior member in age was George Bennett, a former treasurer of Harvard University and treasurer of the Billy Graham campaign organisation.

We had met George in 1984 when he was running State Street Management and Research, a well-known investment management firm in Boston. State Street had just been acquired by the giant Metropolitan Life, which at almost the same time acquired Albany Life, a British direct-selling life insurance company whose unit trusts were managed by Mercury and in which Mercury had briefly had a shareholding when it was formed in 1974. Forthright in his views, and international in his outlook, George thought it would make sense for Metropolitan Life to acquire 50 per cent of Mercury – or even 100 per cent (we were then still owned 100 per cent by Warburgs) – so that State Street and Mercury could join forces and work together to our mutual advantage. They could help us improve our investment performance in American shares, and we could provide global investment management to their clients on some fee-sharing basis.

The idea had some attractions, and both Warburgs and Mercury were initially open-minded as to any proposals that might make sense to all sides. Some of us visited State Street in Boston to meet George's partners, and Hugh Stevenson, Richard Bernays and I had several meetings in New York and in London with Metropolitan Life. The latter's representatives, though pleasant to deal with, proved indecisive, and to George Bennett's disappointment, our talks went nowhere. George, however, joined the board of WIMI and was a natural choice for the board of The United Kingdom Fund in 1987. He occasionally reminisces that, if only Metropolitan Life had listenend to him in 1985, it might have pre-empted Mercury's flotation and captured for itself the large capital profit which Mercury's shareholders made over the following years.

In addition to Tony Solomon and George, the board of The United Kingdom Fund consisted of a number of our other old friends in the US: Leon Levy, Murray Logan of the Rockefeller family office, Jim Martin, previously head of College Retirement Equity Fund (a large pension fund for teachers), and Livio Borghese, who masterminded the launch of The United Kingdom Fund when he was with Bear

Stearns. Then there was our former sparring partner from Wedgwood, Arthur Bryan, and Marietta Tree. The same board was chosen for The Europe Fund, with the substitution of François-Xavier Ortoli, chairman of Compagnie Français des Pétroles and a former Commissioner to the European Economic Community in Brussels, for Livio Borghese, and the addition of myself as a nominee of Mercury, but without Marietta Tree, who died in 1991.

Marietta Tree was born a Peabody, a member of a rich and aristocratic Boston family, but became an active member of the Democratic Party, where she was known as the 'Democratic golden girl'. She was an intimate friend of Adlai Stevenson. A strong anglophile, she married an Englishman, Ronald Tree, owner of Ditchley Park in Oxfordshire, which had a staff of thirty when she first visited it in 1946. Three years later Tree sold it, since when it has been used by the American Ditchley Foundation for its conferences. Marietta was appointed US ambassador to the United Nations by President Kennedy, and was the first woman to hold that post. In her later years, she sat on various corporate boards and added glamour to ours, albeit for only a short period. She told me she believed that 'work is the real fun'.

*

We had a stroke of good fortune in Canada, where in the 1980s we had acquired a small number of institutional clients in Toronto and Montreal, for whom we managed money in global markets. Canadian institutions were, and still are, restricted in the amount they could invest overseas, but they were keen to do it for as much as they were permitted. In 1988, the Parti Québécois, whose main aim is to separate Quebec from Canada, was the provincial government in power, and it was anxious to develop Montreal as a financial centre to rival Toronto. Thirty years earlier, when I first went to Canada, the two cities were of roughly equal standing, but Montreal's position had declined dramatically, mainly as a result of the separatist movement, which scared off outside investors.

An old ally of Warburg was Jean Campeau, an ardent separatist, who had been appointed chief executive of the Caisse de Dépot et Placement du Québec, a substantial provincially owned pension fund which had as an additional agenda the promotion of businesses in Quebec. I had known Jean in the 1970s when he was a very competent as well as welcoming official in the Ministry of Finance in

Quebec City. John Stancliffe, Rodney Ward and I used to visit him there in connection with financings which Warburgs arranged for the Province of Quebec in the eurobond market, and he had been to see Warburgs many times in London. On one occasion, I arranged for him to meet Siegmund Warburg, who put on one of his best performances. 'Mr Campeau, I hear from your admirer Peter Darling here that you are single-handedly responsible for the excellent financial arrangements of Quebec', he told him. Not surprisingly, Jean became a firm friend.

Now, in 1988, he approached me with a proposition. If Mercury would open an office in Montreal, he would make sure we received enough money to manage from Caisse de Dépot to cover our costs and make a small profit. It was a fair deal that worked well for us then and since. We opened an office run initially by James Donald, son of Rodney, our former colleague on the North American side in WIM, who in turn was succeeded by Elspeth Paterson and then by Marc Brillon. These three Canadians have represented us in Montreal and throughout Canada to the highest standard, and have zealously guarded the good relations which Mercury has had with various institutions in Toronto and with the French Canadian community in Quebec, including some with separatist instincts.

When I first spent some time in Montreal in 1957, it was evident even to an outsider that French Canadians were starting to break away from the stranglehold of the church, which had controlled every aspect of their daily lives until then. In the emancipation that followed in the next two or three decades, and as a reaction to the church's previously oppressive influence, the birth rate in Quebec went from the highest in the developed world to the lowest – an almost incredible metamorphosis. As a result, the French Canadian population dropped from 29 per cent of the total Canadian population in 1989 to an estimated 22 per cent today. In the same period, expressions of separatist sentiment, largely unspoken until then, became more frequent and more strident, with emotion sometimes taking precedence over economic reality.

Unexpectedly, I discovered that the separatists, or at least the leaders of the movement whom I met, are not at all anti-British, whatever they may think of Anglo-Canadians. The founding father of the movement and Premier of the province in the late 1980s, Rene Levesque, now deceased, lived in London during the war as a correspondent for the Canadian Broadcasting Corporation, and he liked the place. I heard him make a speech at a lunch at the Savoy Hotel in London in about 1986 – the toast to the Queen had to be given at the beginning of lunch so that he could smoke throughout the entire meal in preference to eating – in which he said, in front of some 400 people, that if Quebec achieved separation under his premiership, he would want it to remain in the British Commonwealth. As far as I know, he never said as much in Canada. Jacques Parizeau, leader of the Parti Québécois at the time of the last referendum on separatism in 1995, used to head for the Cotswolds when he needed a few days' break somewhere he would not be readily recognised. He was an engaging dinner companion, but seems to have fallen out of favour in the province since the failure of the last referendum on separatism in 1995. He told me once that 'Every French Canadian is a separatist at 2 a.m. in the morning, but the difficulty is to keep them that way the next day!'

I have a special affection for Canada from the days in 1958 when I started my Warburgs career in Toronto under Tony Griffin, and as I write these lines in mid 1999, I remain the chairman of the board of Mercury Asset Management Canada, which comprises Marc Brillon, Rodney Donald and Rob Paterson in Canada and Colin Clark from Mercury in London. My career with the Warburg group, which started in Canada forty-two years ago, will thus also end there.

Visiting our colleagues in Canada has always been a pleasure, but I was not happy when the building chosen for our office in Montreal turned out to be on the steepest part of a nearly vertical street known as Beaver Hall Hill, a treacherous place to walk in an icy Canadian winter. Once, Richard Oldfield and I were visiting Montreal and we saw an old man, a tramp almost, fall down just outside the entrance to our office building. We helped him up, for which he expressed his gratitude. 'You're English, aren't you?', he said. 'I wonder if you know Sir Robert Peel, your Prime Minister? He's an old friend of mine.' Old indeed – Sir Robert Peel died in 1850.

CHAPTER 21

Some Name-Dropping at Salomon Brothers

While I was visiting New York in 1990, Leon Levy gave me a copy of Michael Lewis's best-selling book *Liar's Poker*, which is an insider's account of life at Salomon Brothers. When I read it, I became exceedingly grateful that David Scholey had shown no interest in John Gutfreund's offer to buy Warburgs after Siegmund's death eight years earlier. Few if any of us at Warburgs could have endured the macho trading room mentality of Salomon.

In his first chapter, Lewis recounts an anecdote, well known in financial circles, in which John Gutfreund, chairman of Salomon and by then crowned King of Wall Street by *Business Week*, challenged his vice-chairman John Meriwether to a bet of a million dollars on the serial numbers of a dollar bill. The bet was wrapped up in a game they played called liar's poker, similar to liar's dice, and Meriwether, a director of the firm and its top bond dealer, was the acknowledged champion, so it was a brave dare. 'No, John', said Meriwether. 'I'd rather play for real money. Ten million dollars.' Gutfreund withdrew his challenge.

Little could I have realised, when I read this story, that a year later both Gutfreund and Meriwether would resign from Salomon in the wake of a scandal in which Mercury was the innocent victim, or that Warren Buffett, who through his company Berkshire Hathaway had become Salomon's largest shareholder in 1990 by purchasing $700 million of convertible preferred shares, would become Salomon's interim chairman.

The US Treasury introduced a rule in 1990 preventing anyone from bidding for more than 35 per cent of the issue in any auction of new US Treasury bonds. It was thought that the Treasury's move was in part aimed at controlling the activities of Salomon, then the dominant firm in the market for US Treasury bonds, which had been entering the auctions with enormous bids. It seems that Paul Mozer, Salomon's senior government bond trader and a managing director of the firm, was very angry at the Treasury for restricting his activities in the market in this manner. In the auctions which took place in December 1990 and February 1991, Mozer entered a bid for Salomon not only for the firm's allowable 35 per cent, but also for a further 35 per cent, at a potential cost of over $3 billion, in the name of Mercury Asset Management. He entered 'Do not confirm' on his instructions, which meant that the bids in Mercury's name would not be reported to us.

Although Mercury had an active business relationship with Salomon, largely maintained by Nick Ritchie, we had given no instruction to Salomon, knew nothing about the orders he had given using our name, and had no interest in purchasing any bonds in the auction, let alone in the amount of the fraudulent bid made for us in the February 1991 auction. It was a pure case of bid-rigging on Mozer's part, aimed at obtaining an additional but illicit allocation of bonds for Salomon, thereby giving it virtual control of the issue and its price in the after market. When Salomon received the extra bonds, it made a phantom trade, selling them from Mercury to itself.

Unbeknownst to Mozer, it so happened that Warburgs, which was a licensed dealer in the US Treasury market, had applied, legitimately, for bonds in one of those auctions. The US Treasury spotted the relationship between Warburgs and Mercury, and noted that together their application exceeded the newly imposed limit of 35 per cent of any one issue. In April 1991, the Treasury wrote to Mercury and to Warburgs to point out that in concert our two firms were apparently in breach of the rules, and it sent a copy of its letter to Mozer at Salomon Brothers, as the firm which had arranged the purchases. Mozer then telephoned Charles Jackson at Mercury, in the temporary absence of Nick Ritchie, telling him it was all a clerical error and that he would sort it out with the Treasury. Charles took him at his word, a reasonable response given Salomon's position as the leading firm in the market and Mozer's position within it, and the Treasury's letter remained unanswered beyond a mere acknowledgement.

The failure to respond to the substance of the US Treasury's letter fell short of Warburgs' rule that all correspondence should receive a prompt and proper reply, and Mercury was subsequently criticised by the Treasury for it. It was, however, understandable. 'My word is my bond' used to be the dictum in the City of London, and there was no reason for Charles Jackson to assume any lower standard of integrity in Wall Street, as Hugh Stevenson, who was speaking for

Warburgs and Mercury, was later to argue convincingly to the US Treasury. Unfortunately, that code of behaviour belonged to an earlier, less complex and less greedy era of financial history. Despite his undertaking to Charles Jackson, Mozer did not speak to the US Treasury about his 'error'.

Aware that he had been caught out, however, with possibly serious implications both for himself and for Salomon, Mozer did inform his boss, John Meriwether, who told him that his behaviour was 'career threatening'. Meriwether then discussed what he had heard from Mozer with John Gutfreund and with the firm's president and its in-house lawyer. They decided to ask Wachtell Lipton, their lawyers, to investigate, and agreed among themselves that they should inform their regulator, the Federal Reserve Board of New York. But none of them contacted the Federal Reserve. They just sat on the information until August when Wachtell Lipton completed its report – a delay that Warren Buffett, when he learnt of it, described as 'inexcusable'.

Things then moved quickly. Gutfreund and Meriwether resigned from Salomon Brothers, and Buffett took on the chairmanship. Announcements were made in the press, at first somewhat evasively and later, at Buffett's insistence, with full disclosure. Creditors started to desert Salomon, and the Federal Reserve issued an order barring the firm from participating in any future Treasury bond issues. Buffett believed that this move could bankrupt an already crumbling Salomon, with severe consequences for the financial markets, and he spent Sunday 18 August persuading the Federal Reserve to rescind its order. He was eventually successful in reaching a compromise, in which Salomon was permitted to continue bidding for its own account, but not for customers. Buffett described that day as the most important day in his life.

None of this changed the fact that Salomon Brothers had acted fraudulently and that Mercury's name had been used illegally and thereby damaged. Moreover, we had incurred legal expenses, and Charles Jackson had had to travel to Washington with Hugh Stevenson to give evidence to the Securities and Exchange Commission, the US Treasury, the Federal Reserve Board in Washington and the Federal Reserve Board in New York, in each case with multiple lawyers present. I made it known to Charlie McVeigh, Salomon's likeable senior partner in London, that we felt aggrieved and expected something to be done about it.

Warren Buffett appointed an Englishman, Deryck Maughan, as

the new chief executive of Salomon. He had started his career with the UK Treasury in Whitehall and, now in his forties, had recently made a name for himself running Salomon's operations in Tokyo. McVeigh arranged for Maughan to come and see me and a colleague at 33 King William Street. When we entered the meeting room, he stood up and bowed deeply, Japanese style. It was his way of expressing *mea culpa*, and it was impressive.

I met Maughan again shortly afterwards in New York, with his new chairman, Robert Denman, a lawyer. That morning he had been inundated by resignations in a morale-shattered Salomon Brothers, and I admired the phlegmatic manner in which he reacted to what must have been an extremely painful period for him and his firm. Our little difficulty was by then no more than an irritating diversion to him, and we ended up settling it amicably. Maughan went on to rebuild Salomon into a more conventional investment banking firm, which was sold to Travelers Insurance in 1997.

Mozer spent four months in prison, but Meriwether, having been banned from the securities industry for three months, formed Long Term Capital Management, which had to be rescued from collapse with a massive injection of funds from Wall Street houses in September 1998.

*

After episodes like that, one searches for sanity, normality and humour. An abundant supplier of all these was Maureen, our cleaning lady at King William Street. One morning when Maureen was finishing her early morning routine of cleaning my desk, I asked her what she thought of the American sexual harassment case that was in the news that day, involving Anita Hill and Judge Clarence Thomas. Her reply was 'Well, all I can say, Mr Darlin', we could use a bit more of it around 'ere!'

When I told this story at our annual office Christmas dinner party that year, attended by directors and their spouses, it seemed to raise a decent laugh, but two of the wives present were upset that I had mentioned it. I was, they reproached me, making light of an issue that was a serious matter for women. Maureen, of course, had no such concerns, but, unhappily for us, she was transferred by the contract cleaning company for which she worked to 10 Downing Street when John Major was Prime Minister. She was later appointed an MBE (Member of the British Empire).

I will bow to no one in my concern for cases of genuine harassment, whether sexual or otherwise, and fully accept that it is an issue which should not be taken frivolously. Companies employ 'sensitivity consultants' to advise on how to prevent it. I still had a desk at Mercury in April 1998 when Merrill Lynch published an eight-page pamphlet entitled 'A Matter of Respect – Avoiding Sexual Harassment in the Workplace'. Everyone in Mercury, by then a Merrill Lynch subsidiary, received a copy. It counselled men not to pat, hug, kiss, grab or brush up against women and not to address them as 'Honey, Babe or Doll'. One politically incorrect joker submitted to the editor of the house magazine a photograph of three secretaries reading the pamphlet, with the suggested caption, 'Honey, Babe and Doll looking for a bit of Harassment'.

There is nothing new in giving instructions to employees on how they should conduct themselves in personal relationships. The Foreign Office in former times used to counsel its employees in overseas postings not to engage in relationships inappropriate to their rank and status, without further elaboration. Nowadays it is the employers who get the lawsuits for providing an environment conducive to amorous activities. Forget the mistletoe at next year's office party, and better cut out the alcohol too. Merrill Lynch is right to protect itself against possible litigation, but I wonder if its choice of emblem, a charging bull, sends out quite the right signals in this connection. A magnificent bronze of a bull adorns Mercury's entrance hall at 33 King William Street today – a gift to Mercury at the time of Merrill Lynch's acquisition of Mercury in 1998. It is indeed handsome, but to the ancients a bull was not so much the sign of a rising stock market as a symbol of fertility and virility.

There is a price to pay for all this – no more flirting, no more compliments, much less laughter. How far we have moved from an earlier era when Margaret Mitchell, author of *Gone with the Wind*, could write, 'a man who makes improper proposals is a positive necessity in a girl's life'. Anyone today who wants to flirt with someone in his place of work might be well advised first to ask the target of his attention whether he or she would be receptive to a little harassment.

Harassment aside, sex of the not unwelcome kind has always been inextricably intertwined with office life. According to a 1998 report of the Industrial Society, commissioned by a Miss Allcock, four out of ten office workers in a poll of a thousand have had sex with a colleague. The Industrial Society advised that organisations should seek not to ban sex from the office, but rather to apply good management practice, whatever that may mean. It was different when I started my career. Then we were told that affairs in the office were taboo. They happened of course, some consummated and others unconsummated (the latter were the ones most likely to cause problems). There were tell-tale signs of an office affair: the man would appear in a new suit or a more colourful shirt, and a banker's tie would be swapped for one that would not have passed Mr Sharp's test. However, they were usually conducted with discretion and away from the office.

*

There were several changes to Mercury's board during my period as chairman. Paul Bosonnet joined us as our fourth independent director in 1992. He had been chief financial officer at BOC under Ralph Giordano, and was now deputy chairman of British Telecom. The exposure to high salaries which Paul had at BOC gave him an understanding of the sometimes apparently rather generous rewards we had to pay to Mercury's best people in a highly competitive environment, and he proved to be an agile and constructive chairman of the board's remuneration committee. His intelligence and balanced views were also of great value to Mercury during our consideration of the Morgan Stanley merger possibility in 1994, in the discussions which Simon Cairns and David Scholey had with our board. I describe these in Chapter 25.

Our first independent director, Alfred Shepperd, was knighted in 1988. When I rang to congratulate him, Shep said with characteristic but unwarranted modesty, 'Bloody joke, isn't it?' Stephen Zimmerman became deputy chairman alongside David Price. Nigel Hurst-Brown, an excellent business manager who had been on the investment side at Lloyds Bank before he joined Mercury, Charles Jackson and Peter Urquhart, a somewhat eccentric but talented senior fund manager, were appointed to the board.

These additions strengthened the management team and made up for some departures. I was always sad when colleagues who had been with us for a long time decided to leave, and I usually asked them whether they were sure they were doing the right thing, even when they had been offered a larger remuneration package or positions with apparently higher status. Mercury was by then a well-oiled machine which would cope without them, but they would be moving into a new and not always hospitable outside world. I was mindful that one who left us had written to me some years later, 'How I miss my friends at MAM.'

It would at the least be a severe culture shock for them to leave our collegial, if competitive, environment. Jamie Ogilvy resigned in 1989 after three years in our group. He was offered a more responsible job that suited him ideally; his departure was natural and right for him. James Dawnay went in 1990 to a new sort of challenge with Martin Currie in Edinburgh. Richard Bernays, after twenty-two years with Mercury, was offered in 1992 the chief executive position at Hill Samuel Asset Management – an opportunity he found irresistible.

Leonard Licht was with us even longer – twenty-eight years. He often used to come to my desk with a cup of coffee in his hand around 8.30 a.m. to discuss for a few minutes, and often complain about, something that was on his mind. One day in the summer of 1992, there was no cup of coffee. Instead he gave me a letter and beat an embarrassed retreat. It was written in legal language and contained his resignation. I was sorry there was no chance for discussion, and that we had no choice but to respond in a similarly legalistic manner, placing Leonard on 'garden leave' for the contractual period, thus prohibiting him from starting work with his new employer immediately. It was a case of 'we don't want to lose you, but we think you ought to go'.

Leonard had told me often enough that he did not much enjoy committee meetings, a sentiment with which one could easily sympathise, and that he wanted to concentrate on managing money, more or less in his own time. He always had Mercury's interests at heart, and I listened attentively to his perceptive observations on what we were doing right or wrong. But in his own words, while he loved the place, he was not really a company man and he needed a new challenge. It was a pity that we could not have talked about his decision to leave in a civil and constructive way.

He left us to join Jupiter Tyndall, a company that caused us aggravation both before Leonard's departure and at the time of it. It was a small but growing fund management company managed by John Duffield, which incorporated the old Tyndall unit trust group, our client in the 1960s. James d'Albiac, a former Rowe and Pitman partner, an intelligent fund manager and one-time author of Rowe and Pitman's monthly newsletter, had already left us after a few years to join Jupiter Tyndall. Leonard, we subsequently learnt, had received a golden hello of £1 million to join them, as well as a generous supply of share options. He was to resign from Jupiter Tyndall three years later.

On Leonard's initiative, we had bought a 24 per cent stake in Jupiter Tyndall some six months before his departure, but we had overlooked the fact that it owned a small and largely inactive bank in the Isle of Man. Our purchase, involving, in theory at least, a change in control of that bank, required Bank of England permission, which we had failed to obtain. David Price and John Trueman, a top banker in Warburgs, by no means the people to blame for this oversight, had some awkward discussions with the Bank, who eventually decided to let us off with a warning. It was a lucky escape and David Scholey, who was at the time a member of the Court (board) of the Bank of England, pointed out in writing that we might have been discussing my own position 'with considerable difficulty' if the Bank had taken a more stringent attitude.

When Leonard handed in his resignation, his new masters wanted to portray Leonard's move publicly as an amicable transfer on his part from Mercury to a company in which Mercury had a significant investment. They asked for our co-operation in providing a weekend story along these lines to John Jay, an outstanding financial journalist who was then editor of the *Sunday Telegraph* business section. We declined, because it did not seem to us that the manner of Leonard's departure could be described as amicable.

Below board level, we lost the now celebrated Nicola Horlick, incidentally another Trollope reader. Nicola had been a competent organiser for Leonard Licht and his specialist team in MSM, who got on easily with clients and presented well for new business. She left us for Morgan Grenfell, together with two promising members of the team, Charles Curtis and James Goulding, which opened up something of a gap for a while. In the unduly despondent words of Norman Bachop (to be sung to the tune of 'Men of Harlech'):

> Men of Horlick
> Curtis, Goulding
> MSM is close to folding
> Fires gone out and let the cold in
> Bitter times ahead.

Nicola Horlick's subsequent antics at Morgan Grenfell, flying off to Frankfurt with the press and television cameras in tow, and storming into her boss's office there to demand her job back, were entertaining, but they were not in keeping with Mercury's style or for that matter with Morgan Grenfell's. They contrasted sharply with the dignified politeness and low profile which Carol Galley showed to the press when she became a celebrity in the latter part of the 1990s.

If Nicola Horlick managed to attract the attention of the media, her sense of theatre took second place to that of her Morgan Grenfell colleague, Peter Young, who had worked for Mercury for a short period as a fund manager in European shares, before he left to join Morgan Grenfell. Young made some unauthorised investments for Morgan Grenfell's unit trusts between 1994 and 1996, in a notorious case which cost the company and its parent, Deutsche Bank, over £400 million to make good the losses suffered by its clients. He was charged with conspiracy to defraud, and when he appeared in a magistrates' court in November 1998 to answer the charges, he was dressed as a woman with shoulder-length dark hair. He wore a brown jumper with a pattern of violet and blue pansies over a white dress, and beige shoes with two-inch heels. His coral pink handbag matched his lipstick. He let it be known that he wanted in future to be known as Elizabeth. He looked quite attractive in some of the newspaper pictures.

*

As the summer of 1992 arrived and my sixtieth birthday approached, I had the task of identifying and recommending my successor as chairman. Just in case I had any idea of trying to stay on, it was useful to get a reminder from the *Financial Times* that my time was up. 'Mercury is maintaining a stiff upper lip', it wrote in April that year about the chairmanship. 'Peter Stormonth Darling, who has dominated the group for more than a decade, is getting to an age when he should be thinking of retirement.' There was a fifteen-year age gap between me and the two deputy chairmen, and it seemed a good idea for me to be followed by someone whose age came somewhere in between.

The obvious candidate was Hugh Stevenson. Hugh had served on our board since flotation, and he was a faithful attender at the informal monthly management meetings. He knew our people well, and he understood the business. Moreover, his background as a lawyer and a corporate financier would be invaluable to Mercury. The question was whether he was available and whether he would want the job. Hugh was then in a key position in Warburgs, in charge of personnel and administration. I spoke to David Scholey, who wondered aloud if Hugh could be spared, but he realised pragmatically that Mercury was now producing close to half of Warburgs' profits, even though Warburgs had just a 75 per cent holding. And, happily, it transpired that Hugh wanted to take the job.

I like to think that the transition from my chairmanship to Hugh's was almost seamless. Hugh has excellent judgement and a good sense of humour, as well as a superb grasp of organisational detail, and I knew he would make a good chairman. There were farewell dinners, speeches, presents and so on, but by September 1992 Hugh was firmly in charge. At the annual directors' Christmas dinner that year, I thanked everyone for the support they had given me, and for their friendship. I predicted that for Mercury the best was yet to come. It was one prediction of mine which proved to be correct.

CHAPTER 22

Mercury Antiques

A few years ago, I was doing some Christmas shopping and wished the lady in the antique shop a happy Christmas. 'Yes', she answered. 'So lovely when it's over.' Her comment reflected exactly my sentiment when my term as chairman came to an end in September 1992. However good your management colleagues, and mine were very good, you can never escape the awareness that at the end of the day you are accountable to the shareholders for their investment and to the employees for their jobs. Now, at last, I could wake up on Monday mornings without wondering what terrible shocks were in store for me that week. I had developed my own version of Murphy's Law – if anything can go wrong, it will, and it will go wrong on Fridays or Mondays. Colleagues either gave me the bad news on a Friday, so that I could get over it at the weekend, or they kept it until Monday in order not to ruin my weekend. Now, at last, I could forget about that and start behaving irresponsibly again.

I was also glad to say goodbye to some of the routine chores that had gone with the job. As chairman of the largest investment management company in the UK, I was constantly asked to give opinions on matters affecting the investment community and the role of fund managers. I became something of an expert on such rivetingly exciting topics as short-termism – a charge then often levelled at the City by politicians, apparently oblivious that they, with the possible exception of the computer geniuses who failed to anticipate the year 2000, are the ultimate practitioners of it. There is, of course, an endless argument as to what is short term and what is long term. Harold Wilson could note that a week was a long time in politics, whereas Zhou Enlai, when asked to comment on the effects of the French Revolution, could reply that it was still too early to say.

Another topic was corporate governance, which no one had heard of until it was invented by Jonathan Charkham, a consultant to the Bank of England, in the mid-1980s. I spoke often to journalists on these subjects, took part in debates, gave evidence to a House of Lords Select Committee, and wrote papers for clients. Since then, corporate governance has become an industry in itself, with numerous committees, workshops, reports and recommendations. While the guidelines for corporate governance now in place for public companies are mainly desirable, there is a danger of their causing more bureaucracy and less enterprise.

Inevitably, also, I was drawn into activities relating to the City in its wider context. I was asked by Eddie George, then deputy governor of the Bank of England, to join a committee consisting mainly of incredibly intelligent lawyers and chaired by one of them, Bob Alexander (Lord Alexander of Weedon), to review legal risk in financial transactions. Under the able chairmanship of Charles Nunneley, then of Flemings and today chairman of the National Trust and of Nationwide Building Society, I became deputy chairman of the Institutional Fund Managers Association (IFMA), a trade association set up to speak for the fund management community. Investment management was an increasingly visible business sector in the City, and one that was making a growing contribution to the UK's invisible earnings, but until the formation of IFMA in 1985, it had no voice of its own in City deliberations.

Charles Nunneley was also chairman of the Investment Management Regulatory Organisation (IMRO), the self-regulatory body set up to police the activities of fund management companies. Charles suggested in July 1992 that I might succeed him as chairman of IMRO. I pondered whether I should take this on as a matter of duty, and was momentarily intrigued at the thought of chairing the very organisation which I had fought strenuously when it had fined us for a technical breach not so long before. But I knew in my heart that I would not enjoy being a watchdog and would consequently not do the job well.

It sometimes fell to me to give the thank-you speech at annual general meetings (AGMs) of companies in which Mercury had an investment. In those days, a representative of one of the institutional shareholders was asked beforehand by the company's broker to thank the chairman of the company in question for conducting the meeting. It was usual to include a few words of congratulation on some aspect of the company's results, which could present a problem for the speaker in those years when a company had done badly. Then one had to fall back on platitudinous phrases such as 'a good achievement in extremely difficult conditions for the industry', or 'a promising future in his hands'.

At an AGM of Tesco, I defended the level of remuneration of its chief executive, Ian McLaurin – today, as Lord McLaurin of Knebworth, *de facto* chairman of English cricket. Tesco had had a record year, which was reflected in a large increase in the share price, and it seemed to me churlish to attack his bonus, which was tied to levels of performance. Shareholders who had themselves done so well from his efforts should, I thought, be grateful for his efforts. Did any of them really think they could do the job even a fraction as well?

On another occasion, it was my task to thank Anthony Tennant on his retirement as chairman of Guinness. Guinness had had an excellent record under his leadership, and I told the shareholders that, while I personally disliked the taste of Guinness, and could not therefore give an opinion as to whether Guinness was Good for You, I knew that Anthony Tennant had been good for Guinness. I went on to thank him on behalf of the shareholders for his achievements. When the meeting was over, a gentleman wearing an old school tie which was all too familiar to me came up and questioned me as to why I was presumptuous enough to think I spoke on behalf of all the shareholders. I asked him whether he was ungrateful for the substantial rise in the price of his Guinness shares, and got only a grudging grunt in reply. The easiest way of dealing with such people, I had learnt, is to grovel, so I told him I was very sorry for my presumption, and that did seem to make him happier. On similar occasions thereafter, I was always careful to say, 'I believe I speak on behalf of all shareholders . . . .'

Mercury's own AGMs in those days were comparatively tame affairs, but I have observed from attendances at many others over the years that there are almost always a few malcontents who show up. I also noticed that they are seldom the ones to deny themselves the now almost ritual offering of tea and cakes. I used to reflect on a *New Yorker* cartoon depicting a lady in a hat asking a question at a crowded AGM in the US. One of the directors at the top table whispers to another, 'This is the part of capitalism I hate.'

Writing the annual report took up more time than it merited. Many companies' annual reports are written either by outside firms which employ professional authors, or by someone on the secretarial or financial side of the company with a flair for writing. That was not the way at Warburgs, where the art of writing flowingly correct prose that said absolutely nothing about the outlook and not much about the year under review had been perfected over the years.

We aimed to be more informative in Mercury's reports, and I did not want to give up authorship to an outsider. My co-editors Nick Stewart and Charles Farquharson, each at different times an excellent company secretary of Mercury, and I would work our way through up to twenty drafts each year, to the accompaniment of much hilarity during our drafting sessions, only to produce some fairly anodyne language we could all agree on. The effort was out of all proportion to the reward, since probably no more than a handful of shareholders looked at anything other than the results, the remuneration of the directors and the graphics. At least we continued to follow Siegmund's counsel by omitting any photographs and avoiding self-congratulation. But in retrospect we might have done better to employ a professional scribe and spend our time on other matters.

*

When testing for AIDS was introduced, our insurers insisted that every employee take a test. When some people rebelled at this intrusion into their privacy, I was told that, as chairman, I had to set an example and be the first to go for a test. I duly visited a very civil doctor in Harley Street, who telephoned me two days later with the result. 'You're negative', he said to my utter horror, until he explained that in medical jargon negative is good news while positive, in any case with AIDS testing, is very bad news indeed.

A chairman is likely to take an interest in his company's charitable donations and sponsorships. We tended to favour charities, of which there were many, in which members of the firm were involved in some way. In 1994, jointly with Warburgs, we made up the balance needed to donate a new lifeboat to the town of Criccieth on the Welsh coast, near the birthplace of David Lloyd-George, to add to the gargantuan money-raising efforts of Anne Haynes, a senior secretary in Warburgs. Perhaps symbolically reflecting the shifting balance by then between the relative perception of Warburgs and Mercury, the lifeboat was named Mercurius. In a short introductory speech at the launching ceremony, I struggled through a sentence of Welsh, an achievement which instantly paled into insignificance when Shirley Valentine, wife of Michael Valentine, a Warburgs director, gave an entire speech in that language.

Our sponsorships sometimes came close to charity, while at other times they were more in the nature of public relations. Each time they were accompanied by some form of entertainment. We sponsored a concert at the Festival Hall for the Imperial Cancer Research Fund. Once more in partnership with Warburgs, we provided a library for Templeton College at Oxford, and David Scholey, Hugh Stevenson and I went there for the opening ceremony, which consisted of David's pulling a cord to reveal a small plaque and the three of us posing for photographs. There were not many books in the new library; libraries, nowadays it seems, can just as easily consist of computers and software. Even the description 'library' is being superseded by 'resource-based learning centre' or, to those in the know, just RBLC.

I had to be quite firm in declining invitations to join various money-raising committees because the time taken to do such tasks responsibly, which can be considerable, belonged to Mercury. I nevertheless found myself a member or chairman of appeals for the British Olympic and Commonwealth Games teams, for Oxford University, the National Trust of Scotland and the Globe Theatre – the creation of the determinedly persistent Sam Wanamaker, who sadly died shortly before his project was completed. Money raising for charities is today another industry of its own, with executives on private sector salaries with cars and expense accounts. It has become a marketing exercise with the same need for professional and informative presentation as marketing in business. Companies giving to charities will usually ask for the charity's accounts and will look at the ratio of expenses to the amount actually reaching the intended beneficiaries, so there is a check on those which are extravagantly managed.

While sponsorship of events is a legitimate business expenditure as a form of advertisement, I used to wonder whether pure charity was an appropriate function for companies. What can happen is that shareholders' money is spent on the favourite charities of the chairman or other members of the charities committee and their friends in the company. If corporate giving were to be stopped, however, it would have to be replaced by a greater contribution from private individuals, and that is likely to occur only if we in the UK adopt some of the more generous tax incentives available in the US and Canada.

Mercury supported a Youth Enterprise Centre in Brixton, an unfavoured part of London not far from our office in King William

Street, aimed at helping young entrepreneurs who had no money and could benefit from an almost free workplace with communal office support facilities. Paul Marshall devoted a lot of his free time to the centre. It was officially opened by the Prince of Wales on an extremely cold February morning in 1989. The Prince took advantage of the occasion to get some free investment advice from Leonard Licht. He had done his homework thoroughly on the young entrepreneurs and entered into vigorous discussions with some of them, especially two young vegan bakers and Fliss Bee, who made wedding cakes. Others were involved in making curtains and stained-glass windows, repairing computers and providing physiotherapy for skiers under the name Ski Phyzz.

Mercury continued the Warburgs tradition of supporting the arts, with membership of Glyndebourne and Covent Garden, and later the Tate Gallery and the Royal Academy. We sponsored Pavilion Opera and entertained at the Annual Exhibition of the Society of Watercolourists, and various exhibitions at the Tate. These, of course, were useful occasions to invite those of our clients who liked opera or pictures, but we found that many of them, as well as many Mercury people, preferred sporting events. So we broke the old Warburgs rule that encouraged 'culture' but not sport, and took parties of clients to golf, cricket and football. There was even some Mercury entertainment at Goodwood races, not perhaps quite the right image for a conservative investment management house which advocated a long-term approach.

As it grew larger, Mercury had teams to take part in just about every sporting activity from cricket to croquet, go-karting, dragon-boat racing (22 miles from Richmond to Greenwich), skiing (our team was called Mad About Moguls to incorporate the MAM initials), abseiling and broomball, a soft version of ice hockey played on a rink in the City. Some of the teams took part in charity events, others did it for fun, and yet others had as their objective that ghastly expression 'bonding'.

Golf was a passion of some of our senior executives, and we entertained clients who enjoyed the game at the Open Championship every other year when it was held in Scotland. At Muirfield in 1992, we gave lunch to our guests at the ideally situated Greywalls Hotel. The hotel's lawn abuts the tenth tee, giving a close and uninterrupted view of the golfers' tee shots. Most of the players, accomplished at

concentrating intensely on their shots despite the frequently irritating behaviour of the crowds following them, managed to ignore our
party. However, some of our guests, seated on benches only a few
yards from the golfers as they drove their balls arrow-like into the far
distance, were occasionally less than respectfully quiet, which
provoked Rocco Mediate, a leading American professional, to
approach one of our female guests with an invitation. 'Say, lady,' he
said, 'why don't you come and hit the golf ball, and I'll take the
cocktail?'

*

It would be marvellous to shed the burdens of responsibility and give
up the time-consuming, and at times boring, duties of chairman.
However, I did not want to lose my exposure to the daily theatre at
Mercury, and anyway I did not have the self-confidence to retire.
Moreover, I discovered that I was now addicted, for ever perhaps, to
Warburgs and Mercury attitudes and habits. When he gave up the
editorship of *The Times* in 1981 after fourteen years, William Rees
Mogg, now Lord Rees Mogg, wrote of 'a resumption of liberty'
accompanied by the difficulty of being 'left with *Times* like convic-
tions and habits of mind. I have imbibed the *Times* rules of life.'
Warburgs' and, by inheritance, Mercury's rules of life were equally
hard to leave behind. Moreover, I was sure they were good rules.
One of them was never to retire completely.

Hugh Stevenson allowed me to remain on the board of Mercury as
a non-executive, although hardly independent, director, and generously provided me with an office and all the facilities that go with it.
The role of a non-executive director is to advise, encourage, question
and warn, but as the former chairman, it was incumbent on me to
avoid giving advice unless it was sought. Even then, I had to guard
against becoming a focal point for dissenting voices, and I made it
clear right away that if anyone had some complaint or disagreement
with the regime, he or she should talk to Hugh and not to me. A non-
executive director is far from powerless, however, under today's
governance practices. He is likely to be a member, as all non-
executive directors in Mercury were, of the company's remuneration
committee, which has the ultimate power to decide the salaries and
bonuses of the executive directors, including the chairman!

In 1995, after the sale of Warburgs, John Stancliffe became the
next non-executive director of Mercury and moved his office to 33

King William Street. John had joined Warburgs partly at my urging in 1979, after he had had a disagreement with his partners at Credit Suisse White Weld (later CSFB). He made it clear then that he wanted to be involved in the investment management side of Warburgs' business as well as the investment banking side, and he was always a great believer in Mercury. Oscar Lewisohn had transferred from Warburgs to 33 King William Street the previous year, to help us with our Swiss bank, where his banking experience was of great value to Mercury, and to supervise the affairs of a number of Scandinavian private clients whom he had introduced to us.

Mercury was lucky to have the services of these two immensely able Warburgs seniors. For a short period, the three of us, all appreciably older than anyone else in Mercury, shared an office which I referred to as the geriatric ward, or Mercury Antiques after an antique shop of that name in Notting Hill Gate.

One of John's roles at Mercury was to oversee our activities in private equity investment, known previously as venture capital and later as development capital, where his shrewd understanding of business was a great asset. Private equity is a potentially attractive investment sector, in which many of our clients wanted to partici-pate. This business is very ably run by Ian Armitage, who joined us from 3i Group in 1990. Ian, incidentally a fine golfer with a swing reminiscent of Severiano Ballesteros, rebuilt our private equity team following a disastrous leveraged buy-out investment in 1990, for which I was in large part responsible.

Isosceles was the name given to a company formed to buy Gateway, a middle-market supermarket chain, and Mercury was a candidate to buy it. Unfortunately, there was a competing purchaser in Wasserstein Perella, a US leveraged buy-out firm with which we ended up making the investment jointly, but at too high a price. Leveraged buy-outs, which involve the purchase of a company financed substantially by borrowings, were all the rage at the time in the United States, and in many cases resulted in phenomenal capital profits for the highly geared equity-holders.

Disregarding warnings about leveraged buy-outs from Henry Grunfeld, Leonard Licht and I both wanted to get in on the act, and Isosceles was our first opportunity to do so on a substantial scale in the UK. Despite first-class co-ordination of the transaction by Frances Jacob in Mercury's private equity team, I am afraid we allowed our enthusiasm to overtake our judgement, to our eventual cost. At the price of £2 billion that we ended up paying, we had to take on too much debt, and it soon became apparent that Gateway's cash flow was not enough to pay the interest. It was a salutary and painful lesson.

Ian Armitage, who took no part in the Isosceles investment, and the team he put together subsequently, including Frances Jacob, more than recouped the losses on Isosceles in a number of successful private equity deals in the subsequent years, most notably NTL (formerly National Telecommunications), which operates antennae and transmitters for television in the UK. Other successful private investments have included, in earlier times, ASW and Britt Allcroft (which owns the rights to Thomas the Tank Engine), and more recently, Ballygowan (mineral water), Belfast Airport, Leyland DAF Vans, Luminar (theme bars and discotheques) and Sunsail, the yacht chartering company. Roger Llewellyn, who ran our private equity team before Ian Armitage, has for a number of years been chairman of Thomas the Tank Engine.

*

Lovely indeed when it's over, but as Yogi Berra, legendary catcher for the New York Yankees, is alleged to have once said, 'It ain't over 'til it's over.' I had exchanged a part on the stage for a seat in the front row of the stalls, but the soap opera went on. Mercury was getting stronger all the time, and was finding it harder to keep out of the news. A dispute between Mercury and Warburgs over a failed takeover in the oil industry was the next episode to sour the friendship between Mercury and its parent.

Arrogance was never in short supply in Warburgs; nor can I say that it was entirely absent in some quarters in Mercury. While one might hope that a self-confident person would overcome any tendency to arrogance, there is a narrow line to be drawn between this and self-assurance, and no merchant banker would be successful without some degree of the latter. Nor did I ever feel that the level of arrogance in Warburgs matched that of some of the Wall Street houses. There was the story of a chairman of one American firm seeking the views of his younger managers as to how to reduce arrogance in the firm and getting the answer, 'Well, we can always go out and hire some mediocre people.' It was nevertheless, I believe, a factor in the decline of Warburgs in 1994 and 1995.

It was therefore refreshing to find a senior Warburgs director, Piers von Simson, not a total stranger to arrogant behaviour himself, taking the blame for the failure of a bid by Warburgs' client, Enterprise Oil, for Lasmo Oil in the summer of 1994. It took guts for Piers to say publicly, 'It was my responsibility, my shout and I screwed up.'

Enterprise Oil's offer consisted of convertible securities and warrants without any cash, because Enterprise could not afford to offer cash for all of Lasmo's shares. There was evidence that a number of institutional shareholders would decline the offer, but might accept cash if it were offered to them. Enterprise had enough money to buy 10 per cent of Lasmo for cash, and Warburgs approached some, but not all, of those institutions, buying the 10 per cent from just five of them.

Mercury, holder of a sizeable position in Lasmo, was not one of those whose shares were bought by Warburgs on behalf of Enterprise, and it was very angry at being left out. Despite a self-imposed restriction on the amount of Stock Exchange business that Mercury regularly gave to Warburg Securities, it was one of Warburgs' major clients and was offended not to be treated as such. It later voted against the paper offer, which collapsed with Enterprise getting acceptances for only 23 per cent on top of the 10 per cent it had bought for cash.

Equally embarrassing to Warburgs, because it became public knowledge, was Mercury's subsequent decision to cut off Stock Exchange dealings with Warburg Securities for a month. This was, of course, the ultimate demonstration by Mercury of its independence from Warburgs – no longer necessary by then, but exceedingly badly received at Warburgs. Relationships between Mercury and Warburgs reached a new low. A few months later, they were to deteriorate even further over the high-profile failure of merger discussions between Morgan Stanley and Warburgs, for which Mercury was publicly but unjustifiably blamed.

CHAPTER 23

Havens for a Retired Chairman

Once again, this is a chapter which carries a health warning. It concerns activities in 'pooled' investment funds, which include investment trusts, unit trusts and offshore funds, some of the characters who managed them, and some related involvements of my own. I have tried to avoid getting into technicalities, but the subject matter is fairly specialised and may be tedious for readers who are not interested in the details of the investment business. I recommend they move on to the next chapter.

Investment trusts, also known as closed-end investment companies, are different from unit trusts in that they have a fixed number of shares which can be purchased only from an existing shareholder. Unit trusts, by contrast, are similar to mutual funds in the US, in that they are open-ended, which means that their units (shares) can be redeemed at their underlying net asset value from the trust itself. A unit trust accordingly has a variable number of units outstanding at any time, while an investment trust has a fixed number of shares. Each type of structure has its advantages and disadvantages.

The world of investment trusts is populated by people with interesting and informed views on politics, economics and investment, as well as just about everything else, and it is an ideal haven for a retired chairman with a passionate interest in the art of investment. I now wanted to increase my involvement in investment trusts to complement some other investment-related appointments that I had taken on in anticipation of retirement from full-time work, and in search of variety and security. I was already a director of several of Mercury's offshore and American funds, and I had been on the board since its formation in 1989 of a Hungarian investment trust in which George Soros was a sponsor and the largest investor, and of which I was later to become chairman.

After a slightly alarming interview over lunch just before Christmas 1991, with the full board of Scottish Equitable, I was invited to join the board of that company in Edinburgh. Shortly afterwards, I was firmly reminded of my lack of professional qualifications at the company's annual dinner, when one of its top salesmen asked me what else I did for a living. I told him that I was with an investment management organisation in London called Mercury. 'Thank goodness for that', he said. 'I thought for a moment you might be something important such as an actuary or an accountant like the rest of our board.'

Scottish Equitable is one of the best managed of the Scottish life insurers and has now become a wholly owned subsidiary of Aegon, which by almost any statistical measure has been the leading major European financial company in recent years. I have learnt a great deal at Scottish Equitable from the chairmanship of Hamish Inglis, from two outstanding chief executives, David Berridge, who died young, and David Henderson, and from Kees Storm, the brilliant head of Aegon, who discharges his company's ownership of Scottish Equitable with a light touch while never for a moment leaving anyone in doubt as to who is ultimately in charge.

Since 1990 I had been the member from the UK on the investments committee of the United Nations pension fund, which is globally invested and now over $25 billion in size. I have been lucky to have served under three wise chairmen, each with his own distinct style: Governor B.K. Nehru, a former Indian ambassador in Washington, Jean Guyot, chairman of Lazard Frères in Paris and, currently, Chief Emanuel Omaboe from Ghana. Our work has been made more pleasant by the support we have had from the UN's charismatic Secretary-General, Kofi Annan, and the constructive involvement of Under Secretary Joe Connor, a former senior partner of the accounting firm Price Waterhouse, who in his role as *de facto* chief financial officer of the UN has seen that institution through recurring financial crises over the last few years.

We are also well served by Henry Ouma, who directs the UN's internal investment staff, and by seasoned advisers such as Lanny Thomas and David Smart of Fiduciary Trust and Catherine Guinefort of Paribas. The contributions of a congenial and cosmopolitan group of fellow members of the committee always contain some informational gems, even if our discussions do sometimes go on rather a long time for those of us of an impatient disposition. (In the last few years, Consuelo Brooke has managed on behalf of Mercury a high-performing portfolio in European shares for the UN pension fund, which by 1999 had reached more than $200 million in value.)

On its inception in 1990, I was appointed to the international board of the NASDAQ Stock Exchange, where we had two chairmen, David Brooke and Brian Williamson, both of them diplomats with disarming charm. The British contingent has at different times included, in addition to David, Brian and myself, John Manser, chairman of Flemings, and Michael Marks, previously head of Smith New Court, one of London's three main jobbing (market-making) firms, which, like Mercury three years later, was acquired by Merrill Lynch.

From each of these connections, I learnt new and sometimes better ways of running boards and businesses, many of which I wished I had discovered earlier. There was a rule in Warburgs, which we continued in Mercury, that executives of the firm should not normally join outside boards. It was aimed at avoiding conflicts, but perhaps we would all have been less set in our ways and more open to new ideas if we had had some exposure to the methods and styles of other companies.

Mercury's flagship investment trust was Keystone Investment Company (later Mercury Keystone), whose chairman since 1979 has been John Stancliffe. When he came to Warburgs that year, we arranged for him to join the Keystone board, and soon afterwards he became chairman when his predecessor died unexpectedly. John takes a detailed interest in anything in which he is involved, and the subsequent success of Keystone, which puts it right at the top of the UK investment trust long-term performance tables, was in large part because of the way in which he assumed charge. In Stephen Zimmerman, Paul Harwood and, for the last five years, Barry Woolf, he has been well served by three star fund managers. Keystone is now a trust of more than £200 million, and its shares have multiplied about fourteen times under John's stewardship, which continued in 2000.

I was delighted when John asked me to become a director of Keystone on my retirement as chairman of Mercury. The otherwise high-quality board consists of Ian Steers, a successful investor with a canny feel for timing and value, Peter Readman, an international economics adviser with a sense of realism whose other diverse activities include a major commitment to the Chamber Orchestra of Europe, and David Adams, formerly chief executive of the trustees of the British Rail Pension Fund. We may disagree with each other from time to time, but our discussions are always informative and provocative.

*

Mercury had historically been less imaginative than many of its competitors in the creation of new investment trusts, but with the recruitment of Lough Callahan and Julian Baring in 1991 and 1992 respectively, that was about to change. Lough Callahan is an enterprising American lawyer who transferred from Warburgs to Mercury, where he was given a mandate to develop our investment trust business. He had come to England some ten years earlier, and with his artistic wife Mary assembled a fine collection of modern British paintings. Julian Baring, having spent eight years in the mining business in South Africa, became a guru of mining research in the City in the 1970s, and he formed his own small unit trust company which Mercury purchased in early 1992. Unconventional and contrarian, Julian is a larger than life character with a touch of the showman, who fitted surprisingly easily into Mercury's lifestyle in between visits to his vineyard in France.

Lough's first initiative was to launch the Mercury World Mining Trust to exploit Julian's reputation and expertise, with Peter Wilmot-Sitwell as its chairman. It was enthusiastically received by the market and raised £500 million. His next brainwave, in 1993, was a trust to specialise in shares of privatised companies in Europe. Privatisation in the UK had provided rewarding investment opportunities as commercial managements restructured inefficient businesses and made profits undreamt of when the companies were owned by the state. There were similar expectations for companies being privatised in continental Europe. Demand for the shares of Mercury European Privatisation Trust (later Mercury European Investment Trust) was enormous, and the trust was closed at £550 million.

I took on the chairmanship of MEPT and we put together a diversely experienced board with Ed Wallis, the capable and enterprising chairman of PowerGen, who incidentally is a director of Lucas Varity, the old Massey Ferguson; Richard MacLean, then chief executive and publisher of the *International Herald Tribune*, living in Paris; Beatrice Philippe, a distinguished French fund manager with offices in Paris and New York, who had been a trainee in Warburgs' investment department in 1970 and 1971, and whose father, Pierre Philippe, was a director of Selected Risk; Dr Attilio Lentati, managing director of Riunione Adriatica di Sicurta in Milan; Mark Evans, a knowledgeable corporate financier from Credit Lyonnais Laing, who has chaired the trust's audit committee; and David Price. David was by then in the throes of becoming a large-scale farmer in Lincolnshire, where he and his wife Shervie had to rebuild with infinite patience, to its original sixteenth-century architecture, their house, Harrington Hall, after it burnt to the ground in 1991. The trust has been managed by a talented duo in Paul Harwood and Vicky Hastings, and has done well for its shareholders in the five years since launch.

In 1987, Common Market Trust, our offshore fund for investing in Europe, was fifteen years old and we had taken advantage of the anniversary to entertain its directors at a celebratory weekend at Cliveden, which had just opened as a hotel. Some of the continental directors had been amused to stay in the house where Christine Keeler had cavorted with John Profumo and Ivanov, the Russian spy. It had not gone down so well, however, in the upper echelons of Warburgs, and I had been criticised for extravagance. Three years earlier, I had run into similar trouble when I had failed to restrain Andrew Dalton from arranging a board meeting of Mercury Selected Trust (previously Selected Risk) at Palazzo Dorio on the Grand Canal in Venice. When I reached an arguably more mature level of judgement, I came to agree in retrospect with Henry Grunfeld and David Scholey that the expense was hardly justified on either occasion.

Some years later, we amalgamated Common Market Trust with Transatlantic Market Trust under the umbrella of Mercury International Investment Trust (MIIT), which we formed as a Jersey-based investment trust, adding two additional 'spokes' to invest in Japan and the Pacific Basin. It was not a typical investment trust because it was mainly a vehicle for Mercury's smaller pension fund clients to invest in overseas markets, and to start with it had an internal Mercury board of which I was chairman for some years. Its other members at different times were Ross Bunce, Carol Galley, Peter Gibbs and Nigel Hurst-Brown.

The shares of MIIT were quoted on the London Stock Exchange, and a small percentage of them were held by outside shareholders who were not our clients. It was also the largest investment trust on the Stock Exchange, with total assets exceeding £4 billion in value at its peak. It was therefore decided in 1994 that we should appoint some independent directors. The first was John Morrell, a senior member of the City's investment community with original and constructive views on investment methodology. He was followed by Ian Phillips, previously treasurer of the BBC, David Brooke and Donald Macpherson, who had a place in Mercury's history because, as a stockbroker, he had arranged the sale of Mercury's shareholding in Debenhams to Burton's rival, House of Fraser, during the contested takeover in 1985.

It was a happy board which seemed reluctant to depart when, in 1998, a decision was taken to wind up the company following changes in UK taxation introduced by Gordon Brown, which made it unattractive as a vehicle for British pension funds to hold their foreign shares. As my own farewell present, I gave each of the directors a memorandum pad and a packet of smarties – I had wanted to give them liquorice allsorts, but I learnt from his wife that Donald does not like liquorice. Its last meeting was a celebration, or wake, given at Henley one evening in June by John Morrell on his handsome electric motor launch, *Humble*, originally built in 1900. It was attended by the directors and their wives and Mercury's two very able investment trust company secretaries, Amanda Marsh and Tracey Bennett.

As chairman of Mercury, I had believed in the golden rule never to interfere with the company's investment strategy. There were people in different areas of the business appointed to determine strategy, and nothing could be more calculated to undermine their confidence than for the chairman to second-guess their opinions. There were, however, times when I had quite strong views. We consistently underweighted the American stock market in a display of something close to sado-masochism. I thought this was wrong simply because the US has so many of the world's best companies, and I believe that one should select companies to invest in, not countries, markets, currencies or industry sectors. I also felt that many of our fund managers engaged in too much restless and costly switching from one share to another in the pursuit of short-term performance. At the investment trust discussions, I was free to speak out on such matters, and I did so sufficiently often to convince myself, if not the fund managers, of my great investment wisdom!

*

The growth of Mercury's investment trusts, successfully engineered by Lough Callahan, coincided with a comparable increase in our unit trust business under the direction of Richard Royds, who joined us from another unit trust company in 1992. Richard is another extrovert with a flair for salesmanship, and he took Mercury from eleventh in the UK unit trust league tables when he arrived to fourth by 1999 – a remarkable achievement in the highly competitive retail market.

In 1993, Richard enthusiastically announced that he had signed up Brian Lara, the matinée-idol Trinidadian cricketer, who within two months during the previous summer had broken the records for the highest score in a test match and the highest innings in first-class cricket. Photographs appeared in the newspapers of Lara at the Honourable Artillery Company's cricket ground in the City, wearing a pin-striped suit and a bowler hat together with cricket pads and gloves, and carrying a bat.

Under the sponsorship contract, Lara was expected thereafter to wear a Mercury cap whenever the cameras were in sight, except, thankfully for both the West Indies team and Mercury, on the field of play. Too much publicity was given to this controversial arrangement, almost all of it inaccurate. It was reported that Mercury was paying Lara £500,000, whereas in fact he received £100,000 spread over two and a half years. But as I had discovered at the time of their disclosures of my own salary in 1987, the press is not always concerned with accuracy, and once a big number has been printed, there is no going back on their part.

Richard was quoted in the press as saying that Mercury's corporate theme was sporting excellence, which came as a surprise to its ex-chairman, who might have chosen to think in terms of investment excellence. Richard had in mind, I suppose, an advertising campaign that Mercury had run with pictures of a gymnast, a skier, a show jumper and a rugby football player, with slogans such as 'When a leading edge is what it takes'.

It was noticeable that Brian Lara's performance on the cricket field deteriorated from the moment of our sponsorship, and it did not recover to the level of his earlier accomplishments until five years later. There were stories around that success had gone to his head, and he was once spotted using his mobile telephone in a county match while fielding in the slips. However, Richard has assured me that the association with Lara helped considerably in getting

Mercury's name across to retail investors who might otherwise never have heard of us.

*

The old Selected Risk, started by Eric Korner as a Luxembourg incorporated fund in June 1962, with just $3 million in assets and a board including Siegmund Warburg and Dick Dilworth, who were shortly thereafter joined by Giovanni Agnelli and Sir Robert Adeane, languished for a number of years following Eric Korner's death. It had been our first adventure in the byzantine world of offshore funds. An offshore fund is a fund domiciled in a tax haven country, such as Luxembourg, Jersey, Bermuda or the Bahamas, but advised by a fund management company in London, New York or elsewhere, which establishes a subsidiary company in the tax haven to provide the technical management. The fund itself suffers no taxes and typically pays no dividends. Its shareholders, usually an amorphous group who are residents of countries other than that of the tax haven or the adviser, have no taxes to pay until they sell their shares. It is a massive market and a profitable one for investment management firms.

Selected Risk underwent a transformation in the 1980s at the hands of Andrew Dalton. When he is not giving dinner parties for headmistresses or overseeing the selection of Alan Clark as Kensington and Chelsea's parliamentary candidate for the Conservative Party, Andrew is a committed Mercury man who combines investment talent with imaginative new ideas for the business and natural salesmanship. Unconventional, enthusiastic and amusing, he has made a tremendous contribution to Mercury's growth. When he returned from Tokyo in 1984, Selected Risk had assets worth some $30 million and was slowly dying through lack of internal support. Andrew took hold of it, changed its name to Mercury Selected Trust (MST), put in an umbrella structure with lots of different subsidiary funds, managed some of them himself, and went about selling them to as many people as he could get to listen. The value of its assets reached $1 billion in 1995, $2 billion in 1997 and $6 billion in 1999.

The longest-surviving member of MST's board is Jürgen Reimnitz, who joined it in 1971. Jürgen is a highly civilised and multilingual German who, after a career at Commerzbank, is now chairman of Mercury's activities in Germany. In 1987, he was awarded the Légion d'Honneur for services to Franco-German relations; his contribution to Anglo-German relations cannot be any less. Daniel Salem, head of Condé Nast International, joined the board in 1972 and succeeded Eric Korner as chairman in 1974. He presided with understanding and humour over its deliberations, held in various cities on the continent of Europe (meetings cannot be held in London as this could compromise MST's tax status), and he never missed a meeting. I was deputy chairman from 1989, and we had an eclectic group of colleagues, including old friends of Mercury such as Leon Levy and Murray Logan from New York, Tadashi Nakamae from Tokyo, Beatrice Philippe and her brother Alain from Paris, Reg Jeune from Jersey, Eric Roll and several well-known bankers from the Continent.

In 1996, a younger team at Mercury decided that the admittedly sizeable board was a costly luxury, and it fell to me to inform most of its members, including Daniel Salem, that the party was over. I did so with reluctance, not only because I had myself gained so much from meeting this unique assembly of investment experts on a regular basis, but also because I felt there was much wisdom available to Mercury from MST's board, had the relevant members of the firm bothered to tap into it rather than to dismiss it as a talking shop of geriatrics. Investment is one area of business where age can be a positive advantage, for the obvious reason that with the passage of time you have 'been there before'. The board was dismantled and reduced to a minimum, but happily Jürgen Reimnitz is one of the survivors. I chaired the downsized board for a while, but was delighted to be able to pass the chairmanship on to Andrew Dalton in mid-1998 when I left Mercury's offices. As the trust's resurrector-in-chief, no one could be more deserving of the position.

Mercury's other long-running offshore fund, Energy International, was another Eric Korner legacy. He had originally started it with his old Wall Street friend Mark Millard of Loeb Rhoades (now part of Lehman Brothers), who, with a profound knowledge of oil companies, provided the investment management in the early days. Together they assembled a group of big names in the energy industries to form an advisory committee. In more recent years, this was carried on under the guidance of Eric Roll and Herman van der Wyck, one of the senior Warburg directors, who was always helpful to Mercury in introducing new business. The fund has performed well, but it remained quite small, which may in part be a consequence of the divided sponsorship and management of Mercury and Lehman Brothers, which continued in 1999.

CHAPTER 24

Twenty-Fifth Anniversary

A dinner for more than a thousand of Mercury's London staff took place on 28 March 1994 in the Great Room of Grosvenor House, originally built as an ice rink. It was held to celebrate the twenty-fifth anniversary, on that day, of the incorporation of Mercury under its original name of Warburg Investment Management. Despite an aggressively large version of Mercury's burgundy-coloured logo, the ballroom was superbly decorated under John Rodwell's supervision with dark blue tablecloths and candles. The wines, both white and red, were from Mercurey, a parish in the Côte Chalonnaise, whose wines, not quite the best of the burgundies, are nevertheless very drinkable. Hugh Stevenson's invitation included 'partners' for those who were not married – an improvement on an earlier expression, 'spousal alternatives', which I was once told to use but could never take seriously. The invitation accommodated all manner of different arrangements in which some of our colleagues lived their private lives.

In his speech, Hugh mentioned that in the twenty-five years since incorporation, Mercury's business had grown sixty times after allowing for inflation. Henry Grunfeld spoke of the beginnings of Warburgs' investment activities under Eric Korner in the 1930s, and Eric Roll, the first chairman of Warburg Investment Management in 1969, and the only member of its initial board present apart from me, proposed a toast to Mercury's continued prosperity. I found it ironic and amusing that these two senior Warburg figures were celebrating with us the success of a business for which they had apparently shared Siegmund Warburg's low regard when he wanted to give it away fifteen years earlier. As Norman Bachop put it:

> At the Anniversary Dinner the great and the good
> Turned up in large numbers as we expected they would
> And remarked in their speeches upon the success
> Of their own Cinderella, the investment business.

Mr Grunfeld told some stories, and told them very funnily
But we all knew he longed to sell us to Mr Charles Nunneley.

(Charles Nunneley was then in charge of the investment management division of Flemings.)

That two of the three speakers were from Warburgs reflected, I suppose, Hugh's own loyalties at that time. Only a few months later, however, he was fiercely protecting Mercury's interest against the steamrolling attempts of Warburgs to promote a merger with Morgan Stanley. And just over a year after the dinner, he was to become chairman of a newly and totally independent Mercury which had no controlling or dominant shareholder. Indeed, after the spin-off of Warburgs' 75 per cent shareholding in Mercury to Warburg shareholders in 1995, there was no single shareholder in Mercury owning even as much as 5 per cent of the shares. They were spread widely among institutional and private shareholders in the UK, and to a smaller extent overseas, and whereas we had about 2500 shareholders before then, we now had some 12,000. The largest shareholder was Munich Re, which owned 4.5 per cent of Mercury, having held its shares since our flotation in 1987.

Independence did nothing to damage Mercury's business, which continued what now seemed to be an unstoppable growth, fuelled by the bull market of the early and mid-1990s. It was not long before its shares joined the Financial Times Stock Exchange 100 Index, made up of the UK's largest 100 companies in terms of market capitalisation.

*

Derivatives are the exotica of the investment business. With names like naked calls, puts, uncovered strips, straddles and swaps, they sound like a list of services offered by those ladies who leave their colourful cards in London telephone boxes. They are at least as hazardous, and should be avoided by all but the most specialist professional investors, in whose hands they can play a legitimate and useful function in buying or selling large amounts of securities quickly. We were fortunate in Mercury to have two outstandingly able exponents of the art of derivatives trading, Nigel Foster and Graham Dixon. I had a particular opportunity to observe Nigel's skills in a pioneering transaction that engaged us both, and quite a few others in Mercury, during an unusually active four days between

Christmas and New Year in 1993 – more than a year after I had relinquished any executive duties in Mercury.

David Scholey telephoned me one day in December that year, following a conversation he had had with Nigel Althaus, who as a partner in Mullens had been the government broker until Big Bang in 1986 and was now a member of the board of the London Pension Funds Authority (LPFA). LPFA was set up to administer the pension fund of the old Greater London Council, which had been abolished by Mrs Thatcher's government some years earlier, and David wanted to see if I could give it some advice in a personal capacity. On the advice of its actuary, LPFA had decided to split its fund into two sections, the first to take care of pensioners who were being paid their pensions currently, and the second to provide for those who would receive their pensions in the future. Following a substantial rise in the stock market in 1993, their actuary had calculated that the liabilities for the first group could be met if some £750 million worth of shares held by the fund were sold at prevailing market levels and immediately reinvested in index-linked gilts (government bonds where the interest rate is linked to inflation). The beauty of the proposal was that it would eliminate stock market risk: if the sales could be made at current market levels, there would be enough money to provide fully for all the pensions currently in payment.

LPFA's funds were managed by three leading fund managers (which did not include Mercury) and the role envisaged for me was to co-ordinate the sales of equities to be made by the three managers so as to inflict the minimum damage on price levels. There was an obvious danger that any leak of the selling programme would depress the prices of some shares, or indeed the market as a whole. I felt there had to be an easier way of achieving the desired objective with less risk of failure, and knowing that Nigel Foster had experience of moving large sums out of the market through the intelligent use of financial futures, I asked if I could bring him to my first meeting with Cholmeley Messer, chairman, and Peter Scales, chief executive of LPFA.

Although the proposal looked attractive from LPFA's point of view, the decision facing its board was not clear-cut because of the possibility of a fall in the market during the two or three weeks that the sales might take. However, Messer and Scales told us that their colleagues were keen to proceed, while fully appreciating the need for speed as well as the utmost secrecy. Nigel Foster then gave them a brilliant exposition of the opportunities that existed to lock in the current level of the stock market through the sale of stock index futures. The market in stock index futures is more liquid than that in individual shares, and Nigel thought it should be possible to sell an amount of £750 million of futures in three or four days, as compared to the two or three weeks it might take to sell the shares. The shares could then be sold carefully over the next few weeks with offsetting purchases of stock index futures.

LPFA would also need to purchase £750 million worth of index-linked gilts. The problem was that the market in this type of gilt is very illiquid, and the only way to obtain such a large amount was for the Bank of England to issue a new tranche, which LPFA would buy. The Bank, which likes opportunities to raise money with an index-linked interest rate, was co-operative, but it was not empowered to make a private placement with LPFA and had to offer any new tranche to all comers. If, however, it was to make an issue in the quiet period between Christmas and New Year, when many market participants were enjoying a holiday, there was a prospect that we would be able to pick up a large part of it for LPFA.

On Christmas Eve, Messer and Scales gave us the green light to go ahead. My Christmas break was thus disturbed, but I had the privilege of watching the manner in which Nigel and his team, with help from Andy Pickard, Mercury's experienced head dealer, successfully completed this complex transaction in the few days before New Year. Cholmeley Messer had asked me beforehand for our fee indication. When I proposed a fee that he might well have felt was high, but we thought was justified by the complexity of the transaction, I told him that if at the end of the day he felt we had not added value to the process to at least justify the fee twice over, we would be content to charge no fee at all. Cholmeley accepted this idea, and in the event, LPFA was extremely pleased at the outcome and paid our fee readily.

As more and more pension funds took advantage of the stock market gains of the late 1990s by switching into the safer investment haven of gilts, Nigel and Graham Dixon developed a productive business area for Mercury in what is now called transition management. Mercury is the leader in this relatively new activity and has implemented similar transactions for ICI, GEC, Railpen (formerly British Rail), Zeneca, Equitas (the arm of Lloyd's of London which was set up to reinsure the old pollution and asbestos claims) and the

English electricity industry (where the pension fund of the former Central Electricity Generating Board had to be subdivided into funds for each of the regional electricity companies at the time of privatisation). The fee structure that we put in place for the LPFA transaction set the level for future transactions, and transition management is now an important part of Mercury's business, providing a useful diversification from more conventional forms of investment management.

*

The rising star in the 1990s was Carol Galley. Carol joined us in 1971 to provide a press cuttings service for Sir Siegmund Warburg from Mercury's library, which mostly contained research reports and reference books. Quiet and reserved at first, she transferred to the front line a year later and, with encouragement from Bob Arnheim and later Leonard Licht, became an impressive fund manager at first for private clients and later for pension funds. In time, she was promoted to take charge of Mercury's UK pension fund side, a position which carried with it a huge responsibility because of the size of Mercury's holdings. We were, by the mid-1990s, the largest holder of UK equities, owning for our clients about 5 per cent of the total market capitalisation of the London Stock Exchange. Our holdings in many companies were more than 10 per cent, so Mercury sometimes found itself with an awesome power to determine whether a contested take-over bid would succeed or not.

Carol naturally attracted attention from the press for the role she played as the ultimate, although in reality certainly not the only, determinant of the fate of certain companies, and she was sought out by chairmen of companies who either wanted her support or feared the absence of it. When London Weekend Television was taken over by Granada in a hostile bid in 1994, its chairman, Sir Christopher Bland, despite receiving some £9 million for his own shares, was bitter in his criticism of Mercury's role in selling its holding in LWT to Granada, and Carol was the main target of Bland's attack. Against her wishes and instincts, she was to have an even higher profile in 1996, in the much-publicised £3.9 billion take-over battle for Forte, again involving Granada as the acquirer.

I have always found Carol charming, warm and likeable. While she could at times be disdainful of those of lesser intellect, the scurrilous Ice Maiden epithet applied to her by the press during the

Forte affair was unfair and inaccurate. She is a consummate professional, who takes her responsibilities to Mercury's clients extremely seriously and has the courage to do what she believes is right for them. She has a probing mind, sees issues clearly and reacts with intelligence and common sense. She also has reliable intuition – to borrow from Kipling, 'a woman's guess is much more accurate than a man's certainty'.

Her impact on the growth and standards of Mercury over recent years has been of inestimable value. She adheres to the old Warburgs tradition of declining to give interviews to the press, but as a woman she was inevitably in their sights. Since Mrs Thatcher's elevation to Lady Thatcher and her transition to the lecture circuit, Carol has even been billed as the most powerful woman in the country, for example in *Management Today* of March 1999. This you might just believe if you went along with Harold Wilson's characterisation of pension fund managers. When he made a study of the City in 1976 after stepping down as Prime Minister, he wrote about them that 'they are more powerful than the Cabinet and leak less'. Undoubtedly, Carol had and still has a position that could influence the outcome of corporate take-overs, and could bring about changes in top management or in the strategy of companies in which Mercury was invested. But the decisions were seldom hers alone.

*

The Forte/Granada takeover battle of 1996 brought Mercury's name to the attention of a wider public than ever before through the intensive daily coverage in all sections of the British press. It was portrayed as a fight between an admirable old British family-run hotel company and an *arriviste* motorway service station operation which would undoubtedly do away with the fine traditions of high-quality service to customers if it succeeded. The reality was different.

Forte's business had its origins in a milk bar in Piccadilly Circus, opened by Charles Forte in 1935. Charles Forte is a formidable character of Italian parentage and Scottish upbringing, who memorably remarked in 1960 that he could imagine scampi being looked upon by future generations as an English dish. In 1992, by then Lord Forte, he turned over the management of what he had built into the UK's largest hotel and catering company, Trust House Forte (later just Forte), to his sports-minded and recently knighted son, Rocco. Rocco did not have the grasp of detail that his father had, but he followed a sensible enough strategy, with which by all accounts his father disagreed, of selling off non-core activities to reduce the company's debt, thereby unintentionally removing a deterrent to would-be predators. The hotel business, however, can be cyclical, and results in the early 1990s were affected by a fierce recession in the UK. By 1995, Forte's share price was selling for around half of its identifiable asset value. One might have said that Forte was a take-over waiting to happen, but that was apparently not the way Rocco saw things.

Some time after Granada made its bid for Forte in November 1995, Rocco was to admit that he had not expected a take-over. On the day it was announced, he was in Yorkshire for a shoot. He went to catch a train to London, but missed it while using his mobile telephone at the station. He had been taken by surprise and was inadequately prepared, but was none the less determined to fight Granada's bid. Forte by chance was an old Warburgs' client. In 1972, Frank Smith had successfully defended Trust Houses, as it was then called, from an unwelcome approach from Allied Breweries. Now, Rocco was to appoint Warburgs again to defend the company, this time as one of five advisers, which some would say was about four too many.

I had known Rocco when, as chairman of the appeals committee for England's team for the Commonwealth Games in 1990, he asked me to head up the appeal to business. I admired the conscientious and competent way in which he carried out that role, and I enjoyed working for him. In his stewardship of Forte, however, while he was undoubtedly committed to the company's growth, his style was proprietorial, and he continued his father's tendency to run it as a family fiefdom. For example, untypically for a chief executive, he did not himself speak to the company's institutional shareholders, leaving that to his finance director and others, which proved to be a handicap when Forte needed the institutions' support. He was conspicuously involved in London's social life with his attractive wife Aliai, and he was observed travelling around the country in a private jet.

It was a remarkable achievement for the Fortes to succeed in giving the impression that the company was a family business, since the family owned only 8.5 per cent of the shares. Mercury, by comparison, owned nearly 15 per cent for its clients. By coincidence, Mercury owned about the same percentage of Granada, a high achieving company run by the entrepreneurial Gerry Robinson, which had expanded from its original television business into catering and motorway service stations. Mercury thus had divided loyalties as between Forte and Granada, but its first responsibility was to its investment clients, and that meant making the right decision based on an objective and detailed assessment of all relevant aspects of the take-over bid. It was a formidable task for the Mercury team which was put together to hear representations from both sides, not least because of press and public interest.

Almost without exception, press sentiment was on Rocco's side, and there were letters and editorials to *The Times* from the great and the good earnestly pleading that a family business such as Forte, the very essence of the British way of life, should not be broken up by a thrusting motorway service station operator. Their interest focused on Carol Galley mainly because she was a woman. It was no matter to them, apparently, that Stephen Zimmerman, Hugh Stevenson and a number of others were involved in the decision.

Carol handled herself immaculately during the course of the take-over. When Mercury made up its mind to accept Granada's bid, she and Stephen went round in person to tell Rocco of their decision, and to explain their reasons. It was a brave, and correct, thing to do. The tone of their conversation was cool, with Rocco accusing Carol and Stephen, without justification, of putting Forte into play by encouraging Granada to make a bid. In fact, Mercury learnt of the bid only when it was offered the opportunity to underwrite an amount of Granada shares the evening before it was made. It was not all bad news for the Fortes, however. As Lord Forte noted, 'it was thus that a business I had started with a few thousand pounds was sold for £3.9 billion' – a reasonable reward for sixty-five years' hard work.

CHAPTER 25

The Morgan Stanley Affair

In late 1998, at a dinner in a well-known New York restaurant, I found myself sitting next to the chairman of a giant US financial conglomerate. 'That was a terrible thing you people at Mercury did, stopping the Morgan Stanley merger with Warburg', he said to me provocatively. I told him I disagreed completely, that the attempted merger was wrongly conceived and poorly handled, and that it would have been a disaster if it had gone ahead. Moreover, although the press release that Morgan Stanley issued when they called the deal off placed the blame on Mercury, that was certainly not the full story. I explained to my dinner companion what had really happened, and I hope I persuaded him that the perfect merger which he had visualised would have been a catastrophe in practice.

A comprehensive record of that failed merger, which was the investment banking news story of 1994, is contained in Harvard Business School's case study entitled 'Morgan Stanley and S.G. Warburg: Investment Bank of the Future'. It is a brilliantly researched document, published four years later, which gives an objective assessment of the background to the merger discussions and the circumstances of their breakdown. My own account must inevitably be more subjective.

It seems that discussions of a possible merger between the two firms started between John Mack, chief executive of Morgan Stanley, and Simon Cairns, by then in the same role in Warburgs, in September 1994. They had had earlier talks about putting together the back offices of the two firms to save expenses, and combining operations in certain parts of the world. Now the idea of a full merger was put forward by Simon, and John Mack did not reject it.

In October, Dick Fisher, Morgan Stanley's chairman, and Mack had dinner with David Scholey and Simon Cairns at Claridge's, and enthusiasm was expressed on both sides for further development of proposals for a full merger. To underline the secrecy of the discussions, the code name Sparkling was given to the project, with

Morgan Stanley designated as Highland and Warburgs as Spring. Both firms had nurtured ambitions of building a fully international investment banking house, and a combination of one of the *crème de la crème* of American firms with the pre-eminent European one would create a powerhouse with market leadership in almost every important financial centre in the world.

The notion of becoming the first genuinely international investment banking firm was something that had caught the imagination of bankers in the 1980s and gave rise to a guessing game as to who might be the winner. I was at a dinner party for a dozen or so at a London club when the guest speaker was Sam Hayes, professor of investment banking at Harvard Business School. He asked each of the assembled company to say which firm they thought would be the 'first truly global player' in investment banking. The names put forward included Goldman Sachs, Deutsche Bank, Morgan Stanley and Warburgs, my own choice being Merrill Lynch. I doubt whether anyone at the dinner thought for a moment that two of those suggested might actually try to steal a march on the others by getting together. On paper at least, a merger of Morgan Stanley and Warburgs, with their complementary geographical strengths, would indeed constitute the first truly global player.

Simon Cairns is an intelligent person with an understated manner and, until he gave up wearing glasses, a slightly owlish appearance. He was a corporate finance specialist and had built a formidable reputation in the take-over game. He sits as a cross-bencher in the House of Lords, and has devoted a great amount of time over the years to Voluntary Service Overseas, of which he was chairman, and for which he received a CBE. He has a well-developed sense of humour and tells some good stories against, or about, himself. One such story related to Simon's change of title. When he first joined Warburgs at David Scholey's bidding in 1979, he was Viscount Garmoyle, a title which passed to his son, Hugh, when Simon became Earl Cairns on his own father's death in 1992. One day some years later, Hugh came to Warburgs' office to visit Simon. He told the receptionist that his name was Lord Garmoyle, which elicited the reply, 'Oh, yes, we used to have one of those, but somehow he vanished.' On another occasion, when one of our colleagues was disappointed not to be promoted to a certain rank, Simon told him not to fuss about his title – he himself had had one all of his life and it had not made much difference. I am not sure whether this did anything to assuage his listener's unhappiness.

Simon's style is distinctly British and in earlier years he managed to give some of our American partners in Warburg Paribas Becker the impression that he viewed them with a certain indifference. There was no doubt, however, that he had a high regard for Morgan Stanley and for any member of that firm. In this respect, he was doing no more than continuing a Warburgs tradition. Siegmund Warburg virtually deified Morgan Stanley, which he considered the epitome of an upper crust and principled firm with an *haute banque* approach to business. As a young man at Warburgs, I had attended some of Siegmund's lunches for Morgan Stanley's senior partner, John Young, whom Siegmund viewed as a perfect example of the stylish, old-fashioned Wall Street banker. David Scholey, too, had many friends in Morgan Stanley and sometimes spoke of them in almost reverential terms.

Morgan Stanley's immaculate client list was indeed the envy of every other firm on Wall Street. It included many if not most of the US's leading companies, for which Morgan Stanley arranged underwritings of new issues. These were then sold by a group of less distinguished firms, which were only too anxious to be members of Morgan Stanley's syndicates. To David and Simon, the idea of a partnership with such an illustrious firm must have provided a tantalising prospect of realising their fondest hopes for Warburgs.

But there were some problems. The first, and possibly the most serious, was that Warburgs had just announced bad results. Following an excellent year in 1993 (the financial year actually ended on 31 March 1994), when Warburgs had made record profits of £200 million, in the first six months of 1994 they were caught in a squeeze between higher expenses, resulting from some overconfident plans for expansion, and losses suffered in the bond markets. Warburgs' profits in those six months were only £60 million, of which no less than £55 million came from the 75 per cent ownership of Mercury. The tail was now convincingly wagging the dog. Warburgs itself had barely broken even, and it had to issue a profit warning for the full year.

These results were embarrassing, of course, and Warburgs' share price dropped sharply. But more important, they meant that its bargaining position in the talks with Morgan Stanley was weak. Morgan Stanley's results also showed a decline, but it was nothing to compare with the deterioration in Warburgs. In 1993, Morgan Stanley made a huge $786 million profit. Under a new generation, it was no longer the conservative firm of old and had adopted an altogether more aggressive approach to business. In the first nine months of 1994, it made $356 million – down substantially from the pace of the previous year, but still very acceptable.

Secretly, and with the knowledge of only a very small number of people in each firm, terms were drawn up in the weeks after the Claridge's dinner for a combination of the two firms using current market values. The exercise was referred to as a merger, but it was pretty obvious who would be the dominant partner. Shares in a new US holding company would be offered to shareholders of each company. Two-thirds of the equity would be owned by Morgan Stanley shareholders, and one-third by shareholders of Warburgs. Dick Fisher would become chairman of the new company and David Scholey vice-chairman. John Mack and Simon Cairns would each be co-presidents, effectively sharing the chief executive function. There would be a board of thirteen members, of whom seven would be executives and six non-executives. Morgan Stanley would have four of the executive members of the board and Warburgs three, while each side would nominate three non-executive directors. Thus Morgan Stanley would have a majority on the board, as well as its chairman.

Morgan Stanley was also the larger firm in every way. Its revenues ('turnover' in English terminology) were more than four times those of Warburgs, and its profits and equity capital more than double. Warburgs' workforce had expanded exponentially in recent years and had reached 5800 (a figure that would surely have horrified Siegmund Warburg), but it was still well below Morgan Stanley's, which was just short of 10,000. More significant, perhaps, whereas Warburgs' executives owned about 1 per cent of its shares, Morgan Stanley's owned more than 25 per cent of theirs.

One did not need to be a financial genius to see what was going on. Taking advantage of Warburgs' fragile position, Morgan Stanley was planning a take-over under the guise of a merger, thus avoiding the necessity of paying the premium to Warburgs' shareholders which is normal in the take-over of a quoted company. Nevertheless the fiction was continued, at least in London, that it was a merger that was under contemplation. Tellingly, in their discussions in the US with the press and the investment analysts who followed their

shares, Morgan Stanley talked quite openly about the take-over of
Warburgs, but when they came over to London, they changed their
language. A senior officer of Morgan Stanley was apparently left
speechless when it was pointed out to him by Henry Grunfeld that
his firm appeared to be saying different things to different people.

*

There was another problem to be dealt with, and it proved to be
quite a big one – Mercury. Almost two-thirds of the value being
attributed to Warburgs in the proposed merger terms was accounted
for by the market value of Warburgs' 75 per cent holding in
Mercury. What was the attitude of those tiresomely independent
people at 33 King William Street whose business now represented
such an important part of the whole package?

In November 1994, John Mack met Hugh Stevenson, while Simon
Cairns told Carol Galley and Stephen Zimmerman about the
proposed deal. Towards the end of that month, Hugh and Stephen
took the Concorde to New York on a Sunday evening to meet the
following morning with Barton Biggs, chairman, and Jim Allwin,
president, of Morgan Stanley Asset Management (MSAM), Morgan
Stanley's investment management subsidiary. MSAM had been
started only in 1975, and with assets under management of around
$45 billion in 1994, it was about half the size of Mercury. The
purpose of the meeting was to exchange information about the two
businesses and to get to know each other, to see how, if at all,
Mercury and MSAM might be able to work together. The tone of the
meetings on the Monday was polite, but there was no invitation to
stay for dinner. Stephen Zimmerman returned to London on
Monday night, while Hugh Stevenson remained in New York for a
further meeting with Allwin on Tuesday and to attend to other
business.

It became clear that MSAM was run on different lines to Mercury.
One noticeable difference was that not only was Barton Biggs
chairman of MSAM, but, as Morgan Stanley's high-profile chief of
investment research and strategy, his activities also involved the
firm's securities activities. This suggested that there was a less strict
separation of investment management from other functions in
Morgan Stanley, and indeed there was a positive policy of integration of the firm's disparate activities. Mercury, however, believed
that operational independence from its parent had been a key

ingredient in its relationships with its clients over the previous years. Mercury had a protocol of independence agreed by Warburgs at the time of the float, and considered it essential that Morgan Stanley should sign up to this operational independence if the two firms were to be combined.

There was also the question of Mercury's minority shareholders, who owned the other 25 per cent of Mercury. They were originally Warburgs shareholders who acquired Mercury shares in the rights issue in 1987, but by now they were a broad mix of institutions and private individuals, including members of Mercury's management. Press comment highlighted the responsibility that fell on the non-executive directors of Mercury, who were then Alfred Shepperd, Jon Foulds, Paul Bosonnet and myself (Leon Levy having resigned in 1992), to ensure fair treatment for the minority. One newspaper noted that we were hardly ones to roll over for Warburgs' charm.

The UK Take Over Code sets out certain principles as to what happens when a company gains control of another company which itself has a controlling shareholding in a third company. The code states that, where the shareholding in the third company constitutes a substantial part of the assets of the company being acquired, the acquirer is required to make an offer to the remaining shareholders in that third company. While the combination of Morgan Stanley and Warburgs was constructed as a merger and not as a take-over, we were advised that the principle would apply. Either Morgan Stanley, or Morgan Stanley and Warburgs together, would therefore have to make proposals to Mercury's minority.

Discussions continued between the investment bankers and the two firms, but little attention seemed to be given to resolving Mercury's position. Morgan Stanley was later to say that it had relied on Warburgs' indications that it could 'deliver' Mercury. In fact, under Mercury's by-laws, Warburgs was precluded from voting its 75 per cent shareholding where control of the business was at stake. So discussion with Mercury was called for, but there was surprisingly little of it before a leak of the merger proposal occurred on 8 December, the day after a large number of Warburgs' executives were informed of it. Mercury's position, however, was clear. If we were to support the deal, it would be necessary for there to be a renewal of our protocol of independent operation, and there would have to be fair treatment for the minority shareholders.

When you are talking about the merger or sale of a business that is totally dependent on the talents of the pepole who work in it, you certainly have to tell them what is happening and you have to have their support. The simple fact is that you cannot merge or sell a people business without the consent of its people, and no merger partner or buyer will proceed without assurances that all or most of the key ones will stay with the business. You could say that the internal negotiation is at least as important as the external negotiation. David Scholey and Simon Cairns were right, therefore, when they decided that at a certain time approximately 100 people in Warburgs should be informed of the proposals, although it was interesting that Morgan Stanley felt a need to tell only some twenty-five of its senior executives. So it was that on 7 December, the merger plans, which had been known to only a handful of people in each firm until then, were communicated to this wider audience. The intention was to be in a position to announce the merger on 19 December, well ahead of Christmas.

Before the stock market opened in London on 8 December, there were rumours in the market of a take-over of Warburgs. At the opening, there was unusually large volume in Warburgs shares, which rose in the first half-hour from 672 pence at the previous evening's close to 830 pence – an increase of 25 per cent. Someone had been talking. The Stock Exchange pressed Warburgs for a comment and by 11 a.m. London time, 6 a.m. New York time, Scholey, Cairns, Fisher and Mack had agreed, not without considerable reluctance, to announce that S.G. Warburg Group and Morgan Stanley Group were discussing the possibility of combining their businesses, which they believed were 'uniquely complementary'.

Warburgs' shares closed that day at 791 pence, reflecting some disappointment that there might not be a bid premium. This price was nevertheless well above an implied merger price based on previously prevailing market values, suggesting that there were traders who thought Warburgs was now 'in play' and a bid from a third party was possible. Mercury shares rose during the day from 614 pence to 653 pence.

From that moment, the merger negotiations would have to take place in the glare of daily press speculation and comment, with competitors and head-hunters watching every move. 'On the Richter scale of City events, the announcement from S.G. Warburg that it is in merger talks with Morgan Stanley registers a full 10' was a headline in the *Independent* the next day. There were those who thought the deal should have been called off immediately it was leaked because of the near impossibility of negotiating under public scrutiny. But one can well understand the reluctance of the four key participants to give up on their dream.

*

I happened to be flying back from a visit to New York on 8 December, the day of the leak and the consequent announcement, and was due to go to a dinner party that evening at the house of Herman van der Wyck, then deputy chairman of Warburgs. On arrival at Heathrow at about 6 p.m., I was given my mail to read in the car, the first item of which was a large envelope marked 'To be opened by addressee only'. It contained a detailed and up-to-the-minute memorandum from Hugh Stevenson, which set out, with his usual clarity and command of detail, all the aspects of the proposal as it affected Mercury. In his memorandum, Hugh drew attention to the rule of the Take Over Code which would require acceptable proposals to be made to the minority shareholders of Mercury – a view now confirmed by Lazards, which Hugh had called in to provide merchant banking advice to Mercury.

Herman van der Wyck is a tall, amiable, aristocratic Dutchman, who had a major hand in developing Warburgs' European and Far Eastern business over many years. An incurable worker and traveller, sometimes known as the Flying Dutchman, he once said he could sleep anywhere, even standing up. Herman likes to give parties for twenty or thirty of his London friends, who include an interesting mix of continental Europeans, South Americans and Iranians, along with a sprinkling of 'little Englanders', as he sometimes labels the rest of us. His parties are always fun, but this one started off badly for me. Herman himself, whose antennae are unusually sensitive, seemed concerned about the Morgan Stanley proposal when he greeted me on arrival. Already unhappy about the leak, I sensed that he felt something else could go wrong.

I had just started talking to one of Herman's female admirers, the beautiful Shirin Sepahbodi, when I was accosted by Piers von Simson, whom I count as a friend. Piers told me in forceful terms that as a long-time Warburgs colleague, and now a sort of elder statesman on the Mercury board, it was my job to make sure that 'the boys and girls' at 33 King William Street toed the line. It was their and my duty, he told me, to support the merger in the interests of the Warburgs group as a whole.

Much as I have always appreciated Piers' honesty and directness, his approach, to say nothing of his choice of occasion, was a breathtaking piece of chutzpah, and I found myself bristling with defensiveness and reciprocal aggression. Thanks to the briefing contained in Hugh's memorandum, I was able to reply that we needed to see whether Morgan Stanley intended to respect Mercury's protocol of independence and what proposals Morgan Stanley, or Warburgs, would have for Mercury's minority shareholders. Piers told me that Warburgs had studied the Take Over Code and had concluded that there was no requirement for a bid for the minority shares.

It was apparent that Warburgs had only taken its own counsel on this point, and that it was heavily influenced by wishful thinking, which Siegmund used to call 'wishful non-thinking'. There is a saying that anyone who appoints himself his own lawyer has a fool for a client, and it is just as relevant to merchant banking. Warburgs did not appoint another merchant bank, preferring its own advice. Some days later, it was forced to concede that some sort of bid would have to be made to Mercury's minority.

In the following days, it became apparent that the reaction of Mercury's board and management would be critical to the completion of the Morgan Stanley proposal, but we were not the only cause of uncertainty. Press coverage was extensive and it was having a pervasive influence on events, reporting rumours of threatened job losses on a massive scale in Morgan Stanley's London office, where some 2000 employees would in future be reporting to Warburgs, and in the Far East, where the two firms had overlapping operations. Staff at Warburgs' 600-person New York office were clearly concerned for their futures, as were those in Warburgs' fixed-interest business, where Morgan Stanley was in a superior league. While senior people in both firms remained optimistic, there were plenty of stories about unhappiness down the line.

Robert Peston in the *Financial Times* speculated that Siegmund Warburg might have opposed the merger on grounds not only of size, but also of business culture. Peston recalled an interview that Siegmund gave to *Euromoney* in 1980, in which his comments on size were as follows: 'The danger is that the bigger a company becomes, the more difficult it is to deal with it on a personal basis,

and the more you become slaves of a big bureaucratic machinery.'
And about American investment banking attitudes, Siegmund commented:

> One general reservation which I feel about some ... of the US
> investment banking houses is that they put too much emphasis on
> measuring, almost from month to month, what a specific partner
> produces. I don't even like the way they pronounce the word – not
> produce, but 'prodooce'. All this emphasis on producing – that is all
> right for a cow, but not for a human being.

The contact between Morgan Stanley and Mercury in the days
after 8 December increased only slightly from its previously minimal
level. On 9 December, however, Simon Cairns came to meet the
board of Mercury to persuade us of the merits of the merger. When
asked in the nicest possible way by Paul Bosonnet what benefits he
saw in it for Mercury, having regard to the different manner in which
Morgan Stanley handled its relationship with MSAM, Simon seemed
to be short of any convincing answers. He left the meeting looking
rather chastened and angry.

I had to miss a further meeting a few days later when David
Scholey talked to Mercury's board, but apparently he too was unable
to convince its members of the attractions of the merger for Mercury.
The attitude of Mercury's board was still open-minded, but as no
one seemed to be able to address our concerns in a positive way, its
position was hardening. Hopes now rested on a visit which Fisher,
Biggs and Allwin, but interestingly not Mack, were to pay to
Mercury on 13 December.

Those three spent that day in Mercury's offices. It was the first
time most of Mercury's directors had met any of them. The
discussions were inconclusive, but Hugh Stevenson described them as
constructive and amicable, with Mercury maintaining its insistence
on the two issues that it considered fundamental. There were
indications from Fisher that some premium would have to be offered
to Mercury's minority shareholders. Warburgs, however, was reluctant to agree to anything more than a notional premium because any
premium would imply a lower value for the rest of Warburgs under
the agreed merger terms. This problem could be alleviated only if
Morgan Stanley was prepared to amend the terms to give Warburg
shareholders a higher percentage of the combined equity, which it

was pretty clear they were not. There was some indication that Morgan Stanley would be responsive to ways in which Mercury could continue its operational independence.

Another board meeting of Mercury was scheduled for 15 December to consider further our position in the light of those discussions and any reaction we might have had to them from Morgan Stanley. That meeting never took place. Our advisers, Lazards, met with Fisher, Biggs and Allwin early on 14 December. By then it was apparent that they had developed concerns about the deal on a number of fronts. Early in the morning of 15 December, Fisher and Mack, before the opening of the New York Stock Exchange, decided to call off the merger. They informed Simon Cairns of their decision, but declined to make a joint press announcement, which some thought was not exactly sporting behaviour. Not for nothing was John Mack called Mack the Knife. They issued the following announcement:

> While the discussions between Morgan Stanley and S.G. Warburg were proceeding on the basis of a market-for-market merger, the price and terms on which Mercury Asset Management indicated it would be willing to participate in the transaction were unacceptable to Morgan Stanley.

Within hours, Stephen Waters, managing director of Morgan Stanley Europe, with its headquarters at Canary Wharf in London's docklands, added his own rather surprising comment: 'MAM was the reason for us to do this deal.'

Waters' need was to restore the morale of the people under his wing who had expected to be managed day-to-day by Warburgs, and to reassure them that they had not been considered mere cannon fodder for a combined London-based investment banking operation. Mack publicly supported Waters by praising Morgan Stanley's European activity. David Scholey reacted furiously to Waters' version of the rationale for the merger, and Mack's apparent endorsement of it, because he too needed to revive morale, now very low, in Warburgs. David's reaction was understandable because Waters' statement did not tell the full story and was hurtful to Warburgs' people. He had to get the message across that it was the rest of Warburgs that Morgan Stanley had coveted, not Mercury, and that the latter would have been no more than an attractive bonus for Morgan Stanley.

But Mercury took the blame in the public eye. The truth was that Mercury's position was just one of the unresolved problems, the near-revolt of Morgan Stanley's London office, which was profitable at the time whereas Warburgs was not, being among several others. It was also rumoured that there was considerable unhappiness in MSAM at the prospect of merging with Mercury. Once it dawned on the 500 or so directors of Morgan Stanley and Warburgs that about 100 of them were likely to become redundant, the deal was in trouble. If Morgan Stanley's real goal was Mercury, why did it not take more trouble to meet Mercury's senior executives at an earlier stage? Why did it not continue the discussions with Mercury which took place on 13 December, which were never concluded but appeared to be making some progress? And was it just feigning affection for Warburgs over a three-month period?

I believe that Morgan Stanley found it convenient to attach the blame to Mercury as an excuse for pulling out of an audacious but inadequately prepared transaction, which it increasingly realised would involve huge job losses in its own organisation and some severe clashes of business methods and styles. There are few people around today who believe a merger of two such different firms would have worked. Henry Grunfeld, in a message to Warburgs' staff six months later, said that the failure had been a blessing in disguise because of cultural differences.

If Mercury had to take the blame for ending the discussions, it should also be given the credit for sparing the carnage that would have resulted if the merger had taken place.

*

The press had a field day. 'Warburg left at the Altar' was the headline of a feature article in the *Sunday Times*. The 'Marriage of the Century' had been bungled. Warburgs was left in disarray with no credible strategy, according to another story. Moreover, Warburgs had 'hoisted a for sale sign'. Simon Cairns put on a brave face: 'We're comfortable to remain independent', he said. Tom Wyman, head of Warburgs' New York office, put matters differently: 'We're not going to be distracted because a damn pretty girl passed through town and winked at us. The merger was an interesting idea, but it was not crucial.' But there was no doubting Warburgs' humiliation.

Its share price fell by 15 per cent to 699 pence, and Mercury's by 10 per cent to 678 pence.

Relationships between Warburgs and MAM were now severely strained. There was much bitterness towards us in Warburgs. Soon afterwards, according to newspaper reports, Mercury was pressing its parent to sell its holding in Mercury or at least reduce it to 50 per cent. It was claimed, wrongly, that Mercury's non-executive directors, led by Jon Foulds and myself, were leading a campaign for greater independence, and that Hugh Stevenson, previously thought of as a loyal Warburg man, was also pushing for looser ties with Warburgs. Undoubtedly, Hugh had been courageously robust in his defence of Mercury's interests during the merger discussions.

In fact I was one of those who had always believed that we in Mercury had benefited substantially over the years from Warburgs' ownership, and I was not yet ready to change my mind. Warburgs had been a good owner, which had generally handled its position with a sensitive understanding of Mercury's need to demonstrate its independence. The fiasco of the aborted merger was a near mortal blow to it, however, and set in motion a chain of events which led to the resignation of Simon Cairns two months later and the sale of Warburgs the following summer at a distressed price. It was the beginning of the end of the Warburgs that we knew.

CHAPTER 26

Whatever Happened to Warburgs?

The failure of the Morgan Stanley discussions brought about an immediate loss of confidence in Warburgs' top management. As one team leader commented, it was hard to explain to your colleagues one day that the merger was a great idea, and the next day, when it collapsed, that Warburgs was in fine shape on its own. He compared it to being run over by a truck, which then reversed and did it again.

Morale was already low before the Morgan Stanley talks. A badly timed expansion of the firm's activities in global bond markets in early 1994 coincided with the first increase in US interest rates since 1989, initiated by the Federal Reserve Board under the chairmanship of Alan Greenspan. Bond markets, which had been heading higher for some years, declined sharply on the change in direction of interest rates, and Warburgs was caught in a squeeze between higher costs and declining revenues. By December, following a profits warning, Simon Cairns had to take the painful decision to go into reverse and implement cuts in bond trading activities. In January 1995 he announced that Warburgs would exit the eurobond market – an inglorious day for the firm which, through the efforts and imagination of Siegmund Warburg and others, had created that market in the 1960s. It was an agonising admission of defeat in an area where Warburgs had for some years been the acknowledged leader.

In early February, there were defections to Morgan Grenfell of key executives on Warburgs' international equity side, who felt let down by the downsizing of the complementary bond trading activities, followed by a palace revolution on the part of some of the younger executives. A board meeting was held on Saturday, 13 February. Simon Cairns resigned as chief executive and it was agreed that David Scholey, then 59, would step back into the position of chief executive, thus once again combining the positions of chairman and chief executive.

From the time of Warburgs' four-way Big Bang merger in 1986 until 1991, David had assumed the dual roles of chairman and chief executive, thus taking upon himself a huge burden which he discharged with great energy and a strong and effective sense of leadership. There is something to be said for undivided one-man rule. At least it was a change from the almost byzantine governance regime that existed when David first became chairman and notional chief executive of Warburgs in Siegmund Warburg's day. Then David was co-chairman with Eric Roll, but behind them, Henry Grunfeld, who was effectively David's predecessor as chief executive, was still a powerful presence, and then, only pretending to be in the background, there was Siegmund, who seemed to have the last say on all matters of senior appointments and overall strategy (which he called policy). Herman van der Wyck swears that he once heard the following conversation between myself and Henry Kissinger, with whom we were a business partner for a while after his time at the White House:

KISSINGER: Who *really* runs Warburgs?
PSD: Who do you think?
KISSINGER: That's what I thought.

The difficulty I have in believing Herman's recollection is that I can no longer be sure which of several possible candidates I was attempting to indicate; I certainly do not know who Kissinger thought it was.

The problem, of course, arises when the possessor of both roles decides to divide them between himself and another person. Whatever agreement David and Simon had as to the division of their respective functions when Simon was appointed chief executive in 1991, there may have been a tendency for a while on the part of other executives to continue to regard David as the ultimate decision-maker. Whether David strayed too much into Simon's territory, or too little, as might have been his natural and understandable inclination, I cannot say, but the changeover clearly carried with it the risk of ambiguity. It is probable that, having regard to his conscientious sense of a chairman's responsibilities, of which he had reminded me from time to time, David will have offered his resignation to the Board at the time of the February meeting, and will have had it refused. Nevertheless one could feel some sympathy for Simon, in that he was the one to fall on his sword after the failure of the Morgan Stanley talks. He had been unlucky with the timing of the expansion initiative in 1994, which was backed by the board. If he himself sometimes appeared indecisive as chief executive, it must have been awkward for him to take over that role with his predecessor continuing as full-time chairman.

I wrote Simon a note, thanking him for the help he had given to Mercury over the years and for the good times we had had together, and was happy to find that in a period which must have been distressing for him he had not lost his sense of humour. He replied that he had enjoyed a headline about his departure from Warburgs which read, 'Fat Cat Gets Chop', the more so as he was virtually a vegetarian. Not too many months later, Simon was appointed chairman of British American Tobacco.*

*

For a while after Simon's resignation, spirits were lifted when David took charge again, and he was applauded when he spoke on the trading floor. However, good people continued to leave what they saw as a sinking ship, and some odd proposals for senior appointments were contemplated. A new head of equities was recruited from Credit Lyonnais Laing, only to be seen off by those in possession before he could take up the job. And it was reported that within weeks of his resignation as deputy governor of the Bank of England in 1994, following his unusual choice of venue at the Bank of England for the conduct of an extra-marital relationship, Rupert Pennant-Rea had been sounded out as a possible chief executive of Warburgs. It was revealed that he had been intimate with an American journalist, Mary Ellen Synon, on the floor of the governor's dressing room at the Bank of England. Memorably, Ms Synon said of their affair, after it had ended and she had gone public with it, 'If you're going to dump a financial journalist, if you are the deputy governor of the Bank of England, that's dumb.'

David in turn had his share of bad luck with the dramatic collapse of the once mighty Barings,† which came only two weeks after his

---

* He had another moment of fame in 1998 when two five-month-old pigs that he had bred and sold escaped from an abattoir, and to the great delight of Britain's animal loving public defied capture for eight days. The press called them the Tamworth Two. When they were eventually captured, their death sentence was commuted and they were sent to an animal sanctuary.
† In 1818, the Duc de Richelieu said, 'There are six great powers in Europe: England, France, Prussia, Austria, Russia and Baring Brothers.'

reappointment. With Barings' overnight failure, some of the mystique of merchant banking disappeared, to be replaced by a new awareness of the precariousness of even the most prestigious of merchant banks. The need for substantial capital was highlighted, and an alliance with a powerful international bank began to look increasingly likely for Warburgs.

The *Financial Times* reported on 8 March that senior Mercury executives had urged Warburgs to seek a strong merger partner to remove the speculation as to its future, which they felt was capable of damaging Mercury's business. This was certainly a reversal of roles, but perhaps not altogether unjustified if one looks at the change in relative valuations of Warburgs and Mercury on the stock exchange. In 1987, after Mercury's float, Warburgs' 75 per cent stake in Mercury represented about 25 per cent of the market capitalisation of Warburgs. By 1995, that had increased to more than 60 per cent. However, I was not quite sure that, whatever the threat to Mercury's business relationships, it was as yet justified in lecturing its parent, to whom at the end of the day it owed its existence.

In any case, David seemed to be reaching the same conclusion that Warburgs, if it was to survive, should be sold to a major financial institution. As a long-time connection of Warburgs, ING (Internationale Nederlanden Groep), the large Dutch insurance and banking conglomerate, might have been a good candidate to acquire it, but ING's attentions had been drawn to Barings, which it bought soon after Barings' collapse. Three other suitors showed an interest in Warburgs – Swiss Bank Corporation, Smith Barney, the American investment banking firm which later merged with Salomon Brothers, and NatWest Bank. This time Warburgs did not make the mistake of entering into negotiations on its own. It appointed J.P. Morgan and Schroders to give advice. With their appointment, the for sale sign was now pretty clearly up.

Meanwhile, despite steps to cut costs put in place by David, losses continued, and the third profits warning within a year had to be made in April 1995. Defections of Warburgs' employees continued, and the trickle of departures to Morgan Grenfell became a flood, to the consternation of David and others at Warburgs. More than fifty Warburgs people joined Morgan Grenfell during 1995. Perhaps wrongly there was a suspicion that John Craven, a former rival to David Scholey for the top position at Warburgs, who was now chairman of Morgan Grenfell, might have encouraged his colleagues to target Warburgs' employees. David wrote to the head of Deutsche Bank, Morgan Grenfell's parent company, to complain of the predatory behaviour of its subsidiary, while Piers von Simson, outspoken as ever, used the occasion of a meeting at Deutsche Bank, held to discuss the flotation of Deutsche Telecom, to berate his hosts. For ten minutes, he told Deutsche Bank that it should stop stealing Warburgs people.

Two of the three candidates to buy Warburgs were soon eliminated for different reasons. NatWest was not favoured by some Warburgs' directors, who did not like the idea of working for a 'clearing bank'. Snobbery, which I suppose is a branch of insecurity, is unfortunately an occupational hazard among bankers, and it can be seriously damaging to good commercial judgement. It was a pity that it raised its ugly head in this instance because NatWest and Warburgs would have been a strong British combination with synergy to be gained in several business areas. NatWest had a sizeable investment management subsidiary, which had languished and was not profitable. It could have fitted well with Mercury, and NatWest could have provided increased distribution for Mercury's unit trusts. Overall, there would have been interesting opportunities for both Warburgs and Mercury people in a combined operation.

Discussions with Smith Barney were broken off when it leaked its interest to the media, presumably to apply pressure, and David Scholey justifiably responded by cancelling a planned dinner with Bob Greenhill of Smith Barney. Thus he was left with just one potential acquirer, Swiss Bank Corporation, which was not quite the most desirable position from which to bargain.

*

A deal was struck with Swiss Bank Corporation in May 1995. It would pay £860 million for Warburgs' investment banking business, which was equivalent to its book value (the net value of tangible assets) plus about 8 per cent. Swiss Bank Corporation did not want to acquire Mercury because it already owned a major American fund management business, Brinson, which had global ambitions, so it was agreed that Warburgs' shareholding in Mercury would be distributed to Warburgs' shareholders. Thus each Warburgs shareholder would receive cash from the sale of the investment bank and, as it worked out, about half a share of Mercury for each share of Warburgs owned.

There was a smack of desperation to the deal on Warburgs' side. A few days earlier, Mercury was being implored to demonstrate solidarity and speak with one voice with its parent; now Warburgs was about to do a deal which left Mercury out in the cold. Mercury would no longer be permitted to use the Warburg name in its overseas activities – until then, we were still Warburg Asset Management outside the UK and the Swiss bank that we now owned 100 per cent was called Bank S.G. Warburg. After some discussion it was agreed that, to compensate us for the hassle and expense involved in the name change-over, and for the parental desertion, Mercury would receive a payment of £35 million. At the same time, there would be a special dividend of 40 pence per share for the minority shareholders of Mercury.

The Swiss could hardly believe their luck. They had bought London's pre-eminent merchant bank, albeit in decline, without paying any premium over book value. (By the time the deal was finally clinched, Warburgs had returned to profits. The resultant increase in net asset value reduced the 8 per cent premium in the price to a small discount.) Marcel Ospel, shortly to take charge of SBC Warburg in London, was quoted in a Swiss newspaper as saying that they paid practically nothing for it. By any measure, it was a rock-bottom price. No sooner had the ink dried on the Swiss Bank Corporation purchase of Warburgs than Merrill Lynch announced its purchase of Smith New Court at 2.4 times book value. Deutsche Bank had paid 2.7 times book value when it acquired Morgan Grenfell a few years earlier, and Dresdner Bank 2.0 times book value for Kleinwort Benson around the same time as the Swiss Bank/ Warburg transaction. When Swiss Bank Corporation itself bought Dillon Read, a medium-sized American investment bank, just two years later, it paid 3.0 times book value.

It was galling for those who had worked hard for much of their lives to build Warburgs' business and reputation to see it go for a song. One former colleague wrote to me from Geneva, 'The news I hear from our old firm is truly sickening – what a waste of all those years.' Henry Grunfeld would be selling his shareholding without a penny for goodwill after sixty years of total commitment to developing Warburgs. A mischievous internal e-mail message was sent out entitled 'The Zurich Telegraph', which referred to the end of 'World Warburg II and the dream of its leaders that the bank could achieve global domination ... Never in the history of investment banking was so much reduced so quickly to so little.'

While Warburgs' shareholders received no premium over book value for their interest in the investment banking side, those who held on for the next two and a half years to the Mercury shares they received in the distribution would receive a substantial goodwill payment. More than 60 per cent of the value of the package that Warburgs' shareholders received under the Swiss Bank Corporation arrangement was represented by Mercury shares. In late 1997, Mercury was sold to Merrill Lynch for twice its market value at the time of the Swiss Bank Corporation transaction, and the goodwill element in the price was about 90 per cent.

Briefly I returned to the Warburgs board, along with other Mercury non-executive directors, to oversee its last rites. By then Brandon Gough, a former chairman of the large accounting firm Coopers & Lybrand, who had been appointed a non-executive director of Warburgs, had become its chairman, and the board was a shadow of its former self. Bitterness at what had happened and recriminations against colleagues by those who were present for that last meeting were all too evident as we took the final steps to turn over the investment banking business of Warburgs to Swiss Bank Corporation. It was a sad ending to what had been, until the last year or so, a conspicuously successful and unique organisation. By July 1998, the Swiss had completed their purchase, had renamed the investment bank SBC Warburg and were in total control. Mercury, already independent in behaviour, would now be fully independent in its ownership too.

*

The new man in charge of SBC Warburg (to be renamed Warburg Dillon Read in 1998) was Marcel Ospel, a 49-year-old Swiss who had worked briefly for Merrill Lynch in the US, and who was given to informal dress. From now on, executives could forget about Mr Sharp's banking ties, or any other ties, and could come to work in jeans provided they were not meeting clients. One day when he tried to enter Warburgs' building without a tie, Ospel himself was stopped by a security guard who refused to believe that he was the new boss.

Ospel moved quickly to make sweeping changes, and he introduced a new more abrasive style, offensive to many of the old guard in Warburgs' still well-regarded corporate finance business. Some people left, some were sidelined, some were dismissed and others were not told whether the new firm wanted them to stay or depart. One Warburg corporate finance practitioner was sacked, only to be reinstated the same day when it transpired that an important client for whom he was working on a transaction would remove its business immediately. Altogether over a thousand jobs from the combined London operations of Swiss Bank Corporation and Warburgs were lost, and a further 700 systems people were transferred to Perot Systems, the latest flagship of the empire of our old acquaintance Ross Perot, which had established a strong business base in the UK.

Once again Piers von Simson, before resigning, was unabashedly direct in his condemnation of the changes being made. The mood, in the words of the *Wall Street Journal*, was 'rife with division', and there was 'an atmosphere of fear and loathing'. Rodney Ward, one of Warburgs' most able executives, who was in charge of corporate finance at the time of the sale, was the only Warburgs person appointed to the top board of Swiss Bank Corporation, while David Scholey became chairman of its international advisory board.

Henry Grunfeld was one of the few to defend what was happening to his old firm. By then more than 91 years old, but still attending the office regularly, he compared Ospel's arrival to that of Siegmund Warburg and himself when they first came into the City of London in 1935. 'We were an aggressive firm in those days', he said in October 1995. 'Ospel is likely to return the bank to those traditions.' Grunfeld and Ospel were photographed together in front of Raymond Skipp's portrait of Siegmund Warburg, with Ospel wearing an open-necked shirt and a sweater draped casually over his shoulders. Yet again, Grunfeld's judgement was close to the mark. Although Ospel was soon to return to Switzerland to become chief executive of Swiss Bank Corporation itself, Warburg Dillon Read has once again become one of Europe's leading investment banks. But there was a massive cultural shift – the old Warburgs had gone for ever.

*

It had all happened so quickly. At the beginning of 1994, Warburgs was riding on the crest of a wave as the leading European investment bank. Four years earlier, in a poll conducted by *The Economist*, it had been among the UK's 'most admired companies', and its management had been voted third in quality of management. By the middle of 1994, it was losing money and making a spectacle of itself in a rather desperate attempt to link up with Morgan Stanley. In early 1995, its chief executive resigned and its chairman was reinstated as chief executive to rally the troops and restore stability, and by the summer its investment banking side was sold at a give-away price. Whatever happened? How on earth could it all have gone so wrong in little more than a year?

It is a question I am asked and one that I myself put to former Warburgs colleagues. One gets many different answers. When the business editor of the *Independent*, in those days an ailing newspaper, was asked a few months before the sale of Warburgs what had happened there, he replied that it was rather like the *Independent*. 'In the late 1980s it was the best thing in the City, and all the best people wanted to work for it. But now all the best people have left and a lot of third raters have come in.' That analogy, which may have contained a grain of truth at that time, still begs the question – why did Warburgs break down? Here are some of the theories I have heard:

1. Warburgs' global ambition was unachievable without a strong presence in the US. It should have gone ahead with the purchase of Wertheim, a medium-sized but effective US investment banking firm, when it had the opportunity to buy it in 1986.

David Scholey and most of the then younger generation who were involved in those talks wanted to proceed with it, but for reasons which seemed to have been based more on illogical prejudices than on sensible business reasons, we were outvoted. Our earlier venture in the US through Warburg Paribas Becker had failed because Warburgs and Paribas had different objectives and styles, as a consequence of which our American partners were able to divide and rule to the detriment of both firms, and their own too. But by 1986, Warburgs had an active office in New York once again. It had a small capital of $25 million, but some excellent people in Rodney Ward, Nic Millward, Charlie Symington and James Leigh-Pemberton. Together with Wertheim's management, this group would almost certainly have been able to develop a powerful American firm by combining Wertheim's strong American franchise with Warburgs' international relationships.

2. By instinct and background, Warburgs was risk averse. After Big Bang, however, it found itself engaged in risky trading businesses in bonds and equities, which required holding large inventories of securities overnight, financed by borrowed capital. It did not know how to manage these businesses and was temperamentally unsuited to own them. The pull-out from the eurobond market in early 1995 was a signal that Warburgs no longer had the stomach to compete with the large American firms like Goldman Sachs and Morgan Stanley, with consequent defections of talented people who wanted to work in firms which at least had the ambition to be global.

3. With the absorption of three distinctly British firms at Big Bang – Akroyd and Smithers, Rowe and Pitman, and Mullens – Warburgs lost its continental European dimension and became too anglocentric. Its European connections and style had given it an edge over other London merchant banks in the 1960s, 1970s and early 1980s, but now it was swamped by an overwhelmingly British culture.

4. Any institution has a limited time span when it is at its maximum period of dynamism, after which it declines, either gradually or speedily. One has only to look at the demise of so many of the old merchant banks in London and investment houses in New York in the last generation. This is even more applicable where the institution has been the creature of one inspirational and dominating individual, or in Warburgs' case, more than one. They tend to drive away other strong people, leaving a leadership gap when they finally depart the scene.

The younger generation under David Scholey's direction did well in the years immediately following Siegmund Warburg's death, with help in particular from Henry Grunfeld, but after the Big Bang merger, some of the old disciplines seemed to fade.

5. Warburgs should never have agreed to the Mercury float in 1987. There would then have been no trouble in achieving a merger with Morgan Stanley.

Leaving aside the questionable assumption that it was only the existence of Mercury's minority that prevented the merger, and that a merger would have been a good thing, it is doubtful if many of

Warburgs' shareholders would have agreed, in hindsight anyway. Whereas they received £860 million for the investment banking business in July 1995, they got £2.4 billion for the 75 per cent holding in Mercury in November 1997. The latter value would never have been achieved without flotation, mainly because Mercury would not have been able to retain the services of its top management team.

6. Warburgs suffered from the absence of an employee ownership mentality. While its executives were granted share options, their combined ownership of the firm was only about 1 per cent. They seldom behaved like owners in the way that, for example, partners in London or New York Stock Exchange firms were accustomed to doing. The lifestyle was comfortable, at times even lavish, and there was a certain indifference to expenses, which is damaging to any business both financially and psychologically, and especially to one whose cost structure had been too high ever since the Big Bang merger.

That the nature of ownership is important to an investment banking business was shown clearly in the case of Barings. The equity capital of Barings was owned by the Baring Foundation, a charity, while the voting power remained with the board of the bank. Thus none of the executives owned any shares in the bank. To compensate, they were granted an extremely generous share of the bank's profits as a bonus pool. This provided them with every incentive to take risks because if they made profits, the executives would earn valuable bonuses; but if there were losses, they were borne by the foundation. Heads I win, tails I don't lose. When Nick Leeson turned in some large profits from his derivatives trading in Singapore, it was all too tempting for his supervisors to avoid enquiring too closely how they were achieved.

7. Bankers, and especially corporate finance practitioners, are often poor businessmen with limited strategic judgement. This was not so much of a problem for Warburgs when, as in the 1960s and 1970s, it consisted of just a hundred employees and could be managed more or less as a partnership, or even when there were a thousand, as in the 1980s. But it started to show when there

were 5000 in the 1990s. By then, the firm had become too large,
it was inadequately controlled, and the personal touch had gone.

Each of these theories may have some validity, but they do not tell
the full story. My own view is that those in charge simply forgot to
apply some of the rules, never defined as such, which Siegmund
Warburg used to drum into our minds constantly and repetitively.
Collectively, the rules made up the Warburg culture, although
Siegmund would have objected to the use of 'culture' in that context,
just as he complained at the hijacking of 'philosophy' as applied to a
business.

There were rules relating to personal behaviour. We should
acknowledge the predominant importance of people and of our
clients. We were taught the essential virtue of self-criticism, and the
necessity of carrying out our activities with a measured rhythm or
tempo. Good manners, consideration of other employees at more
junior levels and prompt attention to outstanding matters were
requirements of our daily life, while arrogance, self-promotion,
sloppiness, bad writing style and bureaucratic behaviour were
abhorrent to Siegmund and were to be avoided at all costs. To these
one might have added his constant assault on 'telephonitis' (excessive
use of the telephone), if it were not for his having been a compulsive
telephoner himself.

There were also rules for the conduct of the business. As much as
anything, Siegmund wanted Warburgs to avoid becoming a member
of the City establishment. He believed that, if we did so, we would
lose our edge and our originality; we would start to conform and do
all the fashionable things which others did. We ignored his wishes on
this score. Young people joining Warburgs, or even, I am sorry to
say, Mercury, in the 1990s, did not for one moment think of either
firm as being anything other than a true-blue member of the City
establishment. They would not have understood Siegmund's anti-
establishment concerns or his non-conformism. Whereas to most
people not to conform is a right, to Siegmund it was almost a duty.

Another rule that was of paramount importance in Siegmund's
eyes was to stay away from large size and premature expansion. He
believed that small was beautiful, that quality and quantity were in
continuous conflict, and that we should confine our activities
geographically to those few parts of the world where we had some
special knowledge or contacts. This meant the UK, continental

Europe, North America and Japan. He objected, not always successfully, to proposals for expansion in Hong Kong and Australia and Iran, where Warburgs briefly had a representative office in the early 1970s, and was opposed to any venture into Latin America. Do not try to conquer the whole world, he would say, but play to your strengths. His advice was ignored by those directing the firm in the 1990s in their quest for global coverage, so aptly described by Tony Griffin as 'imperial overstretch'.

Another of Siegmund's precepts was that when you have just had a good period in the business it is not the time to expand it, but rather to curtail it. Success breeds failure because it causes complacency, a cardinal sin in his spectrum of bad attitudes. This view has also been stated articulately by Alan C. (Ace) Greenberg, chairman of Bear Stearns, in a little book which is packed with wisdom entitled *Memos from the Chairman*. In one of these memos in August 1985, following one of the best months in Bear Stearns' history, Greenberg wrote, 'Try to cut expenses at all times, but particularly when business is good.'*

Warburgs' big mistake was its expansion in 1994, coming after an excellent and record-breaking year in 1993. Siegmund used to speak about 'expansion euphoria', but by then nobody remembered.

---

* I have two other reasons to pay attention to Ace Greenberg. The first is his original gesture in 1998 in donating $1 million to enable the poor in New York to buy the wonder drug Viagra. The second is his coincidental use of my initials in his writings. In a memo of May 1981, discussing the sort of people he liked to employ in Bear Stearns, he expressed his admiration for people with 'PSD degrees' in preference to business school graduates. PSD, in Greenberg's world, stands for 'poor, smart, and a deep desire to become rich'. Two of the three examples he gave were Cy Lewis and Gus Levy, both of whom I mentioned in Chapter 9. I can think of a few others.

CHAPTER 27

Prince Charming

Mercury continued to make excellent progress in 1996 and 1997, with all cylinders firing under Hugh Stevenson's able chairmanship and with Carol Galley and Stephen Zimmerman effectively acting as co-chief executives. David Price, who was now spending more time on his farm, retired from full-time activity in Mercury in 1997, but continued his membership of the board of Mercury European Privatisation Trust alongside several other board appointments.

Personal relations with Leonard Licht, the other member of the top group ten years earlier, having suffered a period of coolness after his sudden departure in 1992, were now restored to a friendly basis. Donald Macpherson, our colleague on the board of MIIT, invited Leonard and me to lunch at his office in June 1997. With his usual prescience, Leonard told us he thought Mercury would be bid for well before the end of the century. We agreed that, given Mercury's large size, its high stock market rating and its reputation for 'fierce independence', the number of potential bidders could be counted on one or at the most two hands, with the majority of them coming from overseas. There were several American candidates, including investment banking firms such as Goldman Sachs, Salomon, which had by now merged with Smith Barney, and Merrill Lynch, and one or two among the continental European insurance companies which knew Mercury well, with the British possibilities probably limited to NatWest and HSBC (Hong Kong and Shanghai Banking Corporation).

Leonard's prediction proved accurate. After some abortive talks with Putnam, an American fund management company of a size similar to Mercury's, which is owned by Marsh and McLennan, a major US insurance group, Merrill Lynch appeared on the scene in 1997 as the first serious prospective purchaser of Mercury.

Merrill Lynch was popularly known as the Thundering Herd from its 1970s advertising campaign, 'Merrill Lynch is bullish on America', the television component of which showed a herd of cattle stampeding past a fixed-point camera. It had been started in 1914 by Charles Merrill to make investment in shares accessible to middle-class savers unfamiliar with such matters.

I had had dealings with Merrill Lynch from my time in Canada forty years earlier, when it was little more than a retail stockbroker, and had always liked the company. In those days, its name was Merrill Lynch Pierce Fenner and Beane, which gave rise to a disrespectful limerick that I first heard as a rather innocent fund manager in Toronto:

> There was a young girl from Racine
> Who was elected the stock exchange queen
> She stripped to the nude
> And then she was viewed
> By Merrill, Lynch, Pierce, Fenner *and* Beane.

The traders on the Stock Exchange used a cruder alternative word for 'viewed', but neither version outlasted a name change in the 1960s to Merrill Lynch Pierce Fenner and Smith, before this, in turn, was changed in line with the modern fashion for short names to Merrill Lynch.

Merrill Lynch was then and is now, in contrast to some Wall Street firms, quintessentially and proudly a meritocracy, lacking any snobbery, nepotism or patrician aspects. It was a firm of the people determined to reach out to the people, and even as early as the 1950s it was hardly possible to visit a city or town in the US that did not have a Merrill Lynch retail office. Its salesmen were put through a rigorous training programme, and I used to be able to detect 'Merrill Lynch man' of those days from his body language, his walk, his conversation and his dress – dark, almost black, suit with the coat too long and the trousers too short, bright-red tie and brogue shoes with unfashionably large soles, giving the appearance of small boats.

When I returned to London from Canada in 1963, Merrill Lynch was still very much a domestic American firm. It had opened a small office in London's West End in 1960 to deal with retail customers, mostly Americans living in London, and it was making only hesitant overtures to possible institutional clients in the City, such as Warburgs' investment division. In the 1970s, however, Merrill Lynch invested in Selected Risk, our offshore fund, and had a representative on its board. Sometime around then it decided to capitalise on the

huge placing power, nowadays called distribution, which its network
of retail offices provided for it. It expanded its activities into
underwriting new issues of securities and advising on mergers and
acquisitions, and it did not take long for it to become a powerhouse
in almost every field of investment banking. With growing sophisti-
cation and scope, it attracted a different type of professional
employee, and Merrill Lynch man became harder to detect.

*

Some years ago, I was lucky enough to stumble upon the shares of
Merrill Lynch as an investment possibility that met just about all the
criteria I have set for my own investments. Having made every type
of mistake imaginable in my personal investments over the years, and
having carefully observed the methods and strategies of wiser and
more successful practitioners of the art, I developed some rules for
investing which can be stated simply: put as much of your savings as
you can set aside into shares; buy shares in a small number of well-
managed companies which have some unique and desirable product
or service which cannot easily be duplicated by competitors and, as
in any collecting, buy the best; only buy shares in companies you
understand; and hold your shares indefinitely. Do not worry about
timing, currency, country, markets or even price – you will always
have to pay up for quality. Thereafter, benign neglect is the best
policy. Regard your shares as a collection of the world's great
companies. Do not look at the prices every day, or even every week
or month (you will only give in to fear or greed), and sell only if the
share price of one of them seriously underperforms the others over a
long period, because it probably means that the market knows
something negative about the company that you do not.

In a paper he wrote for the finance committee of King's College,
Cambridge, in May 1938, John Maynard Keynes, previously
committed to a market timing approach in his investments, said it all:

> I am clear that the idea of wholesale shifts is impracticable and
> undesirable. Most of those who attempt it sell too late and buy too late
> and do both too often, incurring heavy expenses and developing a too
> unsettled and speculative state of mind.
>
> I now believe that successful investment depends on the careful
> selection of a few good shares which should be held through thick and

thin, perhaps for several years until either they have fulfilled their promise or it is evident that they were purchased as a mistake.

In practice, I have found that the world's leading pharmaceutical companies, some consumer brand name companies and some of the best-known financial service companies, including investment banks and fund management companies, meet these criteria. There are, of course, many others, including technology companies, but I have always had difficulty understanding what they do. Investment trusts or unit trusts with good track records provide a good alternative for investors who have neither the time nor the inclination to select shares of individual companies.

Merrill Lynch stands up to the tests. The service it provides to retail investors and its distribution power, nowadays on a global basis as well as in the US, is unique and should have tremendous growth in the next century as more and more people acquire the necessary funds to provide intelligently for their retirement. Its client relationships, amounting to over $1 trillion, have most of the same characteristics as those which fund management companies have with their clients, such that Merrill Lynch should benefit from the magical economics of investment management which I have described in Chapter 11. Yet Merrill Lynch shares were for a number of years selling on the sort of stock exchange rating of other stockbroking houses, typically some 30 per cent or more lower than the ratings given by the market to the shares of investment management companies.

*

I was delighted that Merrill Lynch turned out to be our suitor, not only because of my high regard for the firm and what it stood for, and because I had a shareholding, but also because I had several friends there from our old Wall Street associate, Warburg Paribas Becker (WPB). In 1985, WPB, from which Warburgs had departed two years earlier, was sold to Merrill Lynch, and a number of talented former colleagues of ours, such as Barry Friedberg, John Heimann and Jeff Peek, were now in senior positions in Merrill Lynch. Another WPB friend, Bill Cockrum, currently professor of entrepreneurism at the Anderson School of Business at University of California at Los Angeles, who has a son in Merrill Lynch, always shared my high opinion of it. These considerations gave me the confidence, long before there was any thought of its acquiring us, to build up a shareholding in Merrill Lynch second in size only to my holding in Mercury.

By the 1990s, Merrill Lynch seemed assured of continuing growth in investment banking and retail stockbrokerage on a fully international scale. The one area of financial services in which it was not directly involved in a major way, however, was investment management, even though the nature of its retail business was so similar. It was something that Merrill Lynch targeted for expansion, and having acquired a Los Angeles-based American domestic institutional fund management firm, Hotchkis and Wiley, in 1996, it now wanted to find a global firm, which almost certainly meant one in London.

Merrill Lynch's search coincided with some introspection at Mercury as to whether independence was still right for us, or whether we needed a big brother shareholder. Mercury reached £100 billion of funds under management in 1997, but its capital was less than £300 million. We had seen what happened to one of our competitors: Morgan Grenfell had had to call on its parent, Deutsche Bank, to commit over £400 million to restoring its clients' losses in the aftermath of the Peter Young affair, referred to in Chapter 21. While we did not believe that the same thing could happen in Mercury, one can never completely guard against fraud, and at least our retail clients, if not we ourselves, might feel more secure if we had a parent with deep pockets.

In late 1996, I happened to meet Barry Friedberg on a Concorde flight from New York to London, and we chatted about old times. Barry is a brilliant investment banker and a member of the inner circle in Merrill Lynch. I was brash enough – it was, after all, four years after I had retired as chairman – to suggest to him that the only financial company in the UK which came close to matching Merrill Lynch in the quality of its management was Mercury, and I told him that my two largest personal holdings were in Mercury and Merrill Lynch. There is no basis for supposing that it had any influence on Merrill Lynch's decision to bid for us, but Barry reminded me of our conversation on the day it announced its bid for Mercury a year later. The idea for that bid in fact arose from a talk that Stephen Zimmerman had in May 1997.

Stephen, who was by then responsible for Mercury's strategic development, while Carol Galley was runing the business day to day, met in New York with Jerry Kenney, Merrill Lynch's chief strategist, for a general exchange of views. During that meeting, he outlined the main strategic questions facing Mercury, such as whether to remain independent, or whether to consider an alliance or merger with a strong financial partner. Kenney told Stephen of Merrill Lynch's wish to make a 'transforming' acquisition in investment management, and it turned out that he had done his homework on Mercury, a prime candidate. In July, Stephen and Carol met with Kenney and Mike Quinn of Merrill Lynch's investment management side in London for further discussions of a possible combination. These were followed by a short pause when a rise in Mercury's share price suggested there might have been a leak.

Negotiations started in earnest in September, and in November David Komansky, Merrill Lynch's chairman, together with Michael Marks, now Merrill Lynch's senior person in London and an old friend and admirer of Stephen and Carol and of Mercury, met the two of them at the Dorchester Hotel in London. Komansky told Stephen and Carol that Merrill Lynch was prepared to pay £17 per share for Mercury or a total price of £3.1 billion, equivalent to $5.2 billion. This was almost four times the price that Swiss Bank Corporation had paid for the rest of Warburgs two years earlier. The offer was favoured by Mercury's management and recommended by its board.

Merrill Lynch was the ideal acquirer of Mercury. Financial strength was one thing, but just as important, with a total workforce now exceeding 60,000 people, it had distribution on a colossal scale. Mercury could create new investment products which Merrill Lynch could then distribute to its clients around the world. And at last Mercury would, through Merrill Lynch, have a real presence in the US. Moreover, with the exception of some activities in fixed-interest management in London, Merrill Lynch had only embryonic investment management activities outside the US, and there would therefore be minimal redundancies. Merrill Lynch was also unlikely to make too many waves in a business that Mercury's people understood well.

*

Merrill Lynch's bid on 17 November 1997 came as a surprise to the market. There had been no leak at all, despite a fair number of people in both firms, in addition to the boards, having to be fully informed. It was a good omen.

It was the largest ever acquisition of a fund management business anywhere in the world, and the consideration was cash. At a stroke, Merrill Lynch would become the third largest active* fund management company in the world after Fidelity and Axa. There were those, including some in Merrill Lynch itself, who felt that the price they were paying for Mercury of £17 per share, which compared to just under £13 at the market's close the previous evening, was high. It represented some twenty-five times the previous year's earnings, whereas Merrill Lynch's own shares were selling at around fourteen times earnings. David Komansky and his colleagues acknowledged that they were paying a 'full' price for what he considered the 'jewel in the crown' of British investment managers. However, when the bid was announced, it did not have an adverse effect on the price of Merrill Lynch shares, which went up from $66 to $68 per share on the day of the announcement. In subsequent months, Merrill Lynch shares continued to rise, passing $100 in the summer of 1998, declining sharply only in the turbulent markets which followed Russia's debt default in August 1998.

Harvard Business School published another excellent case study in August 1998 entitled, 'Merrill Lynch's Acquisition of Mercury Asset Management'. Its main conclusion was that Merrill Lynch was prepared to pay a high price for Mercury's global activities. Mercury had maintained its strength in the UK in both institutional and retail business, with over 900 pension fund clients and some 90,000 clients in its unit trusts and Personal Equity Plans (PEPs), but it was now also the third largest foreign-owned fund manager in Japan, managing funds for twenty-five of Japan's fifty largest corporate pension funds. Mercury also had substantial business from continental Europe, the Middle East, the Pacific, Australia and many other parts of the world. Altogether, non-UK-source business now accounted for about 20 per cent of Mercury's total funds, and the firm had offices in thirteen different countries as well as Jersey and the Isle of Man.

It was as well that the internationally minded members of Mercury's initial senior group had prevailed ten years earlier over

---

* Active fund managers buy individual shares; passive fund managers aim to replicate the various stock market indices by buying the shares that constitute those indices. Funds managed by the latter type of manager are also called tracker funds.

some of our more anglocentric colleagues, who, astute in UK investment policy and brilliant in handling British pension funds, had resisted proposals for international expansion. They had been particularly hard on those who wanted to build a business in Japan. One of them had told me that our efforts in Japan were 'a joke'. Happily, the internationalists had the last laugh.

Another factor in the price was that Merrill Lynch was buying what was by now recognised as a brand name, and brand names these days do not come cheap. I had to acknowledge in retrospect that the time and money we had spent on the branding of the Mercury name, the advertising, however irrelevant some of it had seemed to our business, and even the various logos had all finally paid off. My receipt of two diaries for 2000, one carrying the name of Mercury Asset Management and the other that of Merrill Lynch Mercury Asset Management, suggested that some ambivalence remained as to names, but, in June, to no one's great surprise, the name was changed to Merrill Lynch Investment Managers. The Mercury name will survive in Mercury Selected Trust.

It was hard to deny that Merrill Lynch's purchase was a good deal for Mercury's shareholders. The price of £17 a share was a far cry from our adjusted flotation price of 90 pence in April 1987. Those who held their shares from the flotation ten years earlier had a total return (capital gains plus reinvested dividends) of more than thirty times their investment. Naturally, many members of Mercury's management made some handsome gains, and, furthermore, they would shortly be offered new incentives related to Merrill Lynch shares. According to *The Times*, there were now 300 millionaires in Mercury. This was an exaggeration, but taking account of the various complex incentive schemes ingeniously devised by Hugh Stevenson, and shares that some members of the firm sold in earlier periods, the number certainly exceeded 100, and possibly 200. Although some of these new millionaires will no doubt leave the company over time, the great majority of them are too intelligent to reduce their commitment to the business. They need no reminder that the best things in life cannot be bought with money.

Many old shareholders in Warburgs also benefited, including those members of its senior management who held their Mercury shares when they were distributed to Warburgs' shareholders at the time of the sale to Swiss Bank Corporation in 1995. One former Warburgs colleague wrote that it was the 'deal of the century'; another, recalling that I had told him in 1969 that one way to get rich was to build a small business over a long time and then sell it to a bigger one, contrasted it with the 'shambles of the sell-out of Warburgs in 1995'. He was one of those who started in Warburgs' investment division in 1963, the same year as I did, but had been plucked out of it by Siegmund because he was considered to be too bright to be wasting his time in investment management.

I heard of only one person, a former Siegmund loyalist, who was unhappy with the deal. She suggested to me that we had gone 'down market' and, while it might just be all right to be bought by Morgan Stanley, it was a social disgrace to team up with Merrill Lynch. When she told me that she considered the money she would receive on her shares was 'tainted', I said I supposed she would accordingly give it to charity. Well, she replied, she had not yet quite made up her mind what to do with the money.

Merrill Lynch declared its offer for Mercury unconditional on 22 December 1997 – a handsome Christmas present for Mercury's shareholders and, I believe, its clients and employees. Mercury was now part of Merrill Lynch. I had agreed with Hugh Stevenson some time earlier that the consultancy I had with Mercury would run until 30 June 1998, by which time I would be well beyond my sell-by date, and I was delighted that for the first six months of 1998 I would be a consultant to Merrill Lynch and would have a desk in what was now a Merrill Lynch office. I even managed to take advantage of the Merrill Lynch discount in hotels in New York and Toronto, although in the former city it was my experience that you get what you pay for. You can obtain the Merrill Lynch discount, which is substantial, but the room you get has scarcely any space for the bed and is likely to be situated between an ever-busy gymnasium and some noisy elevators. At the Four Seasons Hotel in Toronto, on the other hand, there was a warm welcome for this Merrill Lynch man, and a valuable saving.

As Mercury was now a subsidiary of Merrill Lynch and no longer a public company, its board was disbanded. The executive directors resigned first, and I thus found myself chairing the last board meeting of Mercury as a public company in May 1998, having chaired its first eleven years earlier. It was held over the telephone and lasted all of five minutes. Hugh kindly organised a splendid farewell dinner of the board for the non-executive directors at the Penthouse in the Dorchester Hotel. An advance copy of the menu produced by the hotel happened to reach my hands, the final item of which read, 'Guests to be offered brandy, pot and liqueurs'. Despite the reluctance most of us instinctively had for any form of self-congratulation or premature celebration as a result of Siegmund's constant indoctrination, it was, we felt, an occasion for some conviviality. The occasion might not, however, have been quite the right one for us to sit around smoking marijuana.

*

Merrill Lynch will not be disappointed with its purchase of Mercury. In 1998, despite some widely publicised losses of UK portfolios as a result of less than sparkling investment performance, new business was at a record level of more than $30 billion. (It was intriguing to see the figure reported in dollars and not pounds, but it did sound more impressive than £18 billion.) Merrill Lynch's distribution power was demonstrated towards the end of the year when, despite troublesome and volatile market conditions, it raised, mostly in the US, nearly $700 million for two new open-ended funds to be managed by Mercury. And, of course, the unique economics of investment management will once again prevail in the years ahead to the advantage of Mercury's new owners.

Carol Galley and Stephen Zimmerman are in charge of Mercury and, together with Jeff Peek, our former colleague in Warburg Paribas Becker and now head of all Merrill Lynch's investment management activities, they constitute an exceptional leadership team. Mercury is blessed with a large number of oustandingly able people, only some of whom are mentioned in these pages, and these people, as Siegmund would have emphasised, are what it is all about.

The hopes and fears of all the years had a happy ending, and a new chapter was beginning. A member of Siegmund's family wrote that Cinderella (his choice of analogy) had thrived by keeping faith with the old king's culture, and that the king would have approved of that. Cinderella had indeed at last found her prince, although for some it may require a leap of imagination to visualise the Thundering Herd as Prince Charming. The old king might also have been pleased, after all, that we had failed to 'get rid of it' in 1979. And it is comforting to know that, in the fairy tale, Cinderella and her prince lived in happiness to a great age.

Postscript: Thank You, MAM

Acts one and two are now over, and all that's passed is merely prologue for the new Merrill Lynch Investment Managers. In the next act the former Mercury will, I believe, scale new heights. Despite some negative publicity earlier in the year about investment performance in one section of Mercury's business, Mercury was named the best investment management group by finance directors of Britain's largest companies in Reuters' annual survey in May 1999. Carol Galley and Stephen Zimmerman, both also members of Merrill Lynch's executive committee, remained at the helm and all the other executive directors who were on the board at the time of Merrill Lynch's acquisition of Mercury in late 1997 were still in place, except Nigel Hurst-Brown, who had moved to Los Angeles to become co-head of Merrill Lynch's American investment management firm, Hotchkis and Wiley. Wisely, Merrill Lynch was taking a 'backstage role' at Mercury, according to the *Wall Street Journal*. I have learnt from the way in which Kees Storm and his colleagues at Aegon conduct their ownership of Scottish Equitable that it is best to use a loose rein when you own a well managed business.

Mercury's alumni, too, appeared to be thriving. Hugh Stevenson was now chairman of Equitas, and a director of Standard Life, among other appointments. He is involved, as he always has been, in a number of charities to which he is generous with both time and money. David Price was appointed chairman of Foreign and Colonial, adding to a variety of positions in the City. Leonard Licht seemed to be enjoying a less formal lifestyle; as always his views on investment markets were original and challenging. Richard Bernays was running the UK operations of Old Mutual, the South African insurance company. Bob Michaelson was chief executive of Sagitta, an investment management company sponsored by Wafic Said, the likeable benefactor of the Said Business School at Oxford, while Richard Oldfield was chief executive of a family office based in an office in Sloane Street. I was delighted to have a continuing business association with Bob and with Richard Oldfield.

Warburg Dillon Read, as it was renamed in 1998 after a period as SBC Warburg, was having a renaissance and, despite some financial setbacks, was once again in 1999 a prime name in European investment banking. Its Swiss owner, Swiss Bank Corporation, itself merged in 1998 with Union Bank of Switzerland to form UBS, has been wise indeed to give precedence to the Warburg name which remains an enduring symbol of quality in the world of investment banking. It was good to read in early 1999 that the two top firms in UK investment research, according to an industry survey, were Merrill Lynch and Warburg Dillon Read, and that Warburg Dillon Read was once again high in the league tables for leading new eurobond issues, as the old Warburgs was in the 1960s and 1970s. More ironically, it was strange to note that while Warburgs no longer carried the initials 'S.G.' in front of its name, its old French partner Paribas was briefly known as S.G. Paribas following a proposed merger with Société Générale which was later annulled.

Warburg Dillon Read continued to occupy the office space at 2 Finsbury Avenue to which the old Warburgs moved to join its Big Bang merger partner firms in the late 1980s. In its large and modernistic waiting area on the seventh floor, one is greeted appropriately by brilliantly realistic portraits of Siegmund Warburg and Henry Grunfeld by Raymond Skipp, painted respectively in 1972 and 1995. Visitors who want to view the portraits at leisure can help themselves freely to mints enclosed in Warburg Dillon Read wrappers, as branding is thus extended to the smallest level.

In June 1999, six of the seven members of the old Warburgs' Chairman's Committee of 1979, together with Renata Propper, met for lunch at Warburg Dillon Read's office to celebrate Henry Grunfeld's 95th birthday (only Geoffrey Seligman, who died in 1994, was missing). Still attending the office regularly, he was in sparkling form, but sadly died a few days later. Eric Roll at 91, David Scholey and Herman van der Wyck until his retirement in April, were still there, while Oscar Lewisohn and I were working elsewhere in contiguous offices in Savoy Street. Bob Boas, Martin Gordon and John Walker-Haworth were others from former days who continued their association with the new Warburgs in 1999. Simon Cairns was chairman of Allied Zurich and of Commonwealth Development

Corporation, while Rodney Ward was in Hong Kong overseeing the activities of Republic Bank of New York in South East Asia.

*

I left Mercury's offices at the end of June 1998 but retained a number of links with the firm. I remained chairman of Mercury Asset Management Canada and continued as chairman of Mercury European Investment Trust and as a member of the boards of Mercury Keystone and The Europe Fund. My own investments, and those of a number of members of my family and friends, have been taken care of very efficiently by David Scott and Richard Nunneley in Mercury's private clients division, and so, one way or another, I found myself in Mercury's offices quite often in 1999. On the surface at least, not a great deal had changed and happily most of the people who made the firm what it is were still there. In a welcome break with merchant banking tradition, female receptionists now sat alongside the males. The dark chocolates offered at lunch were still the best in London.

Satvinder Maan and I moved to Deltec's London office when we left Mercury, thereby re-establishing a long-time friendship with David McNaughtan in London, Arthur Byrnes and John Gordon in New York, and Penelope Dauphinot in Nassau. Tom Colville, late of Warburgs and of Mercury, joined us in London in early 1999. Our office was adjacent to that of Soditic where Oscar Lewisohn, Piers von Simson and Mark Katzenellenbogen, Warburgs alumni, were working. Maurice Dwek, their shareholder and also a director of Deltec, was a frequent visitor from Geneva.

I am hoping before too long to take that 'gap year' which my generation somehow missed out on. However, although I am conscious that retirement is being hailed as the new nirvana, I have not yet had the courage to retire, and so I continue a number of non-executive directorships and consultancies in London, in Scotland and in North America. I also hope to spend more time in Canada, where I have joined the board of Guardian Capital, an investment management company led by the intuitively brilliant John Christodoulou.

One connection which has provided me with special interest and enjoyment, as well as an element of nostalgia, is Scottish Hydro-Electric, of which I became a director in 1994. I remember the exchange of paraffin lamps for electric lights when electricity was first made available to our family house in Perthshire in the late 1940s by the old North of Scotland Hydro-Electric Board, which became Scottish Hydro-Electric on privatisation in 1991.

I recall, too, the vehement opposition voiced in those distant days by those who viewed a hydro-electric scheme on nearby Loch Tummel as an evil which would destroy the environment and ruin a place of great scenic beauty. Engineers working on the scheme were turned away by hotels in Pitlochry, and the Hydro Board's first chairman, Lord Airlie, father of our one-time Mercury colleague Jamie Ogilvy, resigned when friends cut him in the street and his eldest son was blackballed for a local club membership. Today the Tummel Garry hydro scheme is widely regarded by the people of Perthshire as a blessing, and the salmon ladder which is incorporated in it is a major tourist attraction. An accommodation seems to have been reached between justified environmental concerns and the provision of decent living standards.

Scottish Hydro-Electric's territory includes the Highlands and Islands. Under the inspiring chairmanship of David Wilson (Lord Wilson of Tillyorn, formerly Governor of Hong Kong), with support in succession from two first-class chief executives in Roger Young and Jim Forbes, we have held our board meetings throughout the territory, thus affording me the opportunity to visit islands such as Benbecula, Lewis, Orkney, Shetland and Skye. Each visit includes a meeting with the company's invariably dedicated local staff who never fail to respond to calls to go out in the most dreadful weather conditions to fix fallen electricity lines. It has been an education for me to observe such a strong sense of duty and service built on long tradition.

My appointment to the board of Scottish Hydro-Electric in 1994 was unconnected to my directorship of Mercury, and naturally I forswore any exchange of information about the company with my colleagues at Mercury. However, Mercury was at that time, for its clients, the largest shareholder of Scottish Hydro-Electric with a holding of around 12 per cent. Soon after my appointment, Mercury started selling its shares rather noticeably. My board colleagues in Perth were far too tactful to say anything, but it did occur to me that if they accepted at least that I was not feeding negative informtion to Mercury, they might have thought that those in Mercury who knew me must have so little confidence in any board that would have me as a member that they had decided to sell the shares! Happily, in the spring of 1999, Mercury was once again the largest shareholder in

what is now Scottish and Southern Energy, following a merger in
1998 between Scottish Hydro-Electric and Southern Electric.

*

It is always a joy, as well as a duty, for someone at my stage of life to
talk to a young person about his or her career possibilities. Often
they ask whether they should go into the City, not surprisingly
perhaps in view of the increasing recognition of the role which
financial service businesses play in the UK economy, accounting
nowadays for about a fifth of the country's exports, even if they are
described as 'invisibles'. The City has a 'buzz' about it, and lots of
intelligent people work there. Moreover, the financial rewards,
reaching into telephone number proportions for a few, can be a
magnet to those in search of easy riches.

'The City' of course covers a wide variety of different jobs
requiring quite disparate skills, and there is something there for just
about everyone. I am more at ease if I am asked by someone if they
should go into investment management, or fund management as it is
now more often called, because my knowledge of other aspects of
City life is becoming increasingly dated. I feel, as Jack Nicklaus did
when he watched Tiger Woods' victory in the US Masters at the age
of 19, that the latter was 'playing a game with which I am no longer
familiar'. I suspect, however, that the attributes needed for success
have not changed that much.

Investment management was almost unheard of as a career, let
alone as a stand-alone business, when I started out in the 1950s. It
was seen by most as a suffocatingly dull activity within merchant
banking or accountancy, which might have to be tolerated for a year
or so by future executives with grander ambitions as part of a
broadly based training programme. Now, however, fund management is fashionable and many young people have set their minds on
it. But will it work for them, and are they right for it, and how can
they, or I, tell if they are?

It has been said that the art of life is not doing what we like, but
learning to like what we do. In the investment business, I believe one
needs to go a step further. Those who are really good at it, and they
are quite few, actually love what they do. To them it's a drug; they
cannot leave it alone. Every visit to the supermarket is an exercise in
investment analysis. There are others in the business who do not
share this love, and they are condemned to mediocrity. To them,

investment may even be a bit of a bore, and if it is a bore they are likely to do it badly.

I could never have been a good banker, in the conventional sense of that term, and would have been hopeless in corporate finance. But while I claim no exceptional understanding of investment, I was from the start lucky enough to find it fascinating. It involves the study of so many aspects of human endeavour: politics, psychology, financial history, consumer trends, and of course the economy and its outlook. A knowledge of the theoretical science of economics, by contrast, can sometimes be a barrier to good investment judgment, and an understanding of accountancy may be of only occasional help.

The message is 'love it or leave it', but how can a young person with no experience of investing know in advance how much he will like it? Here are some of the qualities which an outstanding practitioner of the art of investment is likely to have:

- an insatiable curiosity as to everything that is going on in the world.

- a capacity to assess people, because businesses are mainly about the people who run them; a sense for psychology will be useful too.

- an awareness of the constant need to question conventional wisdom and a healthy scepticism about what he hears from company spokesmen, stockbrokers and research analysts.

- the ability to accept losses and move on, combined with the patience to stay with winning investments indefinitely.

- a calm temperament – investment can be humbling and stressful.

- common sense.

- intuition.

- a sense of humour – it will be necessary for survival.

- an acquisitive instinct – materialistic as it may sound, the desire to make money for oneself through investing is essential.

If a young person feels he has most of these qualities in good measure, he should try investment management. He will be endlessly absorbed by it, he will enjoy it and he may even make some money.

*

Commenting on the role of luck in sport, Gary Player, the veteran South African golfer still excelling in his sixties, remarked that the more he practised the greater his luck. There is truth in his observation, but there is also no denying the part played by pure chance in the course of a person's career. Denis Greenhill, former non-executive director of Warburgs, called his memoirs *More by Accident* to reflect his view that so many aspects of his life and career occurred as a result of accidental meetings rather than any preconceived plan or intention.

I was extremely lucky that when I went to Canada in 1957 I had an introduction to Tony Griffin, not only because Tony became a great friend of mine as well as a mentor in many ways, but because it was through him that I met Siegmund Warburg on a visit to Toronto in 1958. In turn, I owe a huge debt of gratitude to Siegmund for his kindness, his constant encouragement and his capacity to open up new horizons and possibilities for me. Through him I met a diverse collection of remarkable people, many of whom I have tried to describe in this book. Among many others in Warburgs, I am grateful to Henry Grunfeld and Eric Roll for the values and principles they taught us, and in earlier times to Eric Korner, Geoffrey Seligman and Ernest Thalmann for the interest they took in younger people such as myself. Among my own contemporaries, I was privileged to have colleagues such as Martin Gordon, Michael Gore, Oscar Lewisohn, David Scholey, John Stancliffe, Hugh Stevenson, Andrew Stewart-Roberts, Herman van der Wyck, Rodney Ward and John Walker-Haworth. With all of them I have, I believe, been able to combine a long-term working relationship with the sort of personal friendship which comes from sharing common experiences both good and bad.

There are not, in my experience, many exceptional exponents of the art of investment, but I have been fortunate enough through my career at Warburgs and Mercury to meet a few who seem to have some special flair. Leon Levy has the unique capacity to translate abstract concepts of changes in the economy or in human behaviour into practical investment ideas. Fayez Sarofim, a brilliant investment manager living in Texas, is a believer in buying shares of the world's great companies, and holding them for the very long term. Fayez Sarofim shared with Leon Levy an early insight into the true value of Mercury's franchise – he came to visit us in London in the late 1980s to see if he could buy 100 per cent of Mercury!

Charley Ellis of Greenwich Associates is an articulate advocate of the futility of market timing and the need to tame the false gods of fear and greed which impel so many investors to jump in and out of the market, almost always to their cost. Peter Cundill is a connoisseur of so-called distressed investments – those which for one reason or another are neglected by most investors, but often come good in the end. John Neff, another colleague at Greenwich Associates, is an astute and well-regarded investor who likes to buy shares selling at low prices in relation to their profits.

Robert Brown, who lives in Vancouver, is the only person I know who has any credibility in the study of 'technical' analysis of the market, which broadly speaking involves assessing the likely direction of the market by analysis of the behaviour of the market itself. Robert analyses the daily volume and price movements in the New York stock market, which he calls the money flow, to determine whether the large investors are buyers or sellers. His forecasts of short-term trends, useful if you have new money to invest, are amazingly accurate. Closer to home, Leonard Licht and Ian Steers, a director of Mercury Keystone, are two London-based investors with an unusual nose for investment values. I have benefited greatly from knowing all these gifted people.

*

There were stressful, difficult and even tearful times in Mercury, but it was mostly enjoyable and always entertaining, and I am grateful to my former colleagues there for their friendship and their sense of fun. Hilaire Belloc wrote:

> There's nothing worth the wear of winning
> But laughter and the love of friends.

Alan Clark, once my local Member of Parliament in Chelsea, said there are no true friendships in politics. If he was right, I am glad I chose a career in business, where personal friendships abound. It may be a good rule not to do business with friends – it risks the personal relationship – but there is nothing wrong in allowing friendship to develop with one's business colleagues or clients or competitors.

I had the good luck to be surrounded by a wonderful group of people at Mercury, and to have become their chairman largely because I happened to be around at the right time and to be older than most of them were. It was they who built the business, and to them and the institution they created, I can without false modesty say, Thank You, MAM. As Siegmund Warburg reminded us so often, it is all about the people you have. Mercury had, and has today, the right ones.

Summer 2000
London

Acknowledgements and Sources

Increasingly these days I find myself given to 'senior moments' (those occasions, for example, when you cannot remember whom you had lunch with earlier in the day) as to recent happenings. My memory for earlier events and for people encountered thirty years or so ago, however, while sometimes coloured by a tendency towards hyperbole which can grow with the passage of time, is somewhat better. I have reinforced it with conversations with many former colleagues at Mercury and Warburgs, too numerous to list, and I am grateful to all of them for their willingness to share their own recollections of some of the incidents I have tried to describe. They corrected me on a number of facts, but I cannot guarantee that inaccuracies do not remain. The opinions and interpretations, at least, are all my own.

My warmest thanks are due to Norman Bachop, Hugo de Klee and Richard Oldfield, all of whom read the complete book in draft and made a number of valuable comments. I am grateful also to those who read and commented on various sections, or gave me encouragement or advice of one sort or another, including Sir Arthur Bryan, Mark Cheng, Caroline Cormack, Charley Ellis, Heather Farrar, Charlotte Finlay-Broadbelt, Tony Griffin, John Gordon, Professor Jay Light, Vincent Mai, Elizabeth Rivers-Bulkeley, Candis Roberts, Jonathan Ruck Keene, Peter Scales, Reed Scowen, Wendy Stephenson, Tony Solomon, Shelby White and Andrew Williamson.

Woody Allen says he likes to write his film scripts on his bed at home. Such an idea is anathema to me. I found I could only write when far away from home and from London. I am especially grateful, therefore, to those who provided me with tranquil havens, accompanied by generous hospitality, where most of this book was written: my sister Angela de Klee in Mull, my brother Robin Stormonth Darling and his wife Carola in Perthshire, and Jake and Fiona Eberts in Quebec. Another venue which proved to be conducive to writing was the Kildare Club outside Dublin and near to my mother's old home. It was pleasant to discover that there is a copy in each room there of *Finding the Fairways*, the publication of which was sponsored by Mercury. I am indebted also to British Airways which has supplied me with seats in which to spend many captive hours which passed more quickly, I discovered, when writing than when reading, eating or watching movies.

My assistant, Satvinder Maan, has typed and retyped my frequent revisions with the utmost patience and good humour. Finally, I would like to thank my agent, Jane Conway-Gordon, and my publisher, Benjamin Buchan, for their expert guidance.

*

As a compulsive collector since childhood of postage stamps, cigarette cards, old railway tickets, family crests, postcards and many other items of ephemera, I was unable to resist accumulating a library of magazine and newspaper articles, not only about Warburgs and Mercury and the people who worked in those firms, but also about just about everyone else who plays a part in this story. It has proved invaluable in checking facts and dates and providing additional background on some of the characters I knew less well personally. The following articles and reports, which contained informed original research, were particularly useful:

'The Steinberg Stomp – America's Fiercest Raider Kicks up his Heels', by Hope Lampert, *Manhattan Inc.*, October 1985.

'Hard to be Rich – The Rise and Wobble of the Gutfreunds', by John Taylor (New York, January 1988).

'Warren Buffett's Wild Ride at Salomon', by Carol Loomis, *Fortune*, October 1997. Martin Meyer's 1993 book, *Nightmare on Wall Street: Salomon Brothers and the Corruption of the Marketplace*, was also useful in connection with Chapter 21.

'Warburg – The Morning After' (referring to the Morgan Stanley affair), *Euromoney*, January 1995.

'Morgan Stanley's Global Gamble', *Institutional Investor*, March 1995.

I have referred in Chapter 6 to various interviews which Siegmund Warburg gave. The most revealing of these is 'Confessions of Siegmund Warburg' by Cary Reich, which appeared in *Institutional Investor* in March 1980. An earlier profile in *New Yorker* in April 1966 by Joseph Wechsberg, titled 'A Prince in the City', was informative; but for further reading on Siegmund Warburg, I recommend Ron Chernow's *The Warburgs* (1993), which includes much interesting historical information on the Warburg family and a fascinating account of conditions in Germany before and between the wars, especially as it affected the Jewish community.

I have already mentioned in Chapters 25 and 27 the two excellent Harvard Business School studies which, with their detailed analyses, I found extremely helpful. These were:

'Morgan Stanley and S.G. Warburg: Investment Bank of the Future' (Parts A and B), January 1998.

'Merrill Lynch's Acquisition of Mercury Asset Management', August 1998.

They are, I am told, available on the internet for those with the appropriate skills.

Index